G000078133

WELLINGTON WINGS

WELLINGTON WINGS

*An RAF Intelligence Officer
in the Western Desert*

F.R. Chappell

CRÉCY BOOKS

This edition published in 1992 by
CRÉCY BOOKS LTD
First published in 1980 by
William Kimber & Co. Ltd.

© F. R. Chappell, 1992

ISBN 0 947554 27 0

Printed and bound by Hartnolls Limited
Bodmin, Cornwall

To the memory of
Wing Commander D.T. Saville DSO, DFC
and Wing Commander D.M. Crossley DFC and Bar
and as a tribute to
all the officers, non-commissioned officers and men
who served in North Africa, Malta and Italy
with the bomber squadrons of 205 Group,
Royal Air Force in World War II.

Contents

List of Illustrations

MAPS IN THE TEXT

Foreword
by
Air Commodore C.J. Mount
CBE DSO DFC RAF (Retd)

Roy Chappell — 'Chappie' to us all in 205 Group — was Squadron Intelligence Officer when I came to 104 Squadron in February 1943. On his subsequent posting to Wing Headquarters he continued to take a most active interest in the squadron's activities although responsible for intelligence duties in the wider field of Wing. In this book he recounts the work of the 205 Group squadrons in the Western Desert in North Africa and in Italy from 1942 to 1944. Drawn from diaries made at the time, from personal experience and an ability to observe and report, he combines accuracy with a lively style of presentation.

For me the book recalls people, places and events, which although over thirty-five years ago are still fresh to mind. I was at the time new to bombers and I had to find my feet in new surroundings. But having previously come from Hurricanes in the Western Desert, I was acquainted with the geography and I was accustomed to tactical operations and close support missions.

The narrative refers to the combined operations in Italy of the 205 Group squadrons and those of 15th Air Force. Operations in conjunction with the Americans had, of course, previously taken place. The Bostons and the Wellingtons had combined to harass the Afrika Korps from Alamein to Tunis. But Mediterranean Allied Air Forces was the first combined Headquarters to be set up in the Middle East theatre specifically to co-ordinate the daylight operations of the Fortresses and Liberators with the night operations of the Wellingtons. Later the amalgamation became more marked when the 205 Group squadrons re-equipped with Liberators.

To those who served in 205 Group I believe this book will bring back many memories. To others it gives a vivid insight into operations and conditions in the Middle East at a time described by Sir Winston Churchill as 'not the beginning of the end, but perhaps the end of the beginning'.

C.J. MOUNT

Sources and Acknowledgements

This book is based chiefly on the day to day diaries I kept during the years 1942 to 1945 while serving with the RAF as Intelligence Officer 104 Wellington Bomber Squadron (January 1942 to March 1943) and Senior Intelligence Officer 236 Wing (104 and 462 RAAF and then 40 and 104 Squadrons, for the period March 1943 to August 1944).

I have also consulted the operational record books of 40, 104 and 218 Squadrons, 236 and 238 Wings, at the Public Records Office, London, during 1972 and 1976, and had correspondence and discussions with officers of Adastral House and Air Historical Branch, Ministry of Defence, London.

I have had great help from letters, discussions, reference to flying log books, interchange of documents and manuscript with two experienced aircrew officers of the RAAF, a pilot and navigator, who between them, completed three operational tours with 205 Group squadrons and a part tour on Wellingtons over Germany.

The manuscript has been read by Air Commodore C.J. Mount CBE DSO DFC who commanded 104 Squadron in 1943, by Sir Henry Calley DSO DFC (President of 205 Group Association) who commanded 37 Squadron in 1944–45 and operated in 104 Squadron in 1943, by Squadron Leader Guy Britton (Chairman 205 Group Association) and some chapters by other former officers in the Group, including Group Captain P.I. Harris DFC, Commander of 236 Wing 1943 to 1945 and Squadron-Leader J. Johnson DFC (104 Squadron). To all these officers my grateful thanks. However, reading and discussion does not necessarily signify approval, and the responsibility for facts and opinions expressed must be taken entirely by myself.

I have read many war books and histories of the World War II and compared them with the manuscript in an effort to be accurate. In particular, *The Royal Air Force — The Flight Avails* by Denis Richards and St G. Saunders, *Air War against Germany and Italy 1939–43* by John Herington, *History of the Second World*

War — The Mediterranean and Middle East by Playfair, Molony, Flynn and Gleave, and *The Desert Rats* by G.L. Verney have proved useful in providing background to events.

I am most grateful to all who have helped in this lengthy project — friends, typists, copying services, publishers, editors, readers. No offence or distress to individuals or relatives has been intended and my main intention has been to produce a factual account of how things seemed to be at the time and to record sincere admiration for the brave young men of the squadrons and the courageous commanders who led them over hostile territory in those terrible and urgent days of war.

F.R. CHAPPELL

Introduction

The writing of another book on World War II may require some justification. This one is about the aircrews and ground personnel of a group of night bombers (205 Group RAF) operating in the Middle East and Mediterranean theatres of the war, and the events and personalities are viewed from an intimate angle — that of an Intelligence Officer linked with the squadrons over a three year period and aided by the constructive comments, documents and memories of two of the author's wartime aircrew friends (RAAF officers) who, however, wish to remain anonymous.

Australian participation in 205 Group included No 462 RAAF (Halifax) Bomber Squadron and Australian aircrews and individuals serving in the RAF squadrons Nos 37, 38, 40, 70, 104, 108, 142, 147, 148, 150, 159, 160. Wing Commander Donald Teale Saville DSO DFC, an Australian and a key figure in this book, was Commanding Officer of 104 Wellington Bomber Squadron, RAF from August to December 1942.

It is hoped that the book will provide interest for those who were there and allow relatives and friends to learn something of the conditions under which 205 Group personnel worked and lived or died. Additionally there is the opportunity to pay tribute to some brave and charismatic officers and men whose achievements in North Africa and Southern Europe would otherwise be known only to their comrades.

Apart from the degree of autobiography which seems unavoidable in personal accounts, there are some underlying themes in this book which were not thought of at the time of writing factual diaries,

- the effects of active war service in a bomber squadron upon individuals, both air crews and ground personnel,
- the effects of leadership upon the operational efficiency of a squadron, wing or group,
- the ultimate futility of war with its wastage and misery, balanced to some extent by the heroism and magnificent qualities of many who took part in it.

Historians of the air war have tended to concentrate on Bomber Command and the USAAF in Britain while those writing of the Desert War have dealt mainly with the achievements of the Eighth Army and the Desert Air Force (fighters, fighter-bombers and day tactical bombers) which worked in close day-support of the infantry and armour in North Africa.

The strategical and tactical achievements of the night bombers of 205 Group RAF, a smaller Bomber Command, also deserve attention, for this was a tightly organised and efficient bombing force, flexible enough to be switched in emergency to direct army support in attacking enemy tanks, transport and troops close to the front line. The Group was conscious of its own identity and purpose, with its air and ground personnel appreciative of each other and equally devoted to the task of combining with the Army and Navy to defeat the enemy.

Operating conditions for the men of these night bomber squadrons were very different from the conditions prevailing for Bomber Command crews in Europe. The 205 Group squadrons were units of a mobile bomber force based on tents, trucks and improvised runways scraped from the desert surface or from Tunisian or Italian mud. Airfield equipment was primitive, maintenance of engines and airframes difficult, living conditions always uncomfortable, 'gippy tummy' was common, relaxation in cities with music, dancing and female company was rare indeed; rising sand and *khamsin* conditions, hot humid days and freezing nights were part of the environment.

Targets in general were smaller and more specifically defined necessitating bombing at relatively low levels, frequently 5,000 to 7,000 feet, a range well within the capabilities of both light and heavy flak, and one that left pilots limited room for manoeuvre when caught in concentrations of searchlights and flak, or when attacked by a night fighter. Operational altitudes in excess of 12,000 feet were rare for Wellingtons of 205 Group.

The bomber forces employed were sometimes relatively small in number and in consequence individual attention could be given to some bomber aircraft by co-ordinated radar controlled searchlight and flak batteries. There was no question of saturating the defences, but attacks were planned to stream over a defended target for a limited time period.

On the happier side, weather conditions were settled for longer periods, targets in 1942 and 1943 were usually less heavily defended than in Germany and losses on normal missions were

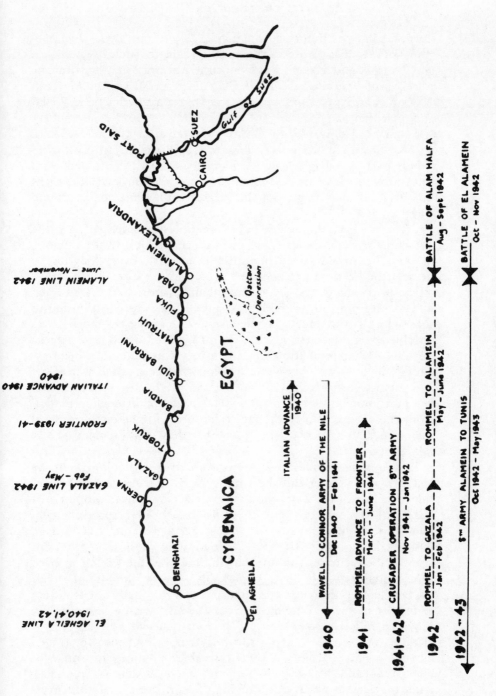

Advances and retreats of forces in desert war 1940—1943

lower than for Bomber Command. Exceptions were the 'Mail
Run' or regular targets frequently attacked, such as Benghazi
and Tobruk; and at certain stages of the war in 1943 other strategic
ports, Tripoli, Sousse, Tunis, Bizerta in North Africa, and Palermo,
Messina and Naples in Italy, became 'hot' targets defended by flak
and night fighters.

From 1944 onwards 205 Group operated with the 15th USAAF
against Southern European targets (some shared with Bomber
Command) in what became a highly successful combined team
effort by American day bombers and Commonwealth night
bombers, all operating from the great complex of airfields around
Foggia.

Critics of bombing policy have sometimes commented upon the
detachment of aircrews from the horrors caused by the bursting
of their bombs far away beneath the aircraft. Everything has to
be seen in its right perspective. Aircrews were directed to attack
cities, ports, factories, ships, marshalling yards, battle areas etc.,
in fact anything that could be bombed and was contributing to
the enemy's war effort. To the airmen doing the bombing it was
purely an impersonal matter. Bombs were aimed at material
objects and in retaliation the enemy shot at material objects —
aircraft in this case. Everyone was involved in a 'total' war effort
and there were various ways and means of contributing to it, and
no questioning of the aim of achieving 'unconditional surrender'
from the enemy. If men thought too much of the consequences of
their war actions it is doubtful whether they could remain sane or
take part in war.

In a bomber squadron aircrews were frequently known to be
lost or were missing and the strains upon the survivors were considerable because they knew they had a definite number of
missions to complete and they also knew that approximately
one-third of the crews were almost certain to be killed or go
missing during their first tour of operations. In spite of the odds
against their survival to the end of the war the young men of
these squadrons stood up remarkably well to the strains of air
warfare and could laugh and joke and talk rationally about a wide
variety of subjects in the mess. 'Stand downs', even of a single day,
provided relief in stress times — periods of leave were enjoyed —
alcohol was a tranquilliser providing temporary relief for frayed
nerves. Strain became more noticeable in times of intensive
operations and was visible in forms such as nervous twitches,
idiosyncrasies of behaviour, greying of hair, use of mascots, over-

indulgence in smoking or drinking. Life in an operational bomber squadron was unnatural and all personnel were affected to some extent.

Bomber Intelligence officers were conscious of their own peculiar and fortunate position in being in the thick of all that was happening without taking the same risks as their aircrew friends. This uneasy feeling or guilt complex may be one of the sub-conscious motivations leading eventually to the writing of this book.

F.R.C.

CHAPTER ONE

Bomber Intelligence – in at the deep end

The decision which led eventually to this book was made by an Air Ministry Selection Board in April 1941 after they had enjoyed pulling to shreds my application for an RAFVR commission as a meteorological officer. At times there were almost fierce interchanges between Board members and myself, so that I was surprised and delighted by the final result. The Board decided that a Cambridge degree in Geography, London Diploma of Education and experience as a schoolmaster (thirty-two years of age) with keen interests in physical education and games were not a sufficiently scientific background for Meteorology but instead they recommended me for a further interview in the RAF Intelligence Branch where I was accepted for training as a Bomber Intelligence Officer.

From my school in Dorset and additional civilian duties as Air Raid Precautions Instructor and Warden I was called up in August to an RAF Officer Training Unit at Torquay with a tight programme of lectures, drills and marching. Then in quick succession came an Intelligence course at Harrow, a brief period at a Bomber Command station (North Luffenham) with two operational squadrons of Hampden bombers, one week of embarkation leave, and posting to HQ RAF Middle East via a convoy leaving Liverpool in November 1941.

Ours was a lucky convoy of sixteen liners and merchant vessels escorted by a battleship and eight destroyers. We encountered no enemy opposition and called at Freetown, Durban and Aden before reaching Port Tewfiq-Suez on 11th January 1942. Some ships of the convoy were diverted from Durban to Singapore in time to be bombed and sunk by Japanese planes.

Personnel and heavy equipment from the convoy were quickly dispersed from the Port Tewfiq-Suez area to various Army, Air Force and Naval camps in the Canal Zone. RAF arrivals were taken by train to Abu Sueir near Ismailia — a well established station with permanent buildings and a Beaufighter squadron. Abu Sueir had recently been bombed by Luftwaffe night bombers and some damage was visible.

On 18th January I was sent to Cairo for an Intelligence course at HQ RAF Middle East. The members of the course were made aware of the problems underlying the Middle East war as the confusions of the sea-sawing Desert campaigns were discussed openly and analysed. The main components were:

1. An Italian advance into Egypt as far as Sidi Barrani in 1940.

2. The Wavell-O'Connor Army of the Nile sweeping westwards in December 1940 in a brilliant campaign, routing the Italians and reaching El Agheila in February 1941.

3. The loss of Desert troops and equipment sent to Greece where they were overrun by the Germans in April 1941 and many lost on Crete.

4. In March 1941 Rommel and his newly formed Afrika Korps retook Cyrenaica and pushed the weakened Army of the Nile back to the Egyptian frontier. A garrison of Australian, British and later Polish troops remained behind the enemy lines in Tobruk.

5. In November 1941 the renamed Eighth Army began Operation Crusader and were able to relieve Tobruk and to reach El Agheila in January 1942 for the second time — but against German troops who retired in good order.

6. With shorter lines of communication and supply Rommel was able to reform in January 1942 and take up a new counter-offensive.

This was the point of arrival of our convoy. The front was soon to be stabilised in February back at Gazala but the Eighth Army had suffered heavy losses in men and tanks in Operation Crusader and its sequel. British tanks were still inferior in reliability and gun power to those of the Germans. Allied forces in the Middle East would be further weakened by the need to send units to India and the Australian 6th and 7th Divisions back for the defence of Australia. The Royal Navy as support for the Eighth Army had suffered a series of shattering blows. The *Ark Royal* and *Barham* had been lost in the Mediterranean and the *Queen Elizabeth* and *Valiant* were lying disabled in Alexandria. Coupled with the earlier losses in smaller ships in the Greece and Crete campaigns and the sinking of the *Prince of Wales* and *Repulse* by the Japanese Air Force, it was difficult to be optimistic from a naval viewpoint. Inter-service relationships were somewhat strained and only the Royal Air Force units appeared to be at good strength and to have relatively high morale. RAF optimism was doubtless due in part to good leadership at the top and to the fact that bomber squadron losses on operations tended to be lower than in

Western Europe while airmen were not so conscious of having inferior equipment to the enemy as were the tank crews and anti-tank gunners. However, Luftwaffe operations against the Eighth Army and the bombing of RAF airfields in the Canal Zone indicated that the enemy air force was active and strong. Air superiority over the Desert had not yet been clearly established by the RAF as it was later in 1942.

The RAF Intelligence course gave further credence to the impressions of the war position that were current among the more thoughtful and knowledgeable service personnel. In spite of now having the USA on our side after Pearl Harbour, it still seemed likely to be a long hard road to victory.

On the convoy I had made a number of friends and had many cheery acquaintances among the officers of the 11th Hussars and an anti-tank artillery regiment. In Cairo it was surprising and annoying to hear RAF personnel referring to Army types as 'pongoes' or 'bloody pongoes' apparently as terms of contempt. There was a distinct tendency to criticise the Army for the recent reverses in the field without realisation of the difficulties arising from inferior weapons and arduous conditions endured to the point of breakdown by battle-tired men.

In return the Army men spoke of the Air Force as 'the bloody boys in blue', with a strong inference that the RAF had all the comforts in their base camps and hardly knew that they were fighting a war.

Fortunately for the morale and efficiency of the Allied fighting services the year 1942 was eventually to be one where successful combined operations of the Eighth Army and Desert Air Force — plus the tactical and strategic bombing of 205 Group Wellingtons at night, the shipping strikes and communications work of other RAF units and the dedicated supply support of the Royal Navy along the coast as ports were recaptured and reopened — would lead to complete and lasting bonds of respect between the three armed services. But more defeats and a further retreat had to be endured before the enemy were to be finally held at Alamein, Egypt's natural defence line between the Mediterranean and the Qattara Depression.

It was a relief for me to be sent to 205 Group HQ at Shallufa for posting to a squadron. The pleasures of Cairo with its dance shows, night clubs, cinemas, good meals at the better hotels, golf, tennis, swimming and drinks at the Gezira Club, and the hordes of Egyptians from extremely rich to extremely poor — all made

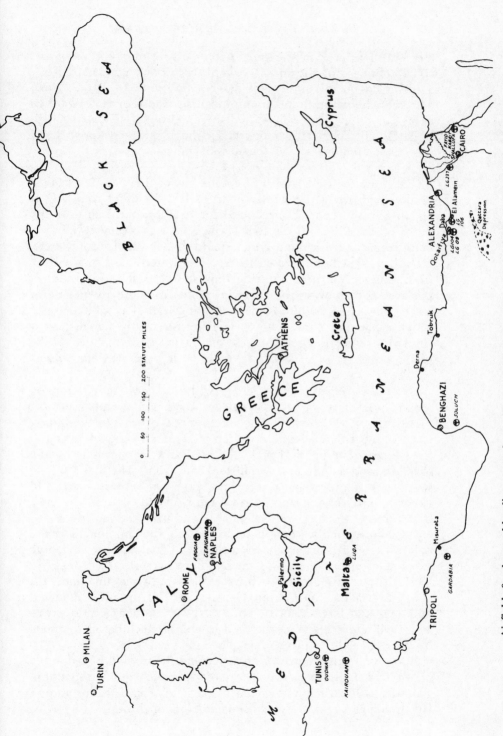

Airfields & advanced landing grounds used by squadrons & wings of 205 Group RAF (1941–1945)

me feel ill at ease in wartime. After hearing of the bravery and resourcefulness of the infantry, tank crews and gunners fighting against odds in the unpleasant desert conditions, I felt that I had had enough of travel and training courses and looked forward to doing something useful in a bomber squadron. I was supposed to be an Intelligence Officer but had enough sense to know that I was still a complete 'sprog' (clueless beginner).

In late January 1942 and on a bright but cool sunny day typical of the Egyptian winter, a motor truck left the 205 Group HQ at Shallufa in the Canal Zone bound for RAF Station Kabrit on the shore of the Great Bitter Lake. The road was bitumen — a dark line through a brown and grey expanse of sand and stony desert. To the right a line of green trees and irrigated fields marked the fresh water canal providing the only source of drinking water in the area and drawing its life-giving fluid from the River Nile at Cairo some one hundred miles to the west. Beyond the fresh-water canal and parallel to it was the Suez Ship Canal, here a straight stretch of twenty miles joining the Gulf of Suez to the Bitter Lakes — natural salt lakes in a depression of the desert surface.

Near the Geneifa army camp with its huts, tents, training grounds, military cemetery, storage areas and motor transport parks, the RAF truck turned sharp right off the main Suez–Ismailia–Port Said road and waited at a rail crossing while an oil-fired locomotive of the Egyptian State Railways puffed across the road drawing a long line of rail tanker wagons. The black smoke stood out sharply against the blue sky. The air was clean and sweet except for the smoke and a faint oily smell from the Suez Oil Refinery which came on the light wind from the south.

As the clanging warning bells ceased the truck bumped over the rail tracks and crossed the Sweet Water Canal towards the blue expanse of water which was the southern part of the Great Bitter Lake. The road turned northwards and followed the line of a concrete walled canal from Geneifa. In the distance appeared buildings and large hangars, a water tower, sandbagged dispersals and their encircled aircraft, recognisable as Wellington bombers by their tall tail fins protruding above the sand walls.

Soon the station fence was reached and the truck driver stopped his vehicle at the gates for the guards to make a quick inspection. This over, the truck ambled on through the camp to the Station HQ building so that the passenger from Shallufa, Acting Pilot

Officer Chappell, could report to the Adjutant and the Commanding Officer.

Documents in the Station Headquarters showed that the newcomer was appointed as Intelligence Officer of No 104 Wellington Bomber Squadron, one of the two squadrons now stationed at Kabrit.

The candidate interviewed at Air Ministry in April 1941 had reached his post with an operational bomber squadron in the Middle East.

RAF Station Kabrit was the home base for two Wellington bomber squadrons, Nos 104 and 148. 104 Squadron had only recently flown out from England via Gibraltar and Malta. Their UK base had been Driffield (Yorks), and from this station 15 aircraft had been sent in October 1941 on detachment to Luqa, Malta, under the leadership of Wing Commander P.R. ('Teddy') Beare and Squadron Leader H.M. Young (known as 'Dinghy Young' because of his successful ditching of bombers in the sea — and later to be one of the famous Dambuster Squadron No 617). After operations from Malta against Italian, North African and convoy targets the 104 Squadron detachment expected to return to Britain.

Instead, the surviving aircraft and crews were posted to the Middle East to reinforce the 205 Group force of night bombers. Eight aircraft arrived as 104 Squadron at Kabrit in January 1942 and were formed under Squadron Leader Young and Squadron Leader Brown into two flights using additional new crews from 205 Group.

Thus, the 'new' squadron at Kabrit included crews experienced in Bomber Command and Malta missions and others starting their first tour of operations. As a squadron the crews were new to the conditions of desert warfare and some of the ex-Driffield types were not pleased to find themselves being regarded as 'new boys'. Even with the experienced leadership of Wing Commander Beare and Squadron Leader Young there was a feeling on the station that No 104 Squadron had yet to establish themselves in the Middle East and the squadron personnel in February 1942 were sensitive about the matter.

By contrast 148 Squadron were regarded by station administration and intelligence as something of a 'gen' (experienced and knowledgeable) squadron under their extremely efficient and pleasant leader, Wing Commander J.D. Rollinson.

The newly appointed 104 Squadron Intelligence Officer was far more of a beginner than any of the squadron aircrews. I still held the rank of acting pilot officer — the lowest and most humble of officer ranks — and the posting to No 104 Squadron was really my first to a unit which I could think of as my own. Apart from the two short Intelligence courses, watching a few briefings, and doing some interrogations, I still had everything to learn about aircrews, their aircraft and bombing operations in general.

I had not yet undertaken an Intelligence briefing on my own and the prospect was somewhat frightening. I had not flown in a Wellington bomber nor in any type of service aircraft. Some of the technical terms used in bombing and flying were unfamiliar to me. The conditions in an aircraft bombing a defended target were mere guesswork or hypothetical images conjured up by my mind after a single viewing of the RAF war film *Target for Tonight*.

At Kabrit I was suddenly plunged up to my neck in a new world of targets, flak information, bomb types and tonnages, flares, flame floats, bomb bursts, searchlights, pinpoints and checks on position, air combats with night fighters, accidents and woundings, questions and answers, the problems of close human relationships with men tired and tense after an 'op' over enemy territory. After interrogation came the final problem for Intelligence of making an analysis of the bombing reports from air crews and assessment of the degree of success of the mission. It was obvious — as had been told me in the past during Intelligence courses — that human factors were vital in getting accurate information from tired crews. An IO had to know his job thoroughly and be respected and trusted by the crews before accuracy of reporting and assessment could be obtained.

In the circumstances of February 1942 of constant bombing operations it was imperative that I learn fast and I was keen to do so. A period of intense and interesting training on the job lay ahead.

On 30th January 1942 RAF Station Kabrit was officially disbanded as such and reformed as No 236 Medium Bomber Wing operating Nos 104 and 148 Wellington Bomber Squadrons. The change meant little at the time but was in keeping with a plan to make the wings and squadrons mobile, ready to move to advanced landing grounds in the Western Desert as and when moves in the front line made it necessary to operate bombers away from the permanent bases in the Canal Zone.

In Intelligence Flight Lieutenant Le Grand became Senior Intelligence Officer of 236 Wing assisted by the two squadron IOs.

The two squadrons came separately to the Station Headquarters Briefing Room for briefing by their own commanders, by the SIO or Squadron IO, by the Wing or Squadron Navigation Officer, Meteorological Officer, Armament Officer, Signals Officer etc. Briefing was a team affair and taken seriously as an essential part of a bombing mission.

The bombing policy for our squadrons originated at the highest level from directives of the War Cabinet which were converted into targets by the target planning sections of HQ RAF, ME and 205 Group HQ. In the Wing we received a Bombing Form (B Form) detailing the target, number of aircraft required, bomb load and type of bombs to be carried, etc. Photo reconnaissance was used to ascertain state of a target area before and after our bombing attacks.

The scale of operations in February was steady at a fairly high level with Benghazi, enemy desert landing grounds used by fighters and Stukas, airfields and ports in Crete and Greece as our main targets together with an occasional shipping strike against an enemy convov to reduce the supplies reaching Rommel from Italy.

My job was to be at Intelligence in the mornings from 09.00 hours to 13.00 hours, answering questions from Group HQ concerning the previous night's operation, arranging material for aircrews to study and read, preparing for the evening briefings on a new target, preparing escape aids and instructions on security, and keeping the records up to date.

After lunch the afternoons were mainly free until 16.00 hours when we returned to Intelligence for the squadron briefings — usually one at 16.00 hours and the other at 17.00 hours. As IOs we prepared blackboard displays of the target and its defences, plus route maps and target maps for issue to the navigators and bomb aimers. One Intelligence Officer was detailed to do the Intelligence briefing in the form of a five-minute description of the target, the reason for its importance, the target defences, relevant background information of the war situation, emphasizing the value of our bombing attack as a contribution to the war effort.

Briefing meant giving this Intelligence information to some 120 aircrew members in front of the group captain commanding the wing or station, the wing commander of the squadron, the two flight commanders (squadron leaders by rank) and the various technical officers of the wing and squadron. The atmosphere in the briefing room could be tense at times when the target was known to be well defended and some of the men in front of you were well aware that this might be their own final briefing. A touch of humour from an experienced and respected leader could help relax the group but the audience could be cynical and deal ruthlessly with any misplaced humour by a lesser man — particularly if he was a non-flying type. In these early days I was conscious of my own ignorance and deficiencies, and became tense and worried by the strain of briefing. As a former schoolmaster I often reflected on the vast difference between talking to a calm respectful school assembly and briefing these groups of young men not much older than sixth-form boys but now involved in the deadly business of war. Flight Lieutenant Le Grand, the SIO, was also a schoolmaster by profession in civilian life — he had been teaching at Radley School near Oxford.

After the second squadron briefing the Intelligence staff went off for a meal at the officers mess and then a duty officer returned to the Intelligence department and went out to the flarepath at any time from 19.30 hours to midnight to see the take-off and deal with any last minute information to be given to crews. Occasionally a last minute change in the target would require us to rush around the dispersals with different target maps and details of any other consequent changes in the mission.

Depending on the number of aircraft operating we were on night duty for interrogations and preparation of a raid report called an OPSUM — an operation summary which had to be phoned to Group HQ and then followed by typed details sent by despatch rider. Before the Opsum was completed we had to study the photographs taken with bombing.

The first crew back would circle the station at about 04.00 hours perhaps and the next three hours would be hectic for the IOs, welcoming and interrogating the crews who were served tea as they came in to our quarters straight from their aircraft. Tables with chairs for the crew members and an IO were set up and each crew interrogation took from ten to fifteen minutes. We sometimes did up to 15 interrogations but an average at Kabrit was about six to eight crews for each intelligence officer on duty. On occasions the group captain or wing commander would do some of the interrogations for us — filling in the necessary bombing reports to avoid crews having to wait for an IO.

Our squadrons each had 24 Wellingtons when at full strength and at normal serviceability some 16 or 20 aircraft might be operating from each squadron. In emergency times every available aircraft might be put in the air for an operation and on many occasions with serious crises and short distance targets such as before and during the Battle of Alamein, we operated double or even triple sorties during one night. [Sorties, strikes, missions, raids, operations — same thing!]

By about 07.00 hours the Opsum had been prepared and phoned and the IOs could get off to breakfast. We often had our meal with the last of the aircrews lingering over their breakfast and talking shop. Then to bed and if lucky we could spend a few hours there before coming back on duty.

When a single IO was operating with his own squadron without help he had to be up again about 10.00 ready for details coming in about the new target for the coming night. In times of severe operating conditions it was thus a desperate matter to get enough sleep. A 'stand down' of squadrons was a blessed relief in the circumstances.

Sometimes a squadron would be required by Group to operate up to nine nights in a row and an IO would average about three hours' sleep during that period. It was pretty ghastly for one's nerves but I always consoled myself that I was lucky because at least my job was a safe one and almost all my friends were aircrew officers or sergeants who were risking their necks nightly, while I was merely missing sleep.

In February 1942 I quickly got to know, like and respect my squadron aircrew colleagues — both officers and sergeants — and found that the more interest I took in flying the more information I got from crews in interrogation. I could see clearly that it was my duty to go on operations with some of our crews and sought permission for this from my squadron commanding officer and group captain. Both agreed that it was a sound idea and they promised to arrange for me to fly on a bombing operation.

The pace of operations began to increase during February and conditions were such that the achievement of going on an operational mission was delayed for me until September 1942.

In order to increase the bomb load or range of our aircraft it was decided that the squadrons should use advanced landing grounds in the Daba area. The Wellingtons took on their bomb-loads at Kabrit with sufficient fuel to reach Daba and have a reserve to return if necessary. At ALG the aircraft were refuelled for the operation. The aircrews got last minute meteorological and intelligence details at a shortened form of briefing at the ALG before going on to their targets.

On returning from the mission the aircraft landed at the ALG for the crews to be interrogated by an IO on the spot before flying home to Kabrit over the Delta.

In a matter of weeks this interim policy changed to a Group decision that all the Wellington squadrons would move up into the desert for operations leaving the Canal bases for repair and maintenance work such as engine changes. At this time there was considerable argument in the squadrons and messes as to the wisdom of trying to maintain and operate bombers as large and complicated as the Wellingtons in conditions of open desert with no protection from blowing sand. As will be seen later the success of the Desert Wellingtons was not proven until 1943 but by then the squadrons were hardened and acclimatised to the conditions and rather proud of their mobility.

*

4th February 1942

After some work on briefing I went to see the bombing-up of aircraft for tonight's operation and was surrounded by bomb trolleys. 'The Beautiful Bomb' is anything but beautiful, but looks efficient and formidable (4,000 lb block buster). At 12.15 we had a visit to Intelligence by the AOC 205 Group (Air Commodore McLean) with Group Captain Kellett (SASO) and Group Captain Fall (Station Commander at Kabrit). In the afternoon I played tennis with Pilot Officer Palmer (pilot) and in the evening some games of table tennis with Pilot Officer Boyers (navigator). Both are nice chaps and aircrew members of 104 Squadron. Jimmy Boyers and I share a room near the officers' mess as single quarters are rare luxuries here. He is an experienced operational type who came out from Driffield with the original detachment of 104 Squadron and has operated over Germany and from Malta, and now will complete his tour in the Middle East.

6th February 1942

We interrogated ten squadron aircraft back from Benghazi. They saw plenty of fires and had little opposition except for about six light A/A, two S/Ls and possibly two heavy A/A guns.

In the afternoon I walked along the shore of the Bitter Lake to the west. It is spoilt by the filthy habit of the Arabs of putting dead or dying animals along the shore. A camel, two dogs, and a porpoise were among the smelly debris. We can't blame the Arabs for the porpoise!

7th February 1942
Briefing for Salamis — the Greek naval dockyard near Athens now used by the Germans. There was an ENSA Show this evening — only fair! The show was opened by a chorus and before pulling back the curtains it was obvious that some females were in the party. Alas for the audience's hopes — they were two middle-aged and plumpish women. However one sang well and the other played an accordion. The poor Station Dental Officer had some terrible moments as he was hauled on to the stage by the singer to be sung to personally — poor chap.

8th February 1942
Interrogation of Salamis crews. No results were seen owing to accurate S/Ls and flak. There was strong opposition from the Dog's Tail peninsula and from Salamis shore but little from the dockyard. In the afternoon I went to Shallufa with the bombing reports.

9th February 1942: Inside a Bomber
This afternoon I went for a walk to Kabrit Point with a very pleasant New Zealand observer from a Whitley bomber which dropped in recently on a special mission from UK. We climbed all over the Whitley — 'Lulu' by name. It's the first time I've been inside a bomber and afterwards I felt even more respect for the quiet chap explaining it all to me. The complicated mechanism and gadgets make it difficult to see how anyone masters them all. In the evening at the cinema it was *Miami — New York* with Claudette Colbert and Clark Gable. It was an old theme and I didn't like seeing reminders of what I'm missing away from home.

10th February 1942
Misty this morning with the ground very damp. However it soon cleared off. The results from Keros were poor. Flight Sergeant Vertican and his crew did marvellously well to get back on one engine and make a safe landing at Kasfareet near here. This afternoon we had briefing for Leros again and also for the Martuba landing grounds. With Le Grand I played tennis beating Hartley and Perkins 6–2, 6–2, and the games were most enjoyable. We

worked late in the evening until 20.00 hours, checking on flak at various targets. Mail came in today but still none for me — I'm getting really fed up about it — nothing since I left UK in November!

11th February 1942
Le Grand had an interview today for flying duties at Shallufa. I was left on my own for once and rather enjoyed the experience. Prepared the briefings for Salamis, Piraeus and Heraklion. Later, operations were cancelled tonight owing to bad weather. A sandstorm is beginning to blow up from the south. The smell of the Suez Oil Refinery doesn't add to the pleasures of the desert — it's a horrible smell!

12th February 1942: First Flight in a Bomber
It was an enjoyable day because I went on a test flight of the Whitley 'O for Orange' with the New Zealanders Pilot Officer Munro (pilot) and Pilot Officer Orchard (navigator — he is thirty-five years old and an architect with wife and two little girls back in New Zealand). They asked if I'd like to come and this was actually my first flight in an RAF aircraft. 'Lulu' flew herself off and rather to my surprise I hadn't any qualms at all. My ears felt the noise and height but otherwise it was most enjoyable and interesting, viewing Kabrit, Fayid and the Bitter Lakes from the air. The Suez Canal dredged area in the lakes can be clearly seen. Afterwards I helped box the compass for 'Lulu' as Munro, Orchard and crew are preparing to go back to UK.

13th February 1942
I completed the Opsum and narrative reports for the Heraklion operation of last night. It proved to be a busy day and not too enjoyable in the office part of it due to an argument over the expression 'bomb tit' (bomb release switch). Boyers says this is the only name he's ever heard for it! He told me the old joke about kit inspection in the DROs at a UK station being misspelt and causing a flurry with the WAAFs.

14th February 1942: Whitley Returns to UK
This was the famous day at Acroma when two Kittyhawk Squadrons No 3 RAAF and 112 RAF attacked 30 Huns and shot down 20. I wrote my twentieth letter to D. — this is to be sent home by the Whitley to England. The Whitley take-off was at 21.30 so I

Wellington bombers over the Nile Delta flying westwards on a bombing mission March 1942

104 Squadron RAF March 1942
Wing Commander P. A. Beare DSO, DFC is seated at the centre, to the left of him are
F/O R. Ginn and Squadron Leader H. M. Young DFC, and to the right Squadron Leader
D. J. Brown DFC.

Arming a Wellington at Kabrit for a bombing operation

Sergeant Wills and his crew crash landed behind the enemy lines but returned safely to Kabrit

Wellingtons of 205 group waiting for their bomb loads.

went out to the dispersal point where Lulu was kept and gave Pilot Officer Orchard my letter. Then we watched her start up and rumble down to the end of the runway. There was a pause and off she went along the flarepath and up into the darkness over the Bitter Lake enroute for home. It was rather romantic and I do hope that they make it safely — they're grand types.
[Pilot Officer Munro later achieved fame as one of the Dambuster Squadron 617.]

15th February 1942
There was rain in the night and it was still gently falling when I got up — the first rain since I came to Egypt. The sand is quite damp and even slippery in parts where it seems to be more like marl when wet. I drew £5 from Accounts — a nasty piece of work there! It was my job to do the Opsum for gardening (laying mines) and bombing Benghazi last night. Pilot Officer Perkins left for Shallufa today after some trouble with his flight commander. His squadron think it's a scandalous piece of work. I don't know the flight commander but Perkins is a very fine chap. [Later Perkins joined a Liberator Squadron.] At the flicks in the evening it was Eleanor Powell and Fred Astaire in *Broadway Melody of 1940*. Rather good apart from poor reproduction by our cinema apparatus.

16th February 1942
During a slack morning I prepared briefing notes for Benghazi, Berca and Benina. Pilot Officer Archer, IO, called to collect his things as he is off to Malta with his squadron. Our Intelligence cat is in the wars — not only is she in a certain condition but her starboard front paw is septic, poor old thing.

At 17.15 hours a flying boat or amphibian shot up the Mess three times and then came in to land — whew!

18th February 1942: First Flight in a Wellington
Rain before 07.00 hours and a light drizzle as we went to breakfast. Le Grand today gave a talk on Intelligence to some new crews. Apparently he has not been accepted for flying duties — but I like the fact that he tried. I prepared briefing notes for Milos. Today I had my first flight in a Wellington (Wimpy) by going on a test flight in 'R for Robert', 104 Squadron, with Pilot Officer Benitz and Pilot Officer Morton. It was good fun and we did some steep turns and shallow dives with pull-ups while viewing the Gulf

of Suez from the air. The Intelligence cat was sent to Sick Quarters but has escaped from a medical orderly as he was getting into the ambulance with her. She is still missing tonight.

19th February 1942
Quite heavy rain fell today early in the morning and pools formed outside the Mess. I started a build-up of 1/1 million maps of Greece, Izmir, Crete and Alexandria before going to a Combined Operations Film dealing with various boats, etc. used for landing purposes. It looked a pretty grim business to me. The Navy and Army were well represented in the cinema for the film.

The Intelligence cat returned today so the SIO and I took her down to sick quarters in a basket. No mistake this time — she's there!

20th February 1942
Operations were cancelled today because of high winds and a sandstorm. This morning I completed the map build-up at the section. In the afternoon I had a grand time on the Link Flying Trainer with Pilot Officer Morton. He very kindly gave me some useful lessons. I had over an hour, climbing, flying straight and level, rate one turns left and right, correcting stalls and spins. The trainer gives one the feeling of being in control of a plane. In the evening after dinner I played table tennis and lost to Grant. Table tennis is great fun with a good opponent and it's something to look forward to instead of the bar.

22nd February 1942: My First Briefing
I gave my first-ever briefing today and it was very brief too! Still it was on my own and very suddenly thrown on me as 104 Squadron appeared for their first ME briefing — to attack an enemy convoy at sea. It was good practice for me as Le Grand has gone up to LG09 an advanced landing ground in the desert near Daba. In the afternoon I went to the Point to assist in mooring one of the club's yachts with Pilot Officer Pope (pilot) who is the skipper of Jimmy Boyers' crew.

23rd February 1942: Mail
Mail arrived today — the first home news for nearly four months. Otherwise it was a hell of a day dealing with bombing reports for both our squadrons who had been sent out in bad weather to

attack a big Axis convoy coming over to supply Rommel. Only
one plane was successful in the difficult conditions and everybody
is badly 'browned off' about the affair. Group were in a flap and
'R for Robert' of 148 Squadron (Sergeant Hamilton) is missing
— the first aircraft and crew lost since I came to Kabrit. We
worked from 08.15 to 13.15 and then from 13.50 to 19.30
with no break. I reached the mess for dinner tired out and a bit
glum — then came the joyful find in the letter rack of four letters.
Afterwards I was inspired to beat Grant three games to nil at table
tennis!

24th February 1942: First Duty Flight
An interesting day. I briefed on Benghazi in the morning and then
was ordered by 205 Group to go up to LG09 to do interrogations
with Pilot Officer Allen of Shallufa. I watched the bombing-up
and we took off at 15.40 in 'B for Bertie' 104 Squadron piloted
by my tennis friend Pilot Officer Palmer, for LG09. The trip over
the Delta was enjoyable and exactly as I had imagined. This was
also my first view of the blue Mediterranean from the air and
details were very clear from 2,000 feet. We arrived at 17.25
making a good landing with the full bombload. I reported to Wing
Commander Beare, 104 Squadron, my commanding officer, who
was in charge of the operation. We had brown stew and rice pudding for 'dinner'. After another briefing I watched one or two of
the aircraft take-off and then went to bed on a table top. It was
very cold during the night and I was very thankful for Pilot
Officer Gray's kind loan of his flying-jacket. LG09 is nothing more
than a runway scraped from a flat piece of desert with a few
tents to accommodate the men stationed here to refuel the Wellingtons. There are some ominous wrecks of aircraft here and there
around the perimeter.

25th February 1942
The first plane came back at about 03.20 and I did about eight
interrogations. It was not too bad a show except for the timing
problem. With Allen, I did the Opsum and phoned it to Wing HQ
or Advanced Group HQ whichever it is, at Qotaifiya near Daba.
We travelled back to Kabrit on 'S for Sugar' 148 Squadron,
(Pilot Officer Harper, an Australian pilot). I thought we hadn't
climbed much from 09 and when I looked out of the astrodome
I saw the desert outcrops and scrub rushing by at fantastic speed.
We were only 50 feet or even less above the ground. We shot-up

motor transport on the Alex-Mersa Matruh road — then rose for
a while. Later we went down over the Delta to shoot-up the wogs
at 50 feet again, causing camels, oxen, donkeys, dogs, sheep,
goats and wogs to scatter hurriedly. One native dived off his bike
as I watched. At one canal we were below the top of the high
lateen sail of a barge and tried to blow the boat over with our
propeller wash. We took off at 07.40 and landed at 09.20 at Kabrit
after cruising at 170 mph most of the way and getting over 200
for a while. The morning was spent at Intelligence checking the
bombing reports. Unhappily, 'E for Edward' (Sergeant Richardson
of 104 Squadron) is missing from last night's operation. This is
the first aircraft and crew to be lost in the Middle East operations
of my squadron.

26th February 1942

Briefing was for Benghazi again and enemy shipping in the harbour
is to be attacked. I was again ordered to LG09 and took off at
15.35 with Sergeant Povey (pilot), Pilot Officer Craig (2nd pilot)
and Pilot Officer Mahood (navigator) in their aircraft 'B' of 148
Squadron — loaded this time with a 4,000 lb bomb. We landed at
LG09 just under two hours later and this time I travelled in the
front turret and was able to map-read the route we were following
via Tanta in the Delta. These pilots think nothing of landing with
their full bomb loads at ALG and Sergeant Povey set 'B for Beer'
down quite gently. Additional briefing was given by Wing Commander Rollinson, CO of 148 Squadron, who is a jolly nice chap
and pleasantly friendly — even to junior intelligence officers. He
offered to help interrogate as there were eleven aircraft operating.
I slept in the Intelligence tent again on a table top. Murray who
was with me is a cipher officer. There was noise of distant
bombing by enemy aircraft on the Fuka landing grounds used by
our own fighters — some twenty miles away towards the front
line. Today I felt rather queer with signs of 'gippy tummy' — a
most unpleasant stomach disorder with violent pains, nausea and
diarrhoea.

27th February 1942

We were aroused at 01.00 hours by a plane returning. It turned
out to be a beginner on a trial flight. Later our planes came in
with a rush and I was thankful for Wing Commander Rollinson's
help. Murray helped do the Opsum which was very kind of him.
We finished at 05.30 and phoned Flight Lieutenant Wise, the SIO,

at Wing HQ. We returned to Kabrit without breakfast as before and in 'M for Mother' 104 Squadron, Pilot Officer Ellis (pilot) and Pilot Officer Proctor (navigator). It was a pleasant journey but I was rather too tired to appreciate it. We breakfasted and then had a hectic morning getting the bombing reports typed and ready, seeing photos and answering questions on the phone.

*

During February 1942 I had flown six times in bomber aircraft and was now accustomed to the experience. This was just as well because the month of March was to provide new variations in flying experience.

CHAPTER TWO

Wellingtons in the Desert

In March I was suddenly posted from the relative comfort of a base station at Kabrit in the Canal Zone to become a desert dweller as resident Intelligence Officer at Advanced Landing Ground No 106. The location was open sandy desert and scrubland close to the road and railway line at Sidi Abd el Rahman, a tiny Arab village with a mosque. We were about two miles from the Mediterranean coast and some eighty-five miles west of Alexandria. Although it appeared unimportant at the time the next station down the line towards Alexandria was El Alamein, about fifteen miles away from LG106.

*

1st March 1942
I briefed — very briefly — on Benghazi, and then flew up to LG09 in 'B for Bertie' of 148 Squadron with another 4,000 lb bomb slung in the bomb bay. Sergeant Dixon was the pilot this time and my friend Pilot Officer Mahood again the navigator. It was bumpy and hazy en route and a sandstorm blew up after we landed. Operations were cancelled and I spent the night on a stretcher in an ambulance — comfortable except for the severe cold and the usual trouble in such conditions — got up twice!

3rd March 1942: RAF Station Kabrit bombed
The day at LG09 started about 03.30 when the first of 25 Wellingtons came in. There was a general rush of crews in at 05.30. Pilot Officer Allen and I finished work at 08.30 and boarded 'O for Orange' 37 Squadron (Pilot Officer Birmingham) as we had had a signal that Kabrit had been bombed in the night and was out of action. [37 Squadron operate from Shallufa.] It was an exciting journey with quite a touch of 'flap'. The aircraft was a Wellington Ic with Pegasus engines one of which kept banging and cutting out occasionally. We made a forced landing at Heliopolis (RAF Station) where we shaved and lunched in state at the officers' mess. The engine fault could not be located so we took off again

and fortunately reached Shallufa safely. Then I went back by MT to Kabrit. There was no apparent damage but I saw a delayed action bomb go up as we arrived. Squadron Leader Baird of 148 Squadron landed back at Kabrit this morning and finished up over an unexploded bomb on the runway.

4th March 1942
There was another Red Warning tonight but the bombing and AA fire was in the distance towards Ismailia. I heard today of the fine escape of Pilot Officer Crossley, Pilot Officer Baron and crew of 148 Squadron who came down in the drink. Their Wellington floated for three minutes just enough for all to get safely into the rubber dinghy. A sea-rescue boat took them to Alexandria. They arrived back here last night by train and were interrogated this morning when Squadron Leader Bartlett (Group Intelligence Officer) and Flight Lieutenant Brown from Group were present to hear the story. Crossley and crew did all the ditching procedures perfectly.

5th March 1942: Combat — Wellington versus Junkers 88
Today I received sudden orders to go to ALG106 via 09. I packed hastily and got on 'G George' 104 Squadron (Pilot Officer Dickenson, pilot, and Pilot Officer Beach, navigator). We had an unpleasant journey with low cloud and rain over the desert west of the Delta. We failed to locate 09 first time and after stooging around decided to find Daba on the road and railway and try again from there. On the way back towards the coast I was in the astrohatch (a plastic dome on top of the fuselage) trying to recognise some ground feature which could be located on the map. We were flying at 1,000 feet above the desert when I saw some bomb bursts on the ground to starboard and shortly afterwards this was confirmed by a radio message repeated over the intercom, that the advanced landing grounds in the Daba area were being attacked by enemy bombers.

Suddenly there was some vibration in our Wellington and the smell of gunsmoke — then I saw tracer coming from the rear direction and flashing by just above the astrohatch. Immediately the source of the tracer became obvious — a Ju88 was slightly above us and overtaking and then sliding away on the starboard side while our rear gunner fired at the enemy with the turret guns.

I hastily ducked down from the plastic dome as if one could find protection within the fabric-covered fuselage of a Wellington and gesticulated and shouted to the navigator, Pilot Officer Beach, standing alongside me. He gave a wry sort of smile and a wave of the hand as if to imply that this crisis was up to the skipper and rear gunner — not us! Together we shut the light steel protecting doors between the dome and the tail and fondly hoped that these would stop the enemy bullets. I also remember doing some rapid praying!

Pilot Officer Dickenson took most violent evasive action, climbing into low cloud and then diving down and circling near the ground when cloud was absent. One diving attack from the rear and another from the port beam were avoided by our quick manoeuvres. Inside the Wellington we were pressed down almost through the floor one minute then flung to one side or found ourselves almost floating with the sudden changes of direction. The Ju88 made another attack and our rear gunner got in several bursts as the enemy lined up astern and then overtook us and broke away to port. He disappeared into cloud and was not seen again. I was interested to note that our tracer looked like water from a hose in a wind and that the Ju had a black diamond painted on the side of the fuselage.

When I saw the Ju88 completely behind and above us on this final attack I fully expected this was the end of 'G for George'. Had the Ju88 possessed forward firing cannon as in the night fighter version he could not have missed us — but it must have been a bomber for he fired only small calibre tracer at us from forward guns and from a position under the fuselage.

We were glad to receive a recall to base and arrived at dusk, making a perfect landing with full bomb load intact. We had not jettisoned our bombs during the combat.

It was a wizard show by the Captain (Pilot Officer Dickenson) and the rear gunner in particular, but the entire crew did well — there was no panic or flap. We did 280 mph at times and were able to turn in smaller circles than the Ju88, but the enemy aircraft was clearly faster than our Wellington.

After my first experience of being under fire I noticed that my mouth was dry and my knees felt weak — either from the strains of evasive action or from sheer funk!

We were interrogated as a crew by Flight Lieutenant Le Grand, the SIO, who filled in a Combat (Bomber) Report about the incident. To have a combat between two bomber aircraft is rare indeed and this one probably occurred because of sheer exuberance and adventurous aggression by the German crew after the excitement of dropping their own bombload on one of our ALGs. 'G for George' countered the attack by equally good defensive action and suffered no casualties or damage.

6th March 1942

Again I was sent to 09, this time flying in 'H for Harry' 37 Squadron, Pilot Officer Pilley (pilot). The weather was still hazy with air conditions bumpy and I didn't feel too happy this time — the result of my last two flying trips involving a forced landing and a combat. At 09 I assisted Hill with interrogations.

7th March 1942

Another change of life for me — I am now to live in the desert at LG106. Flight Lieutenant Wise, the SIO of 231 Wing, picked me up at 09 and took me to Qotaifiya. Then I went by transport to LG106, my new home, which I liked on my first impressions of the place and of the officers — Flying Officer Hambleton ('Tex') in charge of LG106, Pilot Officer James (ciphers) and 'Doc', Flight Lieutenant Anthony. At night I briefed on shipping in Benghazi harbour.

8th March 1942

After interrogations I began the process of settling in. My stomach felt none too good during the morning — change of diet I suppose. I got busy on the Intelligence tent and dug part of a trench near my tent.

13th March 1942

15 Wellingtons turned up today in very pukkah style in formation with mid guns mounted at the ready. They peeled off at the landing ground like fighters. Two of the 148 Squadron lads shot up the Intelligence tent. It's rather funny to think that this formation flying from Kabrit to ALG is due to our combat in 'G for George' 104 Squadron with the Ju88 on 5th March. It has wakened up the squadrons and they are taking measures against possible attacks. At the briefing by Squadron Leader Young he shut me out entirely. He is a very large and formidable man with great experience and fame as a courageous bomber pilot but seems impatient with non-flying types such as IOs. I can understand this.

14th March 1942

Twelve crews were interrogated between 04.00 and 08.30. Two
aircraft went u/s before take-off and one Wellington went back
direct to Kabrit. It was quite a useful operation on the whole and
not unlucky for any crews in spite of being Friday the 13th with
13 aircraft operating — and Sergeant Mayhew on his 13th 'op'
with four of his crew! — he told me this with a cheerful grin while
I was filling in the report for his crew.

15th March 1942: Diversion to LG106

I worked at the files and target information in the morning after
being roused during the night by the diversion of some fifteen
Wellingtons from 37 and 40 Squadrons to our LG. 'Operations'
roused me at 03.15 and I went to bed again after 04.00 as there
was no interrogation needed. They partly wrecked our officers'
mess tent and drank some quantity of drinks but I can't blame
them entirely as I thought we should have had the cooks up to get
them a meal.

In the afternoon seventeen aircraft from 104, 148 and 37
Squadrons arrived and were briefed for Benghazi by Squadron
Leader Baird who was in charge of the operation. His arrangements worked smoothly and efficiently. Pilot Officer Crossley
and his crew arrived to help with operations at LG106. He
becomes Flying Control and Operations Officer and is sharing my
tent.

16th March 1942

The usual interrogations were dealt with in the early morning. In
the afternoon seven Wellingtons from 37 Squadron arrived including my friends Pilot Officer Birmingham and Pilot Officer
Pilley with whom I've flown. A bad Met Report with strong NE
to SE winds caused operations to be cancelled to the relief of all —
ourselves because of the need for a good night's sleep. I slept well
in spite of wind, flapping tent and blowing sand.

17th March 1942: Crash at LG106

Today we had miserable weather with a strong wind blowing sand
in everywhere. You don't have to be irritated to 'grit your teeth' —
the sand sees to that!

At 1600 hours I saw my first crash since joining the RAF —
there have been several others on aerodromes while I've been
present but I've never seen the actual 'prang'.

A special Signals Wellington with aerials mounted on the fuselage was taking off at far end of runway and when it had done half its necessary run the undercart collapsed as we watched. The props came off, the starboard engine caught fire and clouds of white smoke arose as the plane skated along on its belly for 150 yards. The crash lorry put out the fire very quickly and all the crew were found to be safe, thank goodness. It might have been a lot worse. It was terribly dark tonight and very difficult to find our tent from the mess.

18th March 1942

Today it is blowing worse than ever and sand is everywhere in tents and food. After breakfast it rained for a while but nothing would stop the wind and dust. In the afternoon I wrote home and watched the storm. In the midst of this a Wellington came over, circled and by a miracle got down. It was from another squadron and had previously tried to land at LG104.

The evening was clear and cold and I went with Don Crossley to watch the flarepath being laid out — about 1,300 yards of goose neck flares and glim lamps with a Chance light at the landing end.

19th March 1942: Pilot Officer Don Crossley

Over a morning cup of tea in our tent, Don Crossley and I settled the world's problems. He seems to think that there will always be wars and that spiritual improvement matters more than anything else. I argued that wars are not inevitable — that everyone hates war — that there is a need for policing the world just as Great Britain developed its own law and order. Don is doubtful if the world has improved — I'm sure that it has. He obviously has strong fundamental religious beliefs and is a very confident, intelligent and capable man at everything he does — a born leader!

20th March 1942: Aircraft on Fire

Seventeen Wellingtons arrived for northern aerodrome targets and during the briefing an airman dashed in to the tent to report 'An aircraft is on fire'. Sure enough, it was well alight and the glare could be seen through the canvas or gaps in the tent. A bomber on fire means an explosion within minutes so briefing was postponed and we scattered and waited for the bombs to go up. I went to my trench and had several aircrew chaps with me to take shelter. It took quite a time it seemed — then came a series of shattering explosions with the most amazing fireworks I've ever seen — Very lights, flares, ammunition, bombs, sending fragments hundreds of feet into the air — then ominous whizzing noises and thuds as the pieces of metal came back to earth. The Wellington destroyed was 'T Tommy' of 104 Squadron; apparently a flare had been dropped as it was being loaded — it ignited and could not be extinguished. No one was injured.

We resumed briefing and eventually only nine aircraft took off for the missions. The Wellingtons nearest the wrecked aircraft were cancelled as a safety precaution.

21st March 1942: Boyers and Pope

A ghastly day! I finished interrogations with the help of Pilot Officer Allen (on his way to relieve Tennant) and sent in the Opsum and Narrative by 09.30 hours.

To my sorrow, 'R for Robert' 104 Squadron is missing, in which I've flown and in which were my friends Jimmy Boyers (navigator) with whom I shared a room at Kabrit, and Pilot Officer Pope (pilot). There is no news. I can't help feeling depressed. By the way, only the gaunt tail of 'Tommy' remains — the rest was blown to fragments — Don Crossley says aircraft with bombs always go like that, leaving only the tail. I wrote to D. to try to cheer myself and enclosed a drawing of a Wellington for Duncan. In the evening there was a sudden call to help the IO at LG09 — a three hour journey by truck on spine-shattering tracks with thick dust.

22nd March 1942: Aircraft Lost While on Search

I completed ten interrogations and among these was a report by Pilot Officer Watson and crew of a torch flashing from the sea Lat. 33° O1N Long. 27°27E, which could have been the dinghy from 'R Robert' (104 Squadron). The information was passed to Wing and a search was started but the weather was frightfully rough and cold with another sandstorm blowing. Later I heard the terrible news that one of the searching planes had gone into the drink. I had to report the torch sighting and now this extra tragedy has resulted. There is still no news of 'R for Robert' 104 or the crew.

Flight Lieutenant Wise was decent about the matter over the phone but one can't forget it. Fortunately my conscience is reasonably clear in that I was reporting a matter which if unreported would always have meant the possibility that Pope and Boyers and crew were left to drown.

24th March 1942
Back at LG106 I interrogated all thirteen crews back from northern targets and the results were better than recently. Squadron Leader Brown, 'B' Flight Commander of 104 Squadron, was friendly and helpful this morning as always. He suggested that the 'torch signals' seen by Pilot Officer Watson may have been the flickering of a flame float. Still no news of 'R Robert' 104.

In the afternoon we had operations again and seven Wellingtons arrived in formation. A Met Officer turned up from Wing HQ. One aircraft came back early with engine trouble and the weather beat the others. There was much low cloud over the target.

25th March 1942: A Khamsin
My interrogations finished about 07.00 hours and I had breakfast and went to my tent. Sand was already beginning to rise. At 07.45 there was a gale warning and further signal — 'All aircraft to get back to base as soon as possible'. All got off except 'P Peter' who couldn't get started before a terrible dust storm from the south swept over LG106. The hours that followed were the most uncomfortable that I've ever experienced in my life. The wind was hot and stifling — the tent filled with dust which matted the hair, filled the nose and ears, and blocked the corners of the eyes — covering the contents of the tent with a brown layer. The flap of the tent broke loose and I had to don a gas mask to get it fixed. The front of the tent faced the storm and dust simply poured in so I had to open the back of the tent and transfer sandbags to the front and lash everything up to close all openings. Even then the air inside the tent was full of dust and it was most uncomfortable to breathe. I wore my gas mask to get relief. Going outside to fasten the guy ropes on one occasion my hat blew off and I chased it — completely losing sight of the tent. By going upwind against the storm I got back safely but it was quite eerie being unable to see anything but flying sand and dust — and rather frightening for obviously this was a storm in which people could be smothered and lose their lives.

About 10.30 there was the noise of a truck above the storm and an armourer came stumbling in — he was lost. He stayed until there was a slight lull about 12.30 when I lent him an eyeshield and he drove off into the storm to find his tent.

Soon afterwards I made my way, with compass in case I got lost, to the mess tent where I found the other unfortunates including Don Crossley, sitting there choking and coughing with handkerchiefs over mouths and eye shields on. At about 15.00 hours the storm slackened and we got a welcome cup of tea.

Then the wind changed direction entirely and suddenly — within five to ten minutes it veered round to NW and the temperature dropped quickly. The dust wasn't quite so bad as before but we were unable to do anything but lie still.

About 19.00 hours it slackened sufficiently for us to get a meal and at 20.00 I made my way back to my tent — visibility now about a hundred yards instead of less than ten yards. It was impossible to get rid of the sand so I shook my blankets and nearly choked myself — then lay down in my clothes, tired out and with a wretched headache from the storm. My stomach felt none too good from the sand consumed and during the meal I had had to dash outside in case of being sick or having diarrhoea.

26th March 1942
At 07.45 I wakened having slept nearly twelve hours. Thank goodness it's a better day with wind NW cool and a clear sky. We spent the morning cleaning out the tent — sweeping out sand and shaking it out of clothes and from articles.

After lunch we went down to the beach and had our first swim since Aden's glorious warmth at the Goldmour Club. No operations tonight, thank heaven!

Dickie Milburn and a friend came over from Wing to have dinner at our mess and in the midst of the meal our air raid hooter went and we heard a Hun overhead. He circled and came diving down over the mess tent at only 100–200 feet so that we could see the engine exhausts and the cockpit light. It was a Heinkel. He bombed the railway line, came back, circled and bombed again — and we opened up one of our machine-guns at him — foolishly? He then came back to machine-gun us — then up and down the coastal road and also fired at our beacon. Bomb bursts and gunning were also going on just west of us — quite a lively evening for a while. There were some nasty moments as I was twice caught in the open and couldn't find the trench! Life is getting *too* exciting.

28th March 1942
I was wakened at 03.15 but the first aircraft came back about 05.00 hours. There were nine crews to interrogate — one aircraft u/s, and unfortunately 'P Peter' and 'V Victor' are both missing with no definite news of them from the others at the target. No 'ops' tonight.

The mess is annoyed because HQ ME have given an order that bars shall be closed from 18.00 hours tonight to 18.00 hours tomorrow in honour of Mohammed's birthday.

29th March 1942
There is warning of another sandstorm but though the sand is rising it is nothing serious like the *Khamsin*. Twelve Wellingtons turned up but the bad Met Report caused cancellation of the operation. Two postcards from D. She received my 'Whitley' letter which took only ten days and means that Munro and Orchard got back safely to UK.

30th March 1942
Crossley was stung today by a scorpion in his trousers. We found it and killed it and then found two more under a tent flap lying in the ground behind our tent. The sting was very painful and Doc gave a local anaesthetic. Operations at night and this afternoon we had important visitors — Group Captain Gayford and Group Captain Fall. They discussed the pros and cons of the squadrons coming here permanently.

31st March 1942
We went swimming this afternoon, then the truck broke down on the way back and we had to walk from the Mosque (Sidi Abd el Rahman) in the dust, arriving back as sticky and filthy as when we started. A Beaufighter landed today with a big-end gone in one of its engines. In the evening we had enemy aircraft overhead again but they left us alone and concentrated on Daba and LG104.

*

At the end of March I had been in the desert as IO at LG106 for barely four weeks but my relationship with the aircrews from the two Kabrit squadrons had improved noticeably since the combat of 'G for George' 104 Squadron with the Ju88 near Daba. Any stiffness between myself and aircrews seemed to have disappeared. They were amused that an IO had been involved in an air combat and liked to joke that I had become 'operational'.

The general war situation in the desert was becoming a matter of serious unease and it was also very obvious that the Luftwaffe were increasing the scale of their attacks on our airfields and communications.

Number 231 Wing had been established for some time at Qotaifiya, a pleasant camp close to the Mediterranean, and Group plans now required all Wings to become mobile and move to the desert. Our 236 Wing and Squadrons 104 and 148 reached the desert at LG106 only briefly before a new Rommel offensive opened on 26th May against the Gazala Line.

During April and May our squadrons were supporting preparations for an *Allied* ground offensive by sending detachments to Malta against enemy shipping, supply bases and airfields, while the main force of Wellingtons made frequent attacks on Benghazi and the Martuba landing grounds used by enemy fighters and dive-bombers.

The Desert War appeared to be reaching another crisis point and it would soon become necessary to use our fortunate mobility in unexpected retreat.

*

1st April 1942
Another Beaufighter arrived to take off the crew of the damaged Beaufighter which itself remains at LG106 as an object of considerable interest to our personnel, accustomed to nothing but Wimpys.

Friday, 3rd April 1942
Our colourful Texan CO of LG106 (Flying Officer 'Tex' Hambleton) has gone on leave and Pilot Officer Crossley is in charge of the camp. There was an amusing argument at tea time as to what day it was — then we discovered it was Good Friday!

Two Wellingtons arrived to operate with Squadron Leader Brown in charge. It was a pleasant briefing as always with him but the siren went as we finished and Jerry dropped flares a few miles away. Then we heard the crumps of a stick of bombs and saw some Bofors tracer. Our take-off was late as a result of this enemy activity. I asked to go on the 'op' and Squadron Leader Brown was aggreeable but he said that it must be fixed by an order from the Group Captain so that compensation will be OK in the event of any trouble.

7th April 1942
I helped the Doc to shift to a new tent site and in doing so we disturbed a snake, several scorpions and beetles — ugh! Six Wellingtons turned up this afternoon for the usual 'op' to Benghazi —

this is the fifth successive night. Wing Commander Beare, 104, was in charge and operating himself tonight. Briefing was successful owing to my brainwave of getting a copy of Wing Commander Simpson's (70 Squadron) excellent night photograph of the harbour from last night, brought over by Flight Lieutenant Lumsden, the Met Officer.

8th April 1942
We had a Red Warning but it proved to be a raid on Alexandria. Then there was a diversion to our LG106 of three aircraft from 40 Squadron whose crews I interrogated before ours came in. Our 'V for Victor' 104 with a new but very honest skipper achieved an amusing bombing success at Benghazi by aiming at the Central Mole wrecks from 14,500 feet, but actually the bombs hit the base of the Giuliana Mole and started a big fire in a munitions dump or pyrotechnics store. Some crews thought it was an aircraft fire but happily no one was missing. Wing Commander Beare bombed from 7,500 feet and 5,000 feet on two runs across the harbour — what a man! An engineer officer went on the trip with him and probably got some thrills.

In the afternoon I went with Don Crossley into the desert south of LG106 to find an area suitable for laying out a Q Site with dummy flare path to attract enemy bombing away from us. 'Cross' is always thinking of improvements!

9th April 1942
Our Intelligence tent is still being dug out by the Indian soldiers from the Pioneer Corps and it will eventually be three feet below ground level with the tent poles supported on 40-gallon drums cemented into the floor. When finished, the two large EPIP (European Pattern Indian Produced) marquee-type tents linked together will make a fine briefing room — and a safe one, too. This afternoon four Wellingtons of 104 Squadron arrived for briefing on Benghazi.

10th April 1942
This morning I interrogated fifteen crews (from four different squadrons) which is my record so far. Six (148 Squadron) had bombed Heraklion Aerodrome on Crete, seven had attacked Benghazi (four from 104 and three from 37 Squadrons) and two Wellingtons from 40 Squadron had been minelaying. No operations tonight from LG106.

12th April 1942: A Russian Bomber Crew
Today we had fog and then some unusual visitors in the form of
a Russian bomber crew. I interrogated six crews from my squadron back from Heraklion — then four crews from 37 Squadron
who were diverted to us because of fog closing 09. We had large
'money flares' out on our flarepath but the fog reached us before
the aircraft could get down. There were some very anxious
moments and difficult landings. I thought two crews had crashed
from the noise of their 'landings' but they survived and came to
Intelligence quite cheerfully to drink lukewarm tea.

  The Russians arrived later in a four-engined DH86B and were a
bomber crew themselves. We showed them over everything and got
on well. They were more interested in the damaged Beaufighter
with its cannons, than in our Wellingtons. Afterwards Don
Crossley (as Acting CO) said to their captain, when we were
having a drink together in the mess — 'I hope I shall meet you
some day in Moscow'. The Russian replied very firmly, 'I hope to
meet you in *Berlin!*' The interpreter said all Russians were talking
of the day when the British and Russian forces would meet each
other on the continent of Europe. They obviously want us to do
something on the continent and they said what good efforts we
had made at Le Havre and St Nazaire. Afterwards the Russian
crew went off to Qotaifiya to visit 231 Wing and we had a swim.

13th April 1942
The Intelligence tent at LG106 has been completed and I'm rather
proud of it.

14th April 1942
Another duststorm is brewing — commonly called here a 'shit-
storm' — everything is 'shit' — flak is usually referred to by our
aircrews as 'shit coming up'. Breathing was unpleasant at lunch
time but the storm didn't reach *Khamsin* proportions. This evening
I did the map build-up and briefing for the Martuba LGs. Four
Wellingtons of 104 were under the charge of Squadron Leader
Young and the aircraft were afterwards going straight back to
base. The Squadron Leader was more pleasant to me than usual —
it must be the new Intelligence tent.

20th April 1942: Merlins in the Desert
Last night Don Crossley went to sleep very quickly while I was
reading. I heard a plane overhead and went outside but the sound

disappeared. Ten minutes later I heard it again in the direction of our Q site. Presently a truck rushed up and Larry Wells, our Canadian Flying Control Officer, came in and spoke to Crossley who didn't answer. Then Larry said loudly, 'Cross — there are three Wimpys in trouble and I'm going to fire rockets to try to bring them in — are you interested?' Crossley said very clearly and definitely, 'No — not in the slightest!' He then turned over and went to sleep again. I decided to lie awake in case I was needed for interrogation and Larry went off to fire rockets for half an hour or so. Nothing happened. It's rather a joke that this morning Don Crossley remembers nothing of the incident. Actually a Wimpy crew had to bale out last night as they were lost and running out of fuel.

This morning, eight Wellingtons of 104 Squadron — Mark IIs with Merlin engines — arrived for breakfast to avoid the heat of the day with their Merlins. (Merlin engines, so successful on Hurricanes, Spitfires and Lancasters in Britain and Europe, were often a liability in the Western Desert conditions. They overheated easily and developed glycol leaks. In conditions of temperature inversions Merlin Wellingtons found it difficult to climb at take-off. Because of the unsuitability of the liquid cooled Merlins, 148 Squadron were re-equipped with the older and slower radial Pegasus engined Mark IC Wellingtons. However, this did not prevent the RAF from sending Halifax bombers with four Merlin engines to operate in the desert. 462 Squadron (RAAF) joined 236 Wing in November 1942 with Halifax Merlin aircraft. Their serviceability rate in hot weather was very low.)

Today was horrible weather with a strong NW wind with dust and sand blowing everywhere. The Indians of the Pioneer Corps are digging a new tent site for Crossley and myself and finishing another trench as well. We had briefing at 18.45 for 104 Squadron and another briefing at 20.30 for 148 Squadron — ten Mark IC Wellingtons off to Malta. Wing Commander Rollinson did this briefing and also told me that Flight Lieutenant Hill is to relieve me at LG106. A letter arrived for me from Group HQ informing me that I can go on a short air gunners' course in preparation for operational flights. OK!

21st April 1942

A queer birthday — I'm thirty-three today and was wakened before 03.00 hours by the first aircraft back from Benghazi. There were only three interrogations because the others landed

elsewhere and our 'U for Uncle' is unfortunately missing. At
07.00 I got to bed where the flies and the Indians were a nuisance
and sand was already rising again and blowing into the tent.
Crossley was again stung by a scorpion today — this time on a
finger and the finger went numb with pain all up the arm. He also
saw and killed a snake near Intelligence this morning. We moved
into our own new tent later today — very posh and quite roomy
and high with poles raised on petrol tins above the floor — dug
down about two feet below the desert. There were no operations
tonight so I stood drinks in honour of my birthday!

22nd April 1942
Flight Lieutenant Hill arrived to relieve me and he had new information about leave and Intelligence Officers. Le Grand is to go to
Shallufa, Hill as SIO 236 Wing at Kabrit, Allen to 231 Wing, Wise
to start a new wing and myself to return to LG106 after leave.

23rd April 1942
This morning after work and packing up I went back to Kabrit
with Squadron Leader Baird in 'B Bertie' 148 with Peggy engines.
We took off from LG106 at 14.45 and landed at Kabrit at 16.20.
It was an interesting trip and I noted the big changes in the
colouring of the Delta. It's now a golden brown alternating with
green. There is hardly any water in either the Rosetta or the
Damietta — only big pools with little water flowing. Some evidence can be seen of crops being cultivated in the river beds. I had
quite a pleasant welcome at Kabrit from several people I know and
went to the flicks with Pilot Officer Morton who is now captain
of his own aircraft. My old room was available and I'm sharing
with Flight Lieutenant Morris. I thought of Jimmy Boyers.

24th April 1942
Today was mainly a round of visits — firstly to 104 Squadron
office to register with the Adjutant. I got on well with Pilot
Officer Baker and he says Group have put me up for Flying
Officer and our Wing Commander has agreed. Secondly to Accounts
to draw out £35 to send part to D. and to pay for my leave in
Cairo. Next to Intelligence to get up to date and lastly to the
dentist to have my teeth checked. Later I had a swim in the Bitter
Lake which is very buoyant but stings the eyes. Then with Le
Grand I went over to Group to see Squadron Leader Bartlett
(GIO). He was pleasant and says he will return me to LG106 if

possible! I am to go on seven days' leave at once. We returned to Kabrit at 22.30 after a successful day.

25th April 1942 Another Air Raid on Kabrit

I saw the Adjutant again and fixed my leave. The afternoon was spent in writing and mending. In the evening I went to the flicks but half way thro' the picture the lights went out and there was a Yellow Warning — following immediately by Red. We could hear the enemy bombers stooging overhead and realised that we were the likely target! Kabrit's runways and its position on a peninsula jutting into the lake make the station an easy target to locate from the air. The next forty minutes were unpleasant and spent in a trench with Denis Skillings and Chalky White of my squadron among others. Denis enjoyed going to the steps of the trench and putting his head out to see what was going on and reporting back to the rest of us sitting and lying in the bottom of the trench. Five or six planes did their stuff rather too well, we thought. It was interesting for us to see that their tactics were quite different from ours. Wellingtons normally bomb from 5,000 to 12,000 feet while flying reasonably straight and level on the bombing run over the target. The Germans (I think they were Ju88s) came diving down through the tracer of the light flak (Bofors) and bombed at 1,000 to 2,000 feet — then continued over the lake at 500 feet or less.

Some of the sticks of high explosive were unpleasantly close to us and one hoped that they were well spaced to avoid the Mess and our trench near by! Only one man was killed and about ten injured in the raid but the bombers wrote off a hangar, some crewrooms and four Wellingtons completely plus three others damaged. Our station defences put up a good show but didn't shoot down any of the attackers.

26th April 1942

I was up early and away to Shallufa and Cairo by car with Flight Lieutenant Brown and Captain Woodhouse. We put up at the Victoria — not a very bright place but it seems clean. It was an enjoyable day going to the Gezira Club in the afternoon and watching golf, tennis, cricket and swimming. I had tea and cakes by myself on the terrace in some luxury. Then I came back by taxi to the hotel and took a tram to the Cathedral for the 18.30 hours evening service. Coming back I was lost but eventually found the Victoria and had dinner before going to the Cinema Lux to see *Target for Tonight* and *Back Street*. This is the second time

I've seen the RAF film and I thought it was still quite good in giving something of the atmosphere of a bombing raid.

27th April to 1st May 1942: The Qattara Depression
The leave was spent in shopping, watching games, playing golf and swimming at the Gezira Club, dining and going to various picture theatres. A lecture on 28th April attracted my attention and I went to hear Mr W.G. Murray, Director of the Topographical Survey, give an excellent discourse on the *Qattara Depression*, at the Anglo Egyptian Union, Sheria Fouad, Gezira. He described the Depression as a valuable defence to Egypt and a natural tank trap! The Depression had been formed by wind erosion of Miocene Beds and had a high escarpment of 600 feet or more to the north. The floor was almost flat and hummocky with a surface of sand, mud and salt — due to the slight seepage of brackish water. The low areas, which are impassable to cars and unsafe for loaded camels, are up to 60 metres *below* sea level. There was no connection with the Mediterranean nor with the Nile but there are some suggested projects to make tunnels for Med water to flow in and provide HEP — or Nile water to flow in by canal to form a vast inland lake. The dense air and great heat give sultry enervating conditions in the Depression where mosquitoes and flies abound.

[While listening to the lecture I had not the slightest idea that the Qattara Depression and the Alamein Defence Line would soon become world famous. To me as a geographer it was merely a fascinating natural feature which I hoped to see while in Egypt. Without the flank protection of the Qattara it seems certain that Alexandria, Cairo and all Egypt would have fallen to Rommel in July 1942.]

2nd May 1942
We set off for Kabrit by truck via Ismailia — an interesting but tiring journey. The fields contained barley, wheat, marrow plants, maize — the barley and wheat being ripe and ready for harvesting. This was in progress and also winnowing by driving bullocks with rollers attached, round and round in a circle. Plenty of bullocks were also tramping round working irrigation wheels with buckets on them — and I saw *shadufs* in some places. Many sailing boats used the canals for hauling stone as the main cargo. A number of men and boys were swimming in the canals. The busy fertile Delta area is an unbelievable contrast with the surrounding desert of bare sand and stone wasteland.

3rd May 1942
I reported to 104 Squadron Office, to the Accountant Officer and then to Intelligence where I read up the latest reports and prepared for the evening briefing of our squadron for the usual 'mail run' to Benghazi and the Martuba landing grounds as the sub-sidiary target. My briefing went quite well, in spite of Squadron Leader Young starting it by saying that no briefing was necessary. He's correct in some ways, of course, for most crews know Benghazi!

4th May 1942: Back to the Desert
I was up at 04.15 for 06.00 take off with Pilot Officer Ellis in 'Z for Zebra'. It was a good trip and really nice to be back at LG106. Unfortunately a pile of my mail has been sent back to base.

5th May 1942
Interrogations were completed at 08.30 and I had a very light breakfast owing to 'gippy tummy' again — possibly due to change in food and swallowing so much sand. An enjoyable swim in the afternoon was followed in the evening by a terrific series of 'line squalls' which came up suddenly with sand blowing everywhere. Operations were cancelled for 148 Squadron crews who had arrived in the afternoon. We had some fun hunting snakes under petrol drums and also killed some scorpions and centipedes.

In the evening I went round the dispersals with Don Crossley and Larry Wells. Crossley is certainly the most 'clueful' chap I've met in the RAF and this will be a fine landing ground when he is finished with it.

8th May 1942: Air Raid on Daba
I've invested in Tex Hambleton's wireless set for £4 — a bargain but it needs some repairs. It will be useful in getting news bulletins. After a swim in the afternoon I briefed nine crews who are operating tonight. We had a Red Alert during the briefings — this is becoming usual. Tonight the Luftwaffe really got on target — they hit the stores and ammunition depot at Daba fifteen miles west up the road. A whole train of ammunition wagons went up one or two at a time over a period of five hours. There were amazing fireworks and very heavy explosions. One Ju88 was reported shot down.

9th May 1942
Pilot Officer Davis and I did the interrogation of our crews. He's a new IO sent to help me and learn on the job. There were no brilliant results as it was very dark at the target. Ten Wellingtons of 104 arrived in the afternoon and I did the briefing.

10th May 1942
At the interrogations from 03.30 I was helped by Davis and we finished at 07.00 and breakfasted. Then files in the morning and swimming in the afternoon with work again 17.00 to 18.30. After dinner I repaired the wireless set with the aid of the ever-efficient Pilot Officer Crossley — and so we were able to hear Churchill's speech in the mess. It was exciting to think that D. might be listening to the same speech in far-off Dorset.

11th May 1942: 104 Squadron Convoy Arrives
Today I visited Wing HQ to contact the SIO and Met people. We were shown the remains of the Ju88 shot down two days ago and later watched the Met balloon sent up to check upper wind velocities. We came back to dinner and found that the squadron convoy has arrived by road from Kabrit. The change is in process and 104 Squadron will put up their own camp on the western side of LG106.

12th May 1942
Nothing exciting here but there was radio news of our Kittyhawks and Beaufighters today intercepting twenty Ju52s and three Me110s and shooting down thirteen Ju's and two Me110s for the loss of only one Beaufighter — a magnificent effort.

13th May 1942: Test Flight over Qattara
This evening I was invited on a test flight of 'R for Robert' 148 Squadron by Flying Officer Astell (captain) and Pilot Officer Dodds (navigator). Pilot Officer Davis of Intelligence came with me and Bill Astell really put us through it — he did all sorts of stunt flying over the edge of the Qattara Depression. I noted the long sand ridges running NW to SE with blunt ends of dunes facing south. It is wild territory to crash in and we seemed near it at times. It reminded me of the flying by Pilot Officer Dickinson in G104 when we met the Ju88 in this same general area.

[Flying Officer Astell was another 205 Group pilot who later served with the Dambuster 617 Squadron.]

14th May 1942
I did the interrogations of seven of my own squadron and the results were better than usual at Benghazi with at least one ship set on fire. Unfortunately Pilot Officer O'Donnell and crew in 'L for London' are missing and an aircraft was seen to go down on fire.

16th May 1942
I helped the squadron put up their mess tent and then went to Qotaifiya for a meeting of intelligence officers. It was a rush to get back to brief four crews of our squadron for tonight. Flight Lieutenant Hill is here and will do the interrogations tomorrow morning. One of our pilots with greying hair and conscientious nature who hates 'ops' but goes on them, has been taken off at last after completing his tour and will take Don Crossley's place at this LG. Looking around the mess I can see quite a number of young chaps with greying hair — this flak and flying business is no joke! Don Crossley has gone to Group HQ.

17th May 1942
Hill had only three interrogations this morning because our 'M for Mother', Sergeant Baker (pilot) and Pilot Officer Sams (navigator) is missing. Sams is a grand type, thoughtful and pleasant and I do hope he's OK. Their last message referred to engine trouble. The briefing was by Flight Lieutenant Hill tonight and afterwards Pilot Officer Duncan (another new IO in place of Davis) and I listened in to a church service and singing on the BBC.

18th May 1942
I was up at 03.00 for the first planes in and worked hard with Flight Lieutenant Hill until 08.00. Then we had breakfast and carried on afterwards with the new bombing reports which required more time and trouble. Horrible news! — I am to take the place of Flight Lieutenant Hill, IO at LG09, as he is to go to Cairo for posting. I don't like LG09 and it means leaving my own squadron. This afternoon I went over by truck and, as before, hated my first views of the LG with its several wrecks of Wellingtons around the perimeter. My miserable feelings gave way slowly as I met one or two people I knew. A good dinner helped also — but I haven't my camp kit and I'll be back to sleeping on a table top. What of my mail?

19th May 1942
The briefing went fairly well, thank goodness, but there are lots of snags here and very different procedures from my own LG106. I tried to organise things and spent the evening filling in the Bombing Report headings to aid the interrogating. Eleven aircraft (37 Squadron) are operating so I shall be busy. Pilot Officer Wilson who is Regional Control Officer here temporarily, was in my squadron and flight at the Torquay ITW and drilled with me in front of the railway station!

Good news today: Hill and I reported some Very lights seen by 'S Sugar' and 'P Peter' of his squadron on Monday and now we have heard that the entire crew of 'M for Mother' of my squadron have been picked up safely. What a wonderful thing to happen!

20th May 1942: SOS
I did all the interrogations but they were well spaced out. The raid was a complete fiasco due to 10/10 cloud over target, and worst of all, one aircraft, 'D for Donald', is missing. The whole officers' mess is gloomy about it as this was a three officer crew, Pilot Officers Salt, Flitten and Hayworth — good chaps all, and Hayworth had just received news that his wife has had a baby. It made me think of D. also expecting a baby, and the position for her if it had been Pilot Officer Chappell missing in 'D for Donald'. I had to prepare a report about my failure to record news of an SOS on the bombing reports. Apparently one crew reported to their flight commander after interrogation about an SOS which might have come from 'D Donald' but did not mention this to me at interrogation. The crew say they discussed it among themselves at interrogation. I didn't hear it — and nothing went on the bombing report. This sort of thing can unfortunately happen when the crews do not know the intelligence officer and vice versa.

21st May 1942
I worked hard today at a build-up of photographs of tonight's target which is a group of enemy landing grounds. To my relief Flight Lieutenant Hill returned this afternoon having refused a good political job in Cairo. He brought news of the arrest of two of our fellow intelligence officers over some matter of escape purse moneys. I know both well of course and am certain one of them is straight as a die. The briefing was at 18.00 hours and I felt that it went well. In the evening the usual enemy raid occurred with masses of flares over Fuka way and the crump of bombs.

22nd May 1942
Last night was a really good operation at last with fires and
explosions seen and not the slightest doubt that the target area
was reached. Everybody was pleased as punch — myself included.
Later — to my disgust, I was ordered to go further up to yet
another landing ground for an operation tonight. I travelled on the
fire tender borrowed from LG09 and we found the map pin point
with difficulty only ten minutes before ETA for the aircraft.
After briefing I had less than an hour's sleep on hard ground with
mat and blanket under me before the first aircraft returned early.
Another aircraft was missing from the operation and a large fire
seen in Benghazi was very probably our 'X for X-Ray', poor chaps.
We ourselves received another enemy raid and this time the bomb
bursts were too close for comfort. Near bombs have a tremendous
crack while those further away have a longer, more confused
sound like a mass of old iron being dumped. I prefer the latter!

23rd May 1942: 104 Detachment to Malta
I got transport to Wing to see Flight Lieutenant Wise — then had a
mad journey with the Wing Signals Officer back to LG106 for a
special briefing for my squadron which is sending a detachment of
ten Wellingtons off to Malta under the command of Squadron
Leader H.M. Young. I'm glad to be back and I listened to the
briefing and watched the crews take-off with feeling. Then we had
a little party in the mess and watched another enemy raid in the
distance. Every night now there are enemy bombing raids and it
seems that they are working as hard as our own squadrons.

*25th May 1942: Visit of the AOC-in-C, Air Chief Marshal Tedder,
to LG106*
He seemed a very decent clueful chap and shook hands with each
of us and had dinner in the mess. He gave an informal talk to the
sergeant and officer aircrews about any points we liked to raise —
types of aircraft, the possibility of a 'push', Benghazi, other targets
etc. He congratulated us on our squadron's efforts and said they
were most valuable to the war effort.
   The flies are becoming really terrible — they too, seem to be
making all-out attacks. In the evening I saw 'Dicky' Dickenson and
'Doc' Beach off to the Half Way House — as we call Malta. Later
we heard the terrible news from signals that some other real
friends of mine, Pilot Officer Morton and his crew, crashed into a
bomb crater when landing at Malta and were all killed. The news

really hurt. The loss of any of our air crews hurts, but this was Morton. There was no enemy raid tonight — our first free night for some time. Doc Gimson invited me over to the squadron mess tonight with three or four others to a pleasant party to celebrate his birthday.

Today was ETA of our new baby. Do hope D. is well and all is safely over. This morning I wakened with stomach trouble and wondered if it was psychological because of D.

27th May 1942: News of Rommel Offensive
Various clues which I've seen with my own eyes indicate that a push is imminent. I've seen Crusader tanks going up on their trailers — a very large convoy of fifty ambulances — and another convoy of armoured cars and scout cars mainly with Indian crews — all moving westwards. Then tonight came news of a change of target and bomb load for our Wellingtons — it's a push by Rommel instead of by us and we are helping by bombing enemy armour and transport in the battle area.

28th May 1942
I changed over to my own squadron camp. This means leaving my very good tent for a poor one without a fly, but the mess is better with quite good food. In the evening I briefed 148 Squadron for the Martuba landing grounds.

29th May 1942
Interrogation of the crews back from Martuba revealed that it had been a good show with several aircraft set on fire on the ground.

30th May 1942: Enemy Overhead during Briefing
I worked at a new Intelligence tent for 104 Squadron in the morning and then went out to the bomb dump to get bomb boxes to protect my maps and files. At the briefing tonight on Martuba, we could all hear several enemy aircraft stooging right overhead when I was called upon to brief. Group Captain J.H.T. Simpson DFC, our new CO of 236 Wing (formerly CO of 70 Squadron) was present and also the new wing commander of 104 Squadron, Wing Commander J. Blackburn — the aircrews were keyed up and the intelligence officer was trying hard to brief naturally in spite of slight dryness of the mouth. It was quite a tense setting with flares being dropped around us but fortunately no bombs. Our new tents have been sprayed with sump oil and

sand thrown over them to act as desert camouflage — and blackout regulations are carefully observed — so the flares presumably did not reveal the LG106 camps which are now extensive on three sides of the perimeter.

31st May 1942
During the interrogation of the crews back from Martuba two crews reported being attacked by night fighters and one wireless-operator was wounded. I sent in a narrative report giving news of the position of the ground fighting reported by our aircraft and was commended for this. The 'front' must be very fluid. At night we had a hot time for a while from two or three enemy bombers. They dropped some long sticks of about 14 bombs each on the other side of the railway. Some flares were right over our camp and I took shelter in a partly dug hole for a tent while incendiaries and anti-personnel bombs were dropped around our dispersals fortunately doing no damage.

*

At the end of these two busy months our wing and two squadrons of Wellingtons were settled in tented camps at LG106 as a mobile force. Both squadrons had detachments in Malta so we were only at half our normal strength. Wing Commander P.R. ('Teddy') Beare DFC left the squadron sometime in May having been in command of 104 Squadron since the detachment left Driffield in October 1941. With his hard-working flight commanders, Squadron Leader Young and Squadron Leader Brown, the efficient and cheerful wing commander had welded our squadron into an excellent and respected bomber unit of 205 Group.

Squadron Leader 'Dinghy' Young, the veteran operational type so selfless in his complete devotion to the task of bombing efficiently, also left the Middle East at this time by leading the 104 detachment to Malta. There he completed his tour as flight commander with 104 Squadron and returned to the UK for further distinguished service in 1943 as flight commander of 617 Squadron, 'The Dambusters'.

Another magnificent squadron commander to leave us at this time was Wing Commander J.D. Rollinson DFC of 148 Squadron. The new commanders of our desert squadrons were now Wing Commander J. Blackburn DFC of 104 Squadron and Wing Commander D.A. Kerr DSO DFC of 148 Squadron.

CHAPTER THREE

Retreat and Defence

The Rommel offensive beginning on 26th May breached the Gazala Line of 'boxes' (fortified localities generally held by a brigade with supporting arms) and minefields, and by mid-June a withdrawal by the Eighth Army looked inevitable. Tobruk fell on 21st June and after a temporary halt near Mersa Matruh the army reassembled in the defensive position of El Alamein at the end of the month. At the Alamein position both flanks were secured by natural features — the Mediterranean Sea to the north and the Qattara Depression thirty-five miles to the south.

The Wellington squadrons operated from their desert landing grounds until the last possible day — withdrawing behind the Delta to the Canal bases in some cases only hours before enemy tanks arrived. LG106 was evacuated on 27th June after operating double-sorties on the night of the 25/26th.

The whole month of June was a period of intense operational activity for the squadrons as the front crumbled and enemy bombing became more troublesome to our own night missions. In the desperate conditions our night bombers were frequently switched to tactical targets in the battle area.

'Battle Area' operations were quite different in character from other 'ops' and had to be improvised to cope with the quickly changing military situation.

In the main they were directed against tanks, transport concentrations or columns, ammunition dumps etc. and were, in effect, 'seek and destroy' operations as this was mobile war with few static targets. These 'ops' could be protracted and were carried out at low levels in the light of flares from Albacores (naval aircraft) specially assigned to illuminate the target area. Sometimes there was little opposition in the form of flak but on the other hand the target area was a night fighter's paradise with the bombers among the flares and showing up against the illumined surface of the desert.

Although dangerous, these 'Battle Area' operations were popular with the Wellington aircrews because they knew that they were assisting directly in the ground fighting.

1st June 1942

There was a Red Alarm and flares to the east while we were briefing for an attack on enemy aircraft at Derna. I heard tonight from Wing Commander Blackburn in the mess that I am now a flying officer with effect from 25th March.

2nd June 1942

I interrogated all our squadron crews. A large fire was started by our wing commander at Derna LG. Later I cleaned up my tent and myself and went back to work at 10.45. The tents are hot and horrible in this weather which is a moist heat and very trying, but the flies are enjoying it.

A warm front stopped most of Hill's squadron last night with engines overheating or inability to climb.

4th June 1942: War Strain

In spite of my being up again at 04.20 I found that I had missed 'H for Harry' who jettisoned bombs and returned early at 01.00 hours just as he had done on his previous operation. The captain needs a rest and I was thankful to hear later that he is to get one by being appointed CO of the squadron section at base. The operation last night was a poor one with crews apparently bombing north and east of the target which they found difficult to locate.

6th June 1942

After working at erecting the Intelligence tents this morning, Steve Storey and Mick Gray (NZ) kindly helped with shifting my own tent.

Tea-time brought the long awaited cable from home — 'Elizabeth Anne a sister for Duncan arrived 25.5.42 — both well — 7½ lbs — taken flowers from you'.

What a relief!

In the evening we moved into the new squadron tent and prepared for the first briefing. I treated everyone in the bar to drinks in honour of the occasion of the birth of my daughter. Then we had the briefing at 22.45 hours for a battle area operation on an enemy fighter landing ground, with a Red Alert in the middle as usual with flares dropping quite near to us. The take-off was OK in spite of the bombs and flares in the vicinity, but those on the ground spent some anxious moments in a slit trench (a hole dug for a latrine!) while anti-personnel bombs and some larger bombs were dropped all round.

7th June 1942: Target Location

The first aircraft arrived back at 05.45 hours and all our crews are OK but the bombing results are again poor. Wing Commander Blackburn is keen to improve matters and he had a long talk with the Navigation Officer and myself about accurate information for locating a battle area target. At 10.35 hours there was a loud explosion from the dispersal area and the usual cloud of smoke rising up to over 2,000 feet — aircraft 'Z for Zebra' of 148 Squadron had caught fire when bombed up. The photographs from last night by the Wing Commander and by Pilot Officer Cockroft both show planes on the ground so that at least two of our crews got there and their photographs were very good indeed.

9th June 1942

I interrogated our squadron crews and found that they had definitely seen runways so last night's briefing was not in vain. The Wing Commander again has two fine photographs which show the dispersal areas very well. Today I heard of Flying Officer Astell's grim story. His Wellington of 148 Squadron was shot up by a night fighter over Derna recently and four of the crew baled out. Two stuck to the kite and got out OK after crash-landing but 'Bishop' Dodds, the navigator, was too exhausted to carry on and was probably captured. Only Astell got back safely.

10th June 1942

I worked at files and correspondence in morning and afternoon. The briefing for Kastelli (an airfield in Crete) went quite well. This evening we saw a burning tanker off-shore from the mess. There was A/A fire and explosions from the tanker which unfortunately must be one of ours trying to reach Malta or taking fuel supplies up the coast to Tobruk.

11th June 1942: Bir Hacheim Falls

The photos at Kastelli were a great success again and the Wing Commander (Wing Commander Blackburn DFC, 104 Squadron) is a wizard in producing evidence of where he bombed. We could smell the oil from the tanker today — like Suez smell at Kabrit. In the afternoon I wrote letters and was plagued by flies. The usual Red Alert and flares came in the evening and the radio announced the loss of Bir Hacheim. This is a vital box held by the Free French who have put up terrific resistance.

Aircrews of "A" flight 104 squadron. Kabrit September 1942; Squadron Leader I. C. Strutt DFC as flight commander

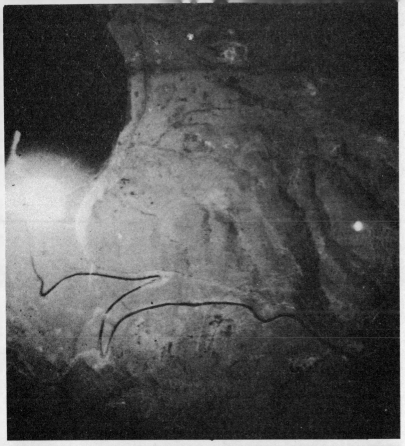

Battle area attack on
persed enemy tanks
transport before the bat
El Alamein

Wellingtons attack the e
retreating along the S
Pass after El Alamein

adron Leader Partington,
adron Leader Turner DFC
Flight Lieutenant Kirkby
36 wing

) Blogg and Squadron
der I. C. Strutt DFC of
squadron on board a
cked enemy aircraft

Group mobile wings and
adrons moving forward
er El Alamein

Former Wellington advanced landing grounds were found occupied by wrecked enemy aircraft

12th June 1942: Return from Malta
The night of the 11th/12th was interrupted by telephone calls
and the return of our Malta detachment. There are new faces in
the mess today as Beach, Palmer, Dickenson, Squadron Leader
Young and others have gone back to England direct from the
island and these new officers are their replacements. The afternoon swim was spoilt by oil in the water from the convoy attack.
Scores of tins of petrol have washed up on the beach and a life-
boat — burned, battered and smothered with oil. It made me hate
this war and the useless waste of everything — and hate the Hun,
too. We found two graves on the beach dated November 1941
which were graves of sailors washed ashore from earlier disasters.
I felt depressed coming back and I don't like my unpleasant hot
little tent with no fly-sheet. Just at the moment, every evening is
interrupted by a raid warning and Jerry's flares and bombs.
Tonight flares were dropped right over the middle of the camp
which was frightening — but no bombs followed so obviously the
camps were not seen.

13th June 1942
'Z for Zebra' (Pilot Officer Shackleton, 104 Squadron) is missing
and a kite was seen shot down over Benghazi, and a fire on the sea
one to two miles SW of the harbour. I knew the crew quite well
and Shackleton was a most pleasant chap. Another filthy duststorm is blowing today but there was a little light relief this
morning. 'B' Flight Dispersal rang up to report a hole and a disturbance around it. One man had put his arm down the hole,
then rang up to know if a bomb disposal squad could be informed.
As a neighbouring landing ground had recently had delayed action
bombs dropped on it I rang the CO, flight commanders etc. and
had armourers go out to investigate. 'A' Flight Dispersal were also
informed and they searched for other holes to line up a stick if
one had been dropped. Later, they found a line of holes but did not
ring up for the Bomb Disposal Squad. The holes were where a line
of telegraph poles had been removed! At briefing tonight I played
a joke on our wing commander. He had groused about the photo
failures of our squadron so I produced Wing Commander
Simpson's photo of Benghazi harbour and a report indicating it
had been taken by Watkins. The joke fell flat and Wing Commander Blackburn was not amused. I suppose it was silly of me to
try a joke when we are all under serious strain. The enemy flares
were over the sea tonight and they must be after the convoy again.

14th June 1942
I worked at files in the morning and in the afternoon salvaged part of the equipment of a boat washed ashore from RFA *Bramble-leaf*. We talked with a coastguard and he said there had been no men in the boat. Our wing commander seems to do nearly every operation — tonight he came back early with engine trouble due to overheating. The other aircraft were diverted because of low cloud at LG106 and I thought how easy it would be to write a tense little radio sketch with an intelligence officer and a phone.

15th June 1942
We worked at putting the EPIP tents into the hole dug by the Indians of the Pioneer Corps. The flies are simply shocking and so bloody persistent. I went round the Bomb Dump with a flight sergeant — a pleasant chap who has been four years away from home and yet he still remains sane in spite of everything. It was a quiet evening in the mess with no CO, no squadron leader and no 'ops'. I listened in to the BBC programme and news. The Libyan news is not so hot — in fact it is very worrying.

16th June 1942
I worked all day without any swimming. The briefing went rather better than usual — just as well because old Wise, SIO of 231 Wing, was there at the back unbeknown to me. He said it was a good briefing. I took him and two others to the bar afterwards. They were Charles Stotesbury, a navigator who was very helpful in Intelligence all day, and Pilot Officer Blogg, his pilot. Both were posted in a few weeks ago. It was very foggy at night and a Wellington 'J Johnny' of 148 Squadron came in to land and crash-landed — catching fire immediately. The crew got out safely but the aircraft burned merrily with ammo and flares, Very lights etc. exploding brilliantly. It was at the end of the runway and in the fog it looked miles away to me. In the morning I got a shock as the wreckage was only 300 yards from my tent.

17th June 1942: Fog Chaos
A nasty clammy fog caused chaos for the squadron aircraft trying to land or get diverted to other LGs. 'S Sugar' (Pilot Officer Cockroft) got down somehow but Micky Gray ran out of fuel and crash-landed safely near LG104. Pilot Officer Watkins (NZ Watty) made the best effort of all. He landed safely in the desert near 104 thro' a gap in the mist. Although there was 'nil petrol' on the

gauges he took off in the morning by arranging to be dragged
1½ miles by tank transporter to a clear spot. He landed at LG05 —
refuelled and changed the rear tyre — then came back to us. A
wizard effort! Wing Commander is mad about the diversion cock-
up and certainly we very nearly lost some good crews.

18th June 1942: Army Back to Egyptian Frontier
I tried a new idea at briefing copied from Flight Lieutenant Hill
by putting ships in red on a half tone map of the target area of
Benghazi harbour. After dinner I had a quiet talk with Watkins
and he helped put the wireless set together again. — We heard
'Mr Muddlecombe' and the news — now we are back to the
Egyptian Frontier — the war position is grim indeed!

20th June 1942
During the night I was sick and generally very sorry for myself —
nothing is more miserable than this stomach trouble. 'Ops' were
cancelled and then an emergency signal came and we were given a
new 'battle area' target. Briefing took place at 19.00 hours. 'A'
Flight are back from leave after Malta. The first plane came back
at midnight — Micky Gray with u/s generator in starboard engine
and overheating. A big inversion of temperature occurred tonight
and it was 32°C at 5,000 feet.

22nd June 1942: Tobruk has Fallen
We are operating with a vengeance now and Tobruk has fallen,
which we held in the last retreat. Jerry seems to be getting the
upper hand in the desert fighting. My day was made happier by
the receipt of a pile of air postcards from D. At our briefing for
Tmimi landing grounds a new method of run-in to target was suggested.

23rd June 1942
It was a successful 'op' last night and everybody is pleased. I
worked all the morning and then took a swim in the afternoon.
Swimming is a blessing in this heat but it's a terribly dusty journey
there and back. At briefing we had a long wait for the target. Now
take-off is at 01.30 tomorrow. It must be difficult to sort out
where the 'front' is to give us a safe 'bomb line'.

24th June 1942: Bombs on LG106
Our aircraft were back at dawn and I worked until 08.30. The

'op' was spoilt by 7/10 low cloud. I had a little sleep in the morning until wakened by the photographers. Worked in the afternoon and evening until briefing. Then we received the most hectic bombing we've had so far. Five enemy aircraft worked on us from 22.30 to 23.15 — bombing, machine gunning and some cannon fire — unopposed. They set some petrol on fire in our dispersal area and destroyed the Wing 'ops' tent. Wing Commander Blackburn called for volunteers to put out the petrol drums burning and I'm ashamed to say that I muttered something about looking after my Intelligence materials — and didn't go with him. The bombers were right overhead and seemed likely to drop more bombs on the fires, but the Wing Commander and a few equally brave helpers got the fires out in about half an hour. Later we had another E/A at 01.30 (25th) for fifteen minutes or so — bombing and machine gunning.

Tonight, John King — a pilot officer navigator — and an old boy from Blandford Grammar School whom I had taught, walked into the mess — posted to 104 Squadron. It was very nice to see him but not the best time to be joining our squadron!

25th June 1942: Double Sortie Operation under Enemy Attack
It was a busy day on the 25th but I managed some sleep in the morning. I was suffering from 'gippy tummy' with no appetite and felt bilious and depressed — not a good beginning for the hectic evening and night of the 25/26th! We did a double-sortie using a neighbouring LG (LG25) for the first landing back refuelling and bombing-up. Jerry was there overhead and dropped flares as our own aircraft landed from the first sortie. Sticks of bombs were then put across the landing ground and one bomb made a direct hit on one of our Wellingtons about to take-off for the second sortie. This was 'N for Nuts' 104 Squadron (Sergeant Sharplin), fully bombed-up and refuelled. The German bombs set 'N' on fire and the bombload went up in a series of tremendous blasts. We had set up a small tent for Intelligence interrogations between sorties and this was very close to the flare-path and the burning Wellington. I scrambled out of the tent and sheltered in the desert a few yards away among small sand humps while the explosions continued and Jerry came down and machine gunned. When the worst of the explosions seemed over I went back to the tent and found that Mason, the clerk, had been knocked over by blast but was unharmed and that Squadron Leader Brown had had a miraculous escape — he was injured in the leg by shrapnel. Of

the Wellington crew four got out injured and Pilot Officer Smith-Windsor and Sergeant Kirby were killed. It was the most shattering incident that I've witnessed so far. Sgt G. Hosford, the Duty Pilot, bravely rescued two of the wounded crew and was later awarded the George Medal.

*

WELLINGTON ATTACKED BY NIGHT FIGHTER,
25th/26th JUNE 1942

While 104 and 148 Squadron Wellingtons were bombing-up for a second sortie at LG25 near Sidi Abd el Rahman and receiving dangerous attention from enemy bombers, other 205 Group squadrons were in action against enemy armour, troops and transport beyond the 'front'. Wellington 'L for London' of 70 Squadron found an enemy convoy of 100 vehicles, bombed it and strafed it thoroughly before itself suffering an attack by an enemy night fighter. This incident has become history because the young Australian observer (navigator), Pilot Officer T.E.W. Howes, behaved with great courage and coolness in the emergency and subsequently received an immediate award of the Distinguished Flying Cross.

A report of the operation and attack given here tells a grim story and is typical of the hazards faced by aircrews on 'Battle Area' operations. The crew of 'L for London' included men from four nations and airforces and was thus representative of the results of the Empire Air Training Scheme as seen in the 205 Group Wellington squadrons. – Captain (Flight Sergeant Stewart RNZAF), Navigator (Pilot Officer Howes RAAF), Second Pilot (Sergeant Brown RAF), Wireless Operator (Sergeant Calvert RAF), Front Gunner (Sergeant Payne RAF), Rear Gunner (Flight Sergeant Wagner RCAF).

Report on attack on Wellington DV.564 'L for London' of No 70 Squadron, on 25th June 1942
'On locating a convoy of approximately 100 vehicles at 23.45 hours, after having searched for an hour and seeing only scattered trucks, we proceeded to bomb it from 4,000 feet running northerly, southerly, easterly and westerly. Fifteen runs, dropping one bomb on each run, were made over the convoy, resulting in three vehicles being set on fire, and the convoy being dispersed. After dropping our 17 x 250lb GPs, we then descended to 2,000 feet above the ground and proceeded to strafe the convoy, receiving no opposition. One of the vehicles appeared to be signalling us with a white signalling lamp. On a number of our bombing runs,

we fired red Very lights, which were the Albacore's signal for a
good target. After making two strafing runs, and having begun a
third attack, we received a burst of machine-gun and cannon
fire, causing temporary failure of the intercom. and lights. A few
moments prior to the attack, the captain saw a Wellington slightly
behind and above us on the port beam, and at the time of attack,
the front gunner says he observed tracer (red) coming from the
Wellington. Both the captain and the observer saw yellow tracer
streaming by them from astern. We immediately swung to starboard, setting an approximate course for base. The aircraft smelt
strongly of cordite and smoke. No second attack was made by the
night fighter, so the observer went from the bomb aimer's position
to the rear of the aircraft to determine what damage had been
done. As all torches had been lost in the attack, the observer
unscrewed the handle of his 06 compass, using it as a torch.

'On arriving at the flare chute, he found that both the second
pilot and the wireless operator who were manning the beam guns,
were wounded in the legs and side, cannon shells having hit the
aircraft close to them, blowing off the end of the barrel of one
of the beam guns. He assisted them back to the cabin, which was
full of smoke, the wireless operator returning to his set and the
second pilot to the navigator's chair. The Type 52 Resistance
caught on fire, flames coming out of it about two feet high and
going up the walls of the cabin. The observer sprayed it with the
extinguisher, but as the flames did not appear to abate, discon-
nected the accumulators. The fire then went out and the
accumulators were re-connected. The second pilot then pointed
out to the observer that the rear turret was on fire. The observer
informed the captain and went aft with three water bottles. One
of these he tipped over the rear gunner, (who was seriously
wounded) as the flames were beginning to catch his clothing, and
extinguished the fire with the other two. Having given the rear
gunner a drink, the observer went forward again and took out the
first aid kits, which the second pilot, who had crawled out of the
cabin, was endeavouring to find. The observer gave one kit to the
second pilot, and obtained the morphine from the other kit.
(This took a few minutes, as the observer was looking for a hypo-
dermic syringe, but he eventually located the ampules.) The
observer then went aft to the rear turret. The rear gunner, who
weighed 13 stone and was 6'2" in height, was able to lift himself
on to the back of the turret and the observer succeeded in drag-
ging him forward as far as the beam guns. He then discovered

that the rear gunner's left leg was shot off and that cannon shells had hit him elsewhere. The observer gave him an injection in his right leg, and then went forward to assist the other wounded men. He returned with a tourniquet for the rear gunner but was unable to apply it owing to the extent of the damage done to the rear gunner's left leg.

'On returning to the cabin, the observer turned the IFF (Identification Friend or Foe) on to stud 3 and informed the captain that the hydraulics had been shot through, and although wounded, the wireless operator was endeavouring to make up a Syko message. The observer then went forward and let the front gunner out of his turret. The front gunner went back into the cabin to assist the wireless operator. It was then discovered that the Syko card had been cut faultily and did not fit the machine correctly. With the captain's permission, a message was sent in plain language, by the wounded wireless operator, asking for medical assistance on arrival, and saying that it may be necessary to crash-land. The observer then went back and gave the second pilot an injection, and on going to the beam guns, found that the rear gunner was dead. The observer then removed the Astro dome.

'We had no difficulty in maintaining height and as the starboard engine appeared to be running a little roughly, decided to climb while we could, reaching a height of almost 7,000 feet. The controls were fairly sluggish due to the damage done, and the fabric lost, from the starboard elevator and the rudder. The machine seemed to be flying quite well, and oil was pumped by the front gunner. From Kanayis Beacon we proceeded to lose height, and arrived over the aerodrome at about 1,000 feet. The undercarriage failed to lock down, so the hand pump was operated. This failed, so the emergency system was tried (supply nil) unsuccessfully. The observer then broke the glass on the hydraulic oil tank and the front gunner operated the pump, while reserve oil was poured into the tank. No results were obtained and we prepared to make a wheels-up landing.

'The second pilot was on the bed with his good leg against the main spar. The wireless operator was sitting on the end of the bed next to the main spar, propped up by Irvin jackets, between him and the spar. The front gunner was in the cabin, while the observer was near the flare chute hanging on to the geodetics. The approach was made at 120 mph, with no flaps and we touched down at about 90 mph, well to one side of the flare path. It was quite a successful belly landing and there was very little shock on impact.

The starboard motor continued running until switched off and exits were made through the astro dome and pilot's emergency hatch. The wounded members of the crew were assisted out of the astro hatch and immediately taken charge of by station sick quarters.'

Notes.

1. The report was signed by the captain, observer and front gunner.
2. The attacking aircraft was clearly identified as a Ju88 night fighter by the wireless operator in the astrodome of 'L for London' before he was wounded. (Statement by Pilot Officer Howes)
3. Pilot Officer T.E.W. Howes DFC completed his operational tour with 70 Squadron and after a brief period of duty at 205 Group HQ, began a second tour on Wellingtons as Navigation Officer and Bombing Leader with 104 Squadron at Kabrit.

*

26th June 1942

Early this morning we dashed back by truck from LG25 to LG106 to interview the second sortie crews. We are all dead tired but must keep cracking as we are striking camp today. At breakfast Charles Stotesbury and Chaldicott were glad to see me — they thought I'd gone for a Burton last night as my tent was so close to the end of the flare-path and the explosion of 'N for Nuts'.

We worked hard clearing up the night's operations and began dismantling the Intelligence tents.

27th June 1942: Retreat to Alamein and Canal Zone

During the morning I got the Intelligence boxes and my kit packed and loaded on a truck ready to move off at 15.00 hours.

[The two squadron aircrew members killed in 'N Nuts' 104 were buried at LG106 by a funeral party before the squadron left.]

In the evacuation back to the Canal Zone the maintenance ground crews travelled in their respective Wellingtons with the aircrews. In the evacuation flurry there was a most glorious, and miraculous, 'prang' in the middle of LG106. Two Wellingtons — one taking off and one taxying — met head on — one was 'Y for Yorker' (Flying Officer Chaldicott, Pilot Officer Blogg and Charles Stotesbury) but both were write-offs. The miracle was that with thirteen men in each aircraft only one was injured.

Flying Officer Ginn, the Squadron Engineer Officer, invited me to travel with him in a Ford Pick-up and after inspecting the two pranged aircraft we set off down the road to Alamein and Amiriya — a staging camp. The road was crowded with vehicles going both ways. Our RAF convoy passed the 9th Australian Division Infantry in trucks going up to occupy the Alamein Defences at the northern end. Some of the Aussies shouted, 'Y'er going the wrong way, mate!' to us as we waved back. In fact we were in retreat, but bombers have to have secure bases from which to operate. The Australians looked fit and cheerful which was most encouraging in these circumstances. Another encouraging sight was that of Hurricanes and Spitfires patrolling low overhead up and down the desert road to prevent enemy bombing attacks in daylight. We reached Amiriya Camp at nightfall and got a meal.

28th June 1942
We were up at 06.00 and after a shave and breakfast went off through the desert to Cairo. It was enjoyable to see green again around Giza and Cairo. Then we went out via Heliopolis into the desert again where our V8 engine developed big-end trouble and I had my turn at driving. We finally entered Kabrit at 5 mph with loud clanking noises from the engine — it sounded as if we had retreated too fast for the Ford!

Within an hour I was at work in Intelligence and the squadrons are operating tonight. After briefing, the Intelligence section worked all night at interrogations and summaries.

29th June and 30th June 1942: Intensive Operations from Kabrit
Operations were on each night with evening briefings and interrogations from 02.00 hours onwards. We are dealing with three squadrons now — 104, 108 and 148 — all stationed at Kabrit and operating at maximum serviceability because of the extremely serious position in the desert where Rommel's armour threatens to break through to Alexandria and the Delta. Our squadrons are doing excellent work bombing and strafing enemy MT and tanks in the battle area. We are given a line beyond which we may bomb or particular areas to attack where there are known targets. Pilot Officer Craig reported a tank concentration of over 100 vehicles SE of Galal — we reported it through to HQ and hope it was dealt with by day bombers. On the afternoon of the 30th I went to Group with Le Grand to see Squadron Leader Brown and coming back Le Grand ran off the road through falling asleep

while driving. It might have been serious but I managed to grab the wheel and get the pick-up back on the road. We are all dead tired.

Flight Lieutenant Haydon (NZ) crashed into the Bitter Lake at take-off on the night of the 30th — only one survivor.

*

In Major-General G.L. Verney's History of the 7th Armoured Division *The Desert Rats*[1] there appears a tribute to the RAF squadrons which is relevant at this point. He writes that by the last day of the month (June 1942) the whole Army was concentrated in the defensive position of El Alamein.

> They owed their survival in large measure to the squadrons of the RAF who had operated from their advanced landing grounds often until the enemy were upon them. Their devoted efforts to hold back the advancing Germans should not be forgotten.

This tribute refers mainly to the fighters, fighter bombers and light bombers of the Desert Air Force acting as a tactical force in direct support of the Eighth Army, but it applies also to the Wellington squadrons of 205 Group who operated against the same enemy targets at night.

A Resumé of the Operational Achievements of 205 Group, produced by the Intelligence Section of the Group at the end of operations from North African bases in 1943, provides these paragraphs:

> During June, one of the most terrific efforts put up by the Group began, culminating in enforced withdrawal of the Wing's, RSUs and ASPs, to the Delta area, but not until the Army's retreat made it a dire necessity. The moves were completed between the 21st and 27th of the month.
>
> Everyone will remember those appalling days at the end of June. Every aircraft was sent on the battle area, mostly on double sorties. Aircrews were literally taken off the boat to participate in operations, and some did not come back. The aircrews were tired, their aircraft were tired, and so were the maintenance personnel, but they carried on and even had

[1] Messrs Hutchinson & Co 1954.

enough resilience to mete out the same treatment when the enemy tried his abortive push in July. The Alamein line was held.

One thing was abundantly clear in those worrying days of retreat and suspense as to whether Rommel could be held out of the Delta — the three branches of the armed services were brought close together in the desperate circumstances and forged new links of mutual respect and appreciation. At this time, too, the first units of the American Army Air Force with Liberators and Mitchell bombers reached Egypt. Providing that Alamein could be held the outlook was not entirely gloomy. Our lines of communication and supply were now short and trouble-free while those of Rommel were long and over stretched. The situation remained critical until the Battle of Alam Halfa (31st August to 7th September) brought success to Eighth Army tanks and infantry supported by intense RAF day and night bombing and strafing.

*

The diary entries for July and August help to show the part played by the Wellington squadrons during these difficult months.

1st July 1942
The briefing at night was for the western battle area where our targets are enemy tanks and transport.

2nd July 1942
I thoroughly enjoyed the night's sleep and after breakfast went to work feeling better than for several weeks. It was a good show last night — but Pilot Officer Retallack and crew were lost and an explosion in the air was seen over the target which probably indicated a night fighter at work over the battle area.

I wonder if we are holding Rommel at last? The RAF certainly are going flat out! The briefing tonight was for the battle area again. The news from the front is slightly more favourable, thank heaven.

3rd July 1942
As duty officer I was interrogating from 03.00 hours and this time the Daba area with trucks, tanks and supply dumps was bombed by our squadrons.

Dick Ellis and his crew are missing and an aircraft was seen to go down on fire near Daba with a smaller aircraft just before — it looks as if a Wellington crew shot down a fighter before being shot down themselves. That would be like Dick and his crew!

4th July 1942: Trip to El Arish by Air

There was the usual interrogating in the early morning and then a pleasant change in the afternoon — a flight with Don Crossley (Operations Staff at Kabrit 236 Wing) in 'E Edward', the wing communications aircraft (a Wellington II) to El Arish in the Sinai Desert. He was taking baggage to the new rear base and invited me to go with him. We went up to 7,000 feet to take a photograph of El Arish landing ground. En route we had good views of the Canal and the Palestine Road. Don made a wizard landing at El Arish and another at Kabrit on our return. He is a very skilful and confident pilot and I enjoyed flying with him.

Briefing was followed by the usual raid at night by enemy bombers on the Canal Area. We bomb them — they bomb us! It reminds me of the play X = 0, but I think we are now giving them more in the air warfare than they are currently giving us.

6th July 1942: Crash at Take-Off

I did the OPSUM and phoned the results to Group this morning. In the afternoon there was a cinema show of RAF instructional films — *Discipline and Morale* which had my favourite 'RAF March Past' included *Tactical use of Cloud, Air Gunnery, Interrogation of Prisoners of War*, etc.

In the evening I briefed two squadrons 148 and 108 and remained on duty all night. There were many troubles in the operation, starting when a plane crashed in flames on take-off. The rear gunner was picked up from four feet of water in the lake, still in his turret and he was the only survivor.

Two other Wellingtons had engine trouble and we also had another Red Alert probably due to more minelaying in the Canal by the Luftwaffe. A letter and snaps from D. arrived today and such things are a pleasant help just now!

7th July 1942: Fatigue

Interrogations were completed and I had breakfast at 08.00, but last night's efforts were not too good. There are definite signs of tiredness among the crews and who can wonder after their terrific efforts? John King has already done six operations in eight days.

Pilot Officer Powell nine in 12 days. Some squadron ours! I slept through lunch and wakened at 16.30.

It was my 'Night-off' so I went to bed early.

10th July 1942
'N for Nuts' 104 Squadron Sergeant Maxfield is missing and Pilot Officer Hoad of 148 Squadron, another friend of mine, has put down in enemy territory at Sidi Barrani, from the operations of the 9th/10th.

11th July 1942
On duty last night and this morning when many aircraft were early back and Pilot Officer Harlton is missing.

I slept in the afternoon and did the briefing at night. The pace of operations is being maintained.

12th July 1942
After a good night's sleep I did the Opsum this morning and dealt with office matters. It was the usual working day — each day is the same. Good news today — Sergeant Maxfield and crew have turned up — they were rescued by a Baltimore crew who put down to help the Wellington crew in distress in the front line area. It must have been a very brave and skilful rescue — and very lucky for our crew.

15th July 1942: Crash at Kabrit
Interrogations went on from 05.00 onwards and unhappily three of our aircraft and crews are missing from the 14th/15th operation — Pilot Officer Horton, Pilot Officer Richards and Sergeant Davies. Later Sergeant Davies' aircraft was found crashed in our territory at the front with three killed. He was involved in combat with a night fighter only ten days ago.

I went to Ismailia to Group HQ with Flight Lieutenant Lawson of HQME and it provided a break in the pressure. We had lunch at the Greek Club and a swim at Ferry Point where the sand was so hot that I couldn't bear it on my feet. Then tea at the YWCA and back in the staff car with a drink at the Officers and Sisters Club at Geneifa.

In the evening during the take-off, Wellington 'W William' returned and crashed into the Chance light at the beginning of the runway and wrote off several trucks. There was a loud explosion and a big fire. All the crew got out safely and miraculously

before the final bang. One or two people were injured by fragments and Group Captain Simpson's car had the back blown off
while he was in it. He was OK to everyone's relief. Several people
came into the bar for whiskies afterwards!

16th July 1942: The Toll of Intensive Operations
Flying Officer Brown was missing from the last night's operation
in which he was flare dropping. The squadron (104) have a stand-
down tonight and they deserve it after the experiences of the last
few weeks. (Losses I can think of include the following captains
and their crews: Haydon, Retallack, Shackleton, Ellis, Sergeant
Cairns, Richards, Horton, Harlton, the crew at LG25, three crew
members with Sergeant Davies, etc. etc. — a pretty ghastly list —
and of course 108 and 148 Squadrons have had similar losses.)

I slept in the afternoon's sticky heat and then in the evening
went to the flicks with Charles Stotesbury to see *The Spider*.
We appreciated the shots of Piccadilly and King's Cross Railway
Station. It's rather moving to see shots of England and all of us
feel the same.

Charles showed me some very fine drawings and crayon
sketches of his — he has real talent I can see.

17th July 1942
I was up at 04.00 hours for interrogations. Breakfast at 08.30
made me wish I could enjoy breakfast as I did in England. I miss
the fresh milk and the different tasting tea — the chlorinated
water here ruins it and affects my mouth. Briefing in the evening
was for only four crews from our squadron — what a change!

18th July 1942: Visit by the AOC-in-C, Air Chief Marshal Tedder
Interrogations began at 04.00 and I worked until 08.30 sending in
reports to Group by phone. After breakfast I slept until the tea-
time shower and shave.

We had a visit from the AOC-in-C, Air Chief Marshal Tedder,
this evening. He congratulated the squadrons and gave some encouraging statements about the war situation. I remembered his
last visit to us in the desert at LG106 and all that has happened
since then in terms of effort and crews lost.

I did the two squadron briefings and was on duty all night.

19th July 1942
The main body of planes came back about 05.00 hours with

rather a rush. Sergeant Cairns and four of his crew returned to camp last evening bandaged and unshaven but cheerful. Unhappily, Sergeant Crozier, the navigator and the nicest Australian I've met, was killed in the crash west of Wadi Natrun in the desert. They were in low cloud down to 500 feet and then ran into a ground mist and hit the ground at 170 mph — and he was in the bomb panel. Crozier was a quiet friendly, delightful chap who often came into Intelligence to chat and read the literature and was always helpful at interrogation. A jolly nice crew — all of them!

20th July 1942

We are now supposed to wear slacks and long sleeved shirts at night owing to the possibility of malaria. There are plenty of mosquitoes around and my net is in my kit at El Arish in Sinai.

21st July 1942: Visit to The Holy Land

A very memorable day — I tried to collect my kit from El Arish at the 'advanced landing ground in the rear'! I went with Flight Lieutenant Harry Beale (NZ) and crew plus Flight Sergeant Cairns and his crew going on leave to Lydda.

The airport at Lydda looked a dream to desert eyes — permanent buildings and green surroundings. After lunch at the airport we flew north over the plain with its orange groves, tree-lined roads, cultivated fields and bare patches with sand belts near the coast — and a bare mountainous area to the east.

About 15.00 we came to Nazareth set in the hills and built up to the heights with monasteries, churches, hospitals, schools. The town looks modern from the air and nothing like the primitive little village I had imagined. We circled three or four times and did a mild shoot-up down into the valley and up over a monastery or school. Then we went past a very high hill with steep sides and a winding track up it. There seemed to be a cemetery on this hill and a monastery on top — we were below the highest point of the hill which probably was Mt Tabor. Then we flew NE between the hills to the Sea of Galilee — a blue oval in the Great Rift Valley with steep brown hills all round it. Tiberias appeared to be the only town and it seemed very small. There were very few villages around the lake and we saw only one boat. A road goes along the west side of the lake. I watched carefully for the point where the Jordan leaves the lake and picked it out. The Jordan meanders over a plain estimated three to five miles wide between the steep sides — and the river appears to be controlled by sluices. The valley contains areas of cultivation and a few trees.

We saw the oil pipe line to Haifa come down from the eastern hills and thought it crossed the Jordan on a bridge but the pipe line was not visible on the western side.

The hills were grey or brown with some patches of green in some valleys. Hill top villages of stone appeared on crests of many hills and other villages in the wadis. Obviously the land is parched except for the Jordan, but it's still marvellously green and fertile to eyes used to the desert.

Coming back we were west of Jerusalem but didn't see it and had only a distant glimpse of the Dead Sea.

And so back via the El Arish landing ground and then across the Sinai to the Canal Zone and Kabrit. We arrived at dusk and had to circle while the last aircraft were taking off for an operation against Tobruk.

We had a wizard view of the take-off of about eight or nine aircraft looking like little models as they gathered speed down the runway and rose slowly at the end and passed out over the lake so low that the slip stream left a track on the surface of the water for 200 yards or so behind each Wellington.

Although I failed to locate my luggage at El Arish it was a very excellent and enjoyable day.

22nd July 1942
I was not called for night duty and breakfasted in comfort after a shower and shave. There is to be proper exodus from 104 Squadron. Following on Pilot Officer Foster, Flight Sergeant Murray, Flying Officer Bradley and Donald Baron — now Neil Blundell (NZ) is off and Steve Storey, Pilot Officer Abbott and others very shortly.

24th July 1942: Accidents
In the afternoon I had a trip with Wing Commander Blackburn, Flying Officer Ginn, Pilot Officer Dodd, and Pilot Officer Powell to Ismailia where we lunched at the French Club — then went further on to the hospital to see the rear gunner of Pilot Officer Horton's crew lost on night of the 14/15th. The plane had engine trouble over the Battle Area and went up in flames immediately on hitting the ground — only the rear gunner got out. Coming back we had tea at Abu Sueir RAF Station now repopulated after a bombing. An accident happened while we were there and an aircraft blew up.

Back at Kabrit there had also been a nasty accident involving three Wellingtons. Someone dropped a 40lb HE bomb and it went off killing five men and damaging three aircraft. Some of these 'accidents' are probably the result of the tensions and pressure of the present intensive scale of operations.

25th July 1942
What a morning! On duty for interrogation and *four* aircraft are missing including our 'R for Robert' with Sergeant Wills and John King in the crew. It was last heard of in the Tobruk — El Adem area with engine trouble — position given as 31.45N 24.40E.

I remember now that John King told me at tea or dinner last evening that this was his thirteenth operation. Also I had a talk in the mess last night with Squadron Leader Brown on the possibility of John rejoining Pilot Officer Tony Crockford who was his former pilot and friend in training.

29th July 1942
After the usual interrogations and morning work I saw Tony Crockford about John King's belongings. Then had a swim although it tastes like . . . In the evening Squadron Leader Sargeaunt, our 'A' Flight Commander, told me that his wireless operator comes from Blandford, Dorset and is the brother of a girl I taught at the Grammar School. A small world?

30th July 1942
I was on duty all night and the main body of Wellingtons came in about 04.45. We had terrible sticky heat in the Intelligence room. After breakfast I saw Charles Stotesbury in the bathroom — he needs a rest too, — not at all his usual cheery self.

31st July 1942
I handed in my kit claim this morning but am not hopeful. A morning off duty was followed by two briefings, one at 16.30 and the other at 20.30. A 'shaky do' for a Peggy Wellington in the evening when he came back with one engine banging and on fire but got down safely. A Red Warning occurred tonight but no bombs were dropped around Kabrit.

1st August 1942
Today is Duncan's birthday at home — he's three — and I'm on

duty tonight in Egypt. Just before midnight a big bang shook
the Intelligence section. A 'sprog' crew returning had jettisoned
their bomb load in the lake. The navigator believed this was what
he had to do and said he jettisoned 'safe'! The next crew flew in
through the balloon defences along the canal and didn't know the
rules of the route in to base. The mosquitoes and bugs are awful
tonight!

3rd August 1942
Up at 05.15 and off at 09.30 for morning. Read and dozed until
16.30 — then to work until 19.00 hours. Back for briefing at
21.00 hours. Bed at 22.30. And so another day has ended. But
this morning Pilot Officer Johnson, the nice Canadian, and his
crew did not come back.

4th August 1942: Change in Squadron Command
It is 4th August — a famous day, but I long for the equivalent of
11th November — some day that will be! I was up at 05.00 hours
as usual and on duty again after breakfast. It was a good 'op'
last night and we have photographs to prove it. Wing Commander
J. Blackburn D F C, Commanding Officer of 104 Squadron since
May, left us today. He went off very quietly and didn't say cheerio
or anything — perhaps wise to avoid farewell parties in these tense
times. He has been a fine squadron commander even if a bit of a
nigger driver! Some of his photographs with bombing have been
superb and absolutely on target. He was impatient for other crews
to follow suit and they did improve under his example and leadership. Now, of course, we have many new crews and the new wing
commander will have to start again, more or less. And I shall have
to get used to a new CO.

5th August 1942: Wing Commander D.T. Saville Takes Command of 104 Squadron
The new wing commander is an Australian, Wing Commander
D.T. Saville, who arrived today and seems OK. He's one of those
smaller, very sharp and alert type of Australians. At 02.00 hours I
had to interrogate a USAAF Liberator crew who landed at Kabrit
and I found it unusual and interesting.

But without a doubt the great thing today has been *the return
of the missing Sergeant Wills crew including John King* — missing
since the Tobruk operation of 24th/25th July. Le Grand, the
SIO, did the special interrogation and one could write a book on

their adventures. What a story and what 'gen' they were able to give. I hope sincerely that they get gongs, for they certainly deserve it. Somehow they got from Sollum to Matruh and captured a car and got through the battle area. I haven't the details yet.

In the afternoon I went with Don Crossley in the Hillman Minx to visit crew members in the 9th General Hospital.

6th August 1942: A Gentleman
Squadron Leader D.J. Brown of 'B' Flight left today and everybody is sorry to lose him but glad for his sake. He's a grand chap and a thorough gentleman. Flying Officer Taylor arrived to join Intelligence — seems OK though an old Etonian! Tonight at briefing we had a large number of American crews at the back listening and getting the atmosphere. They are crews of the Mitchell bombers who are to operate from Fayid. Fortunately visitors no longer worry me too much — we get quite a number to briefing.

[*Note*: Wing Commander James Blackburn DSO DFC and Squadron Leader Donald James Brown DFC were both passengers (returning to UK) aboard HM Transport *Laconia* when this ship was sunk by enemy action on 12th September 1942. Squadron Leader Brown lost his life, but Wing Commander Blackburn survived for further distinguished service in the RAF].

7th August 1942
Some BBC people were here today to interview John King and company. Squadron Leader Sargeaunt was very tired tonight before take-off for Tobruk and I had to get him some caffeine tablets. Apparently in addition to operating four nights out of the last seven he has flown five hours already today to LG224 and 86 to collect a squadron crew. I'm on duty tonight.

8th August 1942: Squadron Leader Sargeaunt Missing
Interrogations began at 03.15 and the last crew came in about 06.00 hours. I completed work at 08.30 feeling in some distress because Squadron Leader Sargeaunt is missing and this is terrible! I hope nothing has happened to him — he's a wonderful chap. Sergeant Thick, the wireless operator with him, is from my home town.

9th August 1942
There is still no news of Sargeaunt except that he sent an SOS.

10th August 1942

I was up before 04.00 for interrogations. It was Flight Lieutenant
Chaldecott's last 'op' and he shot up the Intelligence section to
celebrate — and I heard it and liked it for once! Our briefing in
the evening was attended again by the American crews from
Fayid. Sergeant Maxfield had engine trouble at take-off and came
round again to make a ropey landing due partly to brakes. The
navigator must have thought the aircraft would crash and blow
up because he threw himself out — presumably from the astro
hatch — and was severely injured. This crew has had a rough time
lately. John King is definitely going home — this is presumably
because he has been behind enemy lines and escaped.

[Squadron Leader Sargeaunt, pilot of 'D for Donald' 104 Squadron, made a forced landing behind enemy lines ten miles south of
Sidi Barrani. He and his crew were taken POW.]

11th August 1942: Test Flight

I was required at 06.00 for the second wave only. 'Shortie'
Armstrong is missing from 108 Squadron — another nice chap. In
Intelligence we know most of the crews from all three squadrons
and it hurts when they don't come back. There is often no news of
POW's until months later.

In the afternoon Chaldecott invited Flying Officer Taylor and
me from Intelligence to test-fly 'O for Orange' with him. Rather
foolishly we agreed and had half an hour of pretty risky stunts —
exhilarating but crazy! He did two nearly stalled turns — gave a
low flying exhibition and a quick zoom up to 500 feet. My cap
flew out the window of cockpit on the first steep turn — I may as
well lose *all* my kit!

The low flying made me remember the sad case of a pilot
recently named in DROs for responsibility of causing the deaths
of three people including himself due to a low flying crash in
Palestine. We survived and old Chaldie made a good landing. We
had some excellent views of the Canal and Suez Bay — crowded
with shipping which is encouraging and indicates a major build up
of supplies for a new offensive by the Army. In fact I counted
over 100 ships in the Gulf of Suez, Canal and Bitter Lakes, many
unloading into lighters in the bay or at temporary jetties on the
shores of the Bitter Lakes.

13th August 1942

In the evening I asked Wing Commander Saville about a trip to

Tobruk. He thinks I should go! He and I seem to be developing a rather closer personal relationship than I have had with my previous commanding officers. Perhaps it is because he is my third wing commander and I'm not quite such a raw beginner as I was with the other two. Or is it because he's Australian?

16th August 1942: Stand Down
Today was a 'Stand Down' for our squadron so a party of us went to Ismailia — Chaldie, Basil Blogg, Charles Stotesbury, Squadron Leader Leggate and me. We had a swim at the US Club which was full of nurses, Wrens, ATS and others, suitably surrounded by Army and RAF types. I enjoyed the swim and shower but we got sticky and hot again almost immediately afterwards. Everywhere was so crowded that it took hours to get any food or drink. We visited the French Club, Greek Club, and US Club and then drove back with blazing lights and were told frequently to 'Put those bloody lights out!' There was a drinking party going on in the mess on our return, so we joined in.

17th August 1942: Alcohol
I was up at 07.00 for a nice change and had a leisurely breakfast before day duty began. Talking of drinking, we have a poor old alcoholic among the Admin officers. I saw him drinking at 08.30 this morning when the bar was open after the other two squadrons' flying crews returned. Apparently he appeared at breakfast dressed as a wog, poked his fez-covered head around the door and then spent the whole morning drinking. I don't know who did his work. He was drinking at lunch time and until 15.00 hours when his friends went off to lie down. He stayed on the verandah belching and singing to himself and being sick. At night time he resumed his drinking and I saw him again at 10.00 on Tuesday the 18th as I was on my way to the bathroom. Ye gods! He will have to be invalided out of the service because I can't imagine that he can be cured at his stage. It was a hectic evening with three separate briefings and a long interrogation of 'P for Peter' 148 Squadron crew who had all safely baled out of their aircraft SW of Wadi Natrun. After 30 hours on only aid boxes and 1½ bottles of water between them they were rescued by a Land-Sea Rescue Lysander aircraft.

It was some story and a good effort by very determined chaps. They were also very lucky to be picked up.

Wing Commander Saville is operating again tonight but there is still no arrangement for me to go with him. Today I heard another bar story — Flying Officer Mather, a large and fairly quick-tempered Australian and one of our new captain-pilots, got into an argument with the Squadron Leader Admin in the bar and hit him a beauty on the chin. Tutt tutt! But the said Squadron Leader is not much liked by any of us so we hope Mather is not punished. We have quite a number of Australians in the three squadrons at Kabrit including our new wing commander of 104 Squadron who has taken over so well.

18th August 1942: Crash at Deversoir
Up at 03.30 for the usual duties and later after breakfast, back to bed where I found it very hot under the fly netting!

Pilot Officer Aubyn James of Intelligence came in on a visit to our section. The briefing went well fortunately for me. Unhappily that was the end of good fortune for the night. After the briefing Wing Commander Saville very kindly offered me his room and desk as he knew I intended to write some letters. I settled down in comfort with an electric fan and had just told D. of my friends Basil and Charles, when the Wing Commander came in quickly and said 'Blogg has crashed in the lake and the navigator is killed — coming?' We dashed off in the Wing Commander's car with the Doc and found it all too true. We could see the burning aircraft on the shore of the Bitter Lake near Deversoir from ten miles away. Basil Blogg was marvellously composed and looking after his crew — he's a grand lad. Five were safe but dear old Charles Stotesbury was killed with a fractured skull. 'O for Orange' had an engine cut-out and could not maintain height to get back to Kabrit. Knowing they would have to crash-land, Charles had gone to defuse the bombs or make sure they could be jettisoned safely, so was in or near the bomb panel when they made what was really a good belly landing on the beach. The aircraft caught fire but they got Charles out. I've never felt worse — and when we returned, old Chaldecott who was well oiled in the mess took it very badly and was nearly weeping. Squadron Leader Leggate told him to shut up. I went to bed in complete misery. Chaldie, of course, had Basil Blogg as his second pilot and Charles as his navigator until Basil took over as captain when Chaldie completed his tour.

19th August 1942: Wing Changes!
It was moving day at Intelligence today and 236 Wing are moving

to a landing ground on the Cairo—Alexandria road with two squadrons 148 and 108 — leaving us (104) at Kabrit to be joined by
40 Squadron under a new Wing 238 with a new group captain,
Group Captain J.A.P. Harrison, who visited the Intelligence
section today with Group Captain Simpson, our old CO. The
latter was pleasant as usual — he's a very fine chap — no side or
bull! The new group captain also seems a very nice type and he
appeared today still with his wing commander stripes.

20th August 1942

Charles was buried at Geneifa this morning.

At the night briefing twenty American Intelligence Officers
came to listen and watch our methods. The AOC and the new
G/C also came but they fortunately arrived late just after my
piece. I'm on night duty tonight.

21st August 1942

Today I wrote to Mrs Stotesbury. I also wrote D. a letter on
matters in the event of my own death on operations or by some
other way. Somehow, with Charles being killed and so many crews
missing recently, death seems unpleasantly close and possible.

24th August 1942

I saw the Doc and got a medical certificate for operational flying.
It's good to know that medically I'm up to flying crew standard
and this is one more step towards going on operations.

*

July and August 1942 continued a tense period for the squadrons
and with the high tempo of operations, activity by enemy night
fighters and a heavy concentration of flak at Tobruk, our losses
increased. 104 Squadron lost seven crews from 28 operations in
July and two crews from 30 operations in August. With similar
losses in the other two squadrons and the usual occasional accidents, one became very conscious in Intelligence of the war
drain on the lives of cheerful bright young men.

From July Tobruk became Rommel's main supply port and
thus a main target for 205 Group bombers. Its strong defences
included a barrage of heavy and light anti-aircraft guns and night
fighters which between them caused regular losses among the
attacking bombers.

One dangerous and effective battery of heavy guns at Tobruk

was christened 'Eric' by our crews and Flying Officer A.B. Read, 108 Squadron Intelligence Officer (later squadron leader and GIO of 205 Group), drew a cartoon of 'Eric' as a fat, bespectacled and cunning Hun waiting with clock in hand to give the order to fire on the attackers. In the cartoon the guns were depicted as firing strings of German sausages at the aircraft overhead.

To counter the strong defences at Tobruk the 'Maw Plan' — put forward by Wing Commander Maw of 108 Squadron — was adopted to provide a 'blitz' time on the target. Bombers arriving early circled outside the flak zone until the agreed time of attack when all aircraft went over the target on a given heading. The limited period of intense bombing was an attempt to swamp the defences and lessen the casualties among the bombers.

Unhappily, on the night of 19th/20th September one of two 236 Wing Wellingtons missing believed shot down over Tobruk was 'W for William' 108 Squadron, piloted by Wing Commander Roger Maw DFC. A man of great personal charm who looked older than most flying men because of his greying hair, he was a most popular and efficient squadron commander, liked by everybody at Kabrit. Later, we heard with pleasure that he was a prisoner of war.

CHAPTER FOUR
Alamein Night Bombers

As the front at Alamein stabilised it was possible to release aircrews who had completed their operational tours and there were big changes in squadron personnel. 104 Squadron now had its new commanding officer, the Australian Wing Commander Saville (who had joined the RAF Reserve in peace-time), and two new flight Commanders — Squadron Leader I.C. Strutt and Squadron Leader A.C. Leggate.

The squadron was teamed with 40 Squadron (Wing Commander R.E. Ridgway DFC) and controlled by 238 Wing under the command of Group Captain J.A.P. Harrison DFC with effect from 19th August 1942. 236 Wing with Squadrons 108 and 148 had moved to a landing ground outside Cairo (LG237).

The successful Battle of Alam Halfa (31st August to 7th September) raised the morale of the Allied forces and gave ground troops a close view of what our night bombers could do in army support operations. Major-General Verney in *The Desert Rats* writes:

The 22nd Armoured Brigade . . . were in positions south of Alam Halfa Ridge and the enemy reached them in the evening of the 31st August. The German attacks were repelled and as night came on the RAF bombers, who had not been able to act previously on account of the great clouds of dust, began to hammer the enemy.

Major H. Woods of the KRRC described the scene:

At 12.30 a.m. our bombers . . . found his whole strength had moved eastwards and located him with flares in the valley below us. It was one of the most awe-inspiring sights I shall ever see, I think, — there were seldom less than 20 flares in the air at any one time and the whole valley with its mass of the Afrika Korps stationary was lit up like a huge orange fairyland. All the time, red—orange, white—green tracer was darting hither and thither like 100 mph coloured fairies. The huge flash of the bombs, which included two of 4,000 lbs, also inspired the whole thoroughly warlike scene, with little figures silhouetted against their vehicles as they tried to find cover from our bombs. The bombers were so accurate that they bombed right up to the minefield beyond which, 2,000 yards away, was another of our companies.

205 Group bomber crews would have enjoyed reading this at the time!

After the Battle of Alam Halfa the morale of the Army continued to rise under the new leadership team of Generals Alexander and Montgomery. At Kabrit we also considered Alam Halfa a crucial turning point in the war and were encouraged by seeing large numbers of ships unloading in the Bitter Lakes and Suez area. We knew that the Scottish 51st Division had arrived in Egypt among other new divisions for the Eighth Army, and that supplies of new equipment included the US Sherman tanks said to be equal to the best German tanks. War is largely a matter of logistics and plainly we were witnessing a determined and successful effort to win the battle of supply.

In September and early October, following the Alam Halfa peak, our bombing operations continued at a high level but below that of the maximum efforts and furious pace of June, July and August. Tobruk, enemy landing grounds and the battle area were the main targets and the intensity of operations again mounted sharply before the opening of the Battle of Alamein on 23rd October.

A Resumé of the Operational Achievements of 205 Group 1941–1943 states:

> On the night of 22nd/23rd October 1942 another period of the most intense operations began at Alamein. On the night of 23rd/24th October crews reported that our guns were in action from the sea to the Qattara Depression. Operations alternated between the battle area and the enemy's landing grounds. In General Von Thoma's own words, 'The constant bombing by day and by night proved more than one could stand.'

*

3rd September 1942

I started work again at 03.50 hours this morning after returning from leave in Cairo last evening. In the afternoon I had a quick trip with some pals to Suez for a swim and tea at the French Club. There were encouraging sights in the port area and out in the Bay I recognised some of the liners as old sea friends from the 1941 convoy. The Suez area is crowded with shipping of all kinds. The briefing in the evening was attended by the commanding officers of Wing, Squadron and a neighbouring establishment but unfortunately there was at first little 'gen' to brief on. Last minute target alterations led to some dashing about after midnight with new battle area information for the crews already waiting by their aircraft and ready for take-off. The Battle of Alam Halfa is still in progress and for once the Army news is encouraging. We are tonight supporting the Army by again bombing enemy armour and transport.

6th September 1942
A busy morning passed quickly, putting files in order, map building and getting ready for briefing. A letter from D. at lunch time was heavenly after a long wait for mail.

In the afternoon I went to 'M for Mother' with Stan Dodd to see how an hydraulic gun turret works. Johnny Johnston started up his engines and I could then move the turret and the guns. There are three controls to operate — one for hydraulic pressure — twist grip control for turret movement and the other is the gun trigger. It's remarkable how anyone in the squadron will give up his own time to show me a gadget on an aircraft and this turret practice was in preparation for my promised operation to Tobruk.

7th September 1942
We had a visit by Air Chief Marshal Barratt in the morning. At night there was a Red Alert and some enemy planes were over the Canal Area dropping incendiaries and laying mines in the Canal. One enemy plane was reported shot down.

9th September 1942
At 00.40 hours I was on duty for interrogations. 'Z Zebra' 104 Squadron is missing with Sergeant Anscomb (who has been taken off 'ops' once), Sergeant Maxfield (noted for his escape) and Sergeant Rowley — a very good navigator. A plane was reported by the other crews as being seen shot down in flames over the target. This was appalling luck for an experienced crew who must be almost at the point of completing their tour of 'ops', made longer because of the emergency.

11th September 1942
In the evening I took one of our clerks down to the flarepath to see the take-off which I always find exciting. The third plane off — one of ours — had engine trouble on take-off and over-ran the runway and was bogged well and truly. The flarepath had to be

changed before the others could take off. It was a nasty thrill watching the tail light go down the flarepath — still go on — and still on, never rising as it should — expecting a fire or explosion at any minute and finally seeing the tail-light waving violently about as the Wellington tipped up on its nose in the soft mud and sand — then fell back. All the crew were perfectly safe — but it took a special caterpillar tractor and much digging to get the plane out.

12th September 1942

All our aircraft came back safely and it was a good 'op' after all the flap at take-off last night — a flap not without reason because the whole operation, a double sortie, depended on timing. Anyway the precautions taken worked successfully. We finished work at 05.30. In the evening the Wing Commander told me that I may go with him tomorrow on my first operation!

13th September 1942: Bombing Mission to Tobruk

I've just noticed that this is the 13th. But it's Sunday and I can't say that 13 has been particularly unlucky or lucky for me in the past. The morning was occupied with normal work and the afternoon spent in preparation for briefing — the target is Tobruk. The Wing Commander is taking 'X for X-Ray' and Flying Officer Mather's crew and I am operating as front gunner. The crew: Wing Commander Saville (captain), Sergeant Lynch (second pilot), Sergeant Corten (navigator), Sergeant Hayes (wireless operator), Flying Officer Chappell (front gunner), Sergeant Symonds (rear gunner).

[Continued on the 14th after the 'op']

The take-off at 17.20 hours was excellent, with the large 4,000 lb bomb, a full crew and also as passengers, Mason, one of our clerks and his luggage and a fitter, both going to join 236 Wing at LG237. I travelled as tail gunner and manipulated the turret to get used to it.

The Delta area looked green and luxuriant with muddy water filling all canals and drains and overflowing from the River Nile on to the neighbouring fields here and there. We had a wonderful view of the Delta Barrage and its twin walls across the Rosetta and Damietta distributaries.

We made an absolutely perfect landing at ALG with our heavy load — no jarring or jolting — the Wing Commander is undoubtedly a wizard pilot. He was a civilian pilot in Australia with ANA and is said to have flown over 10,000 hours so perhaps his good flying is understandable — it's very different from some young pilots I've flown with! I had a pleasant time with Le Grand and A.B. Read of Intelligence at the officers' mess with drinks and dinner.

Then at 21.30 we took off smoothly into the night and this was it! Looking out of the astrohatch I was surprised to see the tracer-like sparks from the engine exhausts — Rolls Royce Merlins on this Mark II Wellington. For a brief moment I thought we were involved with a fighter firing tracer at us — remembering the Ju88 encounter of 5th March.

After half an hour I was told to go into the front turret and did so, entering a dark but just visible world of stars above and incendiaries like stars on the ground — these were thrown out for estimate of wind drift by the aircraft ahead of us. I put Le Grand's blanket around my legs and made myself as comfortable as possible. Everything in the plane was very orderly and comforting — I hadn't the slightest qualm because of the Wing Commander and what seemed a good crew — all Australians except me! The navigator was working hard at his desk — wireless-operator was recording messages and tinkering with his set — the rear gunner was giving wind drift information — the pilot and second pilot were busy in front in the cockpit and only the front gunner was clueless!

Before Sollum we could see the flash of guns at Tobruk. Later as we approached nearer and nearer to the flak barrage and bomb flashes I could see that the flak was formidable — bursts well above us — up to 15,000 or 16,000 feet at least. We were then flying at 8,000 feet. I could not distinguish the coastline to be sure of it — just a dark line which was probably the coast. We stooged around the target just out of the flak and watched the party. I saw several bombers caught in the searchlights and flak and also noted an aircraft flying around outside the flak with strong downward light as if to identify itself to the gunners and searchlights. This was probably a night-fighter and I reported it to the captain. He had already seen it. Later we went inland to see our own target — a gun control position near the Tobruk–Derna road and believed to have radar equipment feeding information to the AA batteries of the port. I saw the road clearly as a dark line through the lighter coloured sand and revealed by the light of flares dropped by our aircraft and others. I could see the wadis defined clearly and also saw numbers of bomb bursts and craters in the sand which looked like wasted efforts.

After an hour around the Tobruk area we dropped our special bomb from 7,000 feet and felt it give us a hearty bump underneath. We then set course on the first leg of the return to base. There was a line of incendiaries and we dropped a few as well — then I saw a curious line of lights which popped on and off continuously. I don't know what they were. It was cold in the front turret but I stayed on until we reached the Delta area and then went back to the astrohatch position.

The navigation was excellent in spite of the darkness making pin-points difficult to locate. We took drifts constantly and with these adjustments the navigator took us accurately along track hitting navigational aids each time. Cloud would have made this impossible and wireless aids and dead reckoning would have had to suffice.

I could recognise some landmarks in the Delta and along the canals, and eventually I saw our home flarepath and red lights. We made one circuit while another aircraft landed — I saw the Chance Light go on and the aircraft passing it and landing in its beam. Then it was our turn and we went in and lowered in stages to a final hold-off and a good landing.

After landing ('X for X-Ray' had been air-borne for 7 hours 20 mins plus 47 mins Base to ALG — total time 8 hrs 07 mins operational time) I filled in the Sortie Report with our crew and assisted with some other interrogations — there was quite a crowd in the Intelligence room as this had been a special maximum effort operation with the bombing of Tobruk as part of a combined land—sea—air operation. Then we went off to breakfast and I had a chat with the Wing Commander and Harry Beale (NZ) and his brother — about the operation and the war in general — and so to bed. My impressions, when looking back on the operation next morning were these:

(1)   This operation was not to be taken as a fair sample of the experiences of a Tobruk raid because we did not go through the worst of the flak barrage.

(2)   I began to get a little anxious over the target when we were constantly stooging over and under flares — and I felt sure that we were very visible to possible fighters or ground defences.

(3)   Tobruk flak looked very formidable — especially horrible streams of red tracer — large stuff — not at all a pleasant sight in spite of the colouring.

(4)   The long journey makes one sleepy and it's difficult to keep awake. It's very cold in the front turret.

(5) It's difficult to recognise land marks in the dark conditions and eyes must be accustomed to the darkness. The front turret is not a good position for visibility — the captain, second pilot, and navigator were able to recognize things much better from the cockpit.

(6) Night bombing is no joy ride. My previous conceptions of the dangers, discomforts and anxiety for aircrews were confirmed or increased and I admire my aircrew friends even more than before.

[The big night on Tobruk of 13th/14th September 1942 was an abortive raid because of heavy naval losses of two destroyers, one light cruiser and several small craft. The landing parties met heavy opposition and failed to take their objectives, although a land raiding party temporarily captured the inlet of Mersa Sciause and destroyed coastal guns. 101 aircraft from 205 Group attacked Tobruk and the Senior Air Staff Officer, Group Captain R. Kellett who planned the air part of the operation was unfortunately forced down and taken prisoner. It was learned, subsequently, that the unusually heavy air attacks, designed to occupy the enemy's attention, aroused the suspicions of the German general who alerted all the troops in Tobruk. Another raid about this time on Benghazi also failed but a Long Range Desert Group attack on Barce destroyed sixteen Italian aircraft and did other damage.]

14th September 1942
I slept until 13.20 and then had a swim and a talk on the beach with Flying Officer Mather's crew about last night's operation. In the evening I worked in Intelligence and then went to the station cinema to see *Snow White and the Seven Dwarfs* — it is good to enter the world of fantasy and forget the war occasionally.

17th September 1942
I was up at 02.30 and after interrogations had a long talk with the Wing Commander and 'A' Flight Commander ('Strutty') in Intelligence about recent operations and future possibilities here and in the war generally. It was very interesting and as a result we didn't breakfast until 06.00.

The morning was spent in bed and having a sunbathe. Then back to work to give a lecture on 'walking back' aids.

A parcel of books sent to me from home are already popular and going the rounds. I had another talk after dinner with Tony Crockford about flying and operations. He is a very good bomber-pilot and has sound and sensible views which I respect.

18th September 1942
Flight Lieutenant Williams today took over as SIO 238 Wing from Flight Lieutenant de Saumaris ('Sos') who goes to Group HQ. After work and dinner there was a very good ENSA show, *You're Welcome*, with eight girls and four men, in their correct ratio for service entertainment!

20th September 1942
At briefing in the evening the Station Commanding Officer, the Wing Commanding Officer and both Squadron Commanders were present — both the latter are operating tonight but 'G George' 104 Squadron had magneto trouble which eventually prevented our Wing Commander from going.

23rd September 1942
A talk with Basil Blogg before he went on 'ops' as second pilot with Squadron Leader Leggate, was interesting in providing some new information on aircrew psychology.

24th September 1942
I realised today that a year ago I went to North Luffenham on my first posting to Bomber Intelligence in the RAF, it seems an age ago. At the afternoon swim at the Point we watched some amazing cutter races with army teams competing and every man rowing for himself. We' gave suitable encouragement from our concrete pile. Then we played tennis doubles and relaxed because 104 have a squadron 'stand down' tonight. A single 'stand down' here is something like being suddenly given a week's holiday in peace time because we can temporarily forget the war.

25th September 1942
I was up at 02.00 until 04.30 because 40 Squadron was operating. In the afternoon I plotted gun positions on target maps and had some tennis with Johnny Martin against Pilot Officer Proctor and Bunny Ramage. Briefing in the evening and my night duty.

Personnel of 238 Wing, 40 and 104 Squadrons, relaxing between operations on the island of Malta GC, January 1943. (*Left*) The author and Sergeant Pilot Somerville at Luqa airfield. (*Right*) At the Modern Imperial Hotel, Sliema: seated at the front are Flight Lieutenant Stewart DFC and Flight Lieutenant Baker, Adjutant of 104 Squadron. Standing behind them are Pilot Officer Daeppen, Squadron Leader Jacklyn, DFC and bar, and the hotel proprietor

Aircrew enjoying a visit to Leptis Magna

Flight Lieutenant Peterson and Flying Officer Fuller of 104 Squadron at Leptis Magna

Flight Lieutenant K. Loveless and crew, 104 squadron

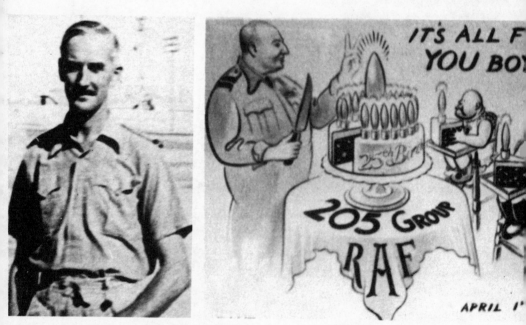

Flt. Lt. A. B. Read, Intelligence officer 108 squadron, SIO 236 wing and GIO 205 group and, (right) one of his cartoons

27th September 1942
Last night there were good results at Tobruk and good photographs including an excellent one by Basil Blogg's crew. We had enlargements made and sent to Group HQ by special despatch rider. A convoy outside the harbour was attacked by our 'M Mother' and 'S Sugar' (Wing Commander Saville) but without any direct hits being claimed. It's very hot today and there's an absolute plague of ladybirds, wasplike flies, and cockroaches — it appears to be Insect Swarming Time!

28th September 1942
The insects are terrible again and it's most unpleasant walking about or even sitting in a room because the ladybirds bite! E.R. Cro, Cypher Officer, friend from the convoy out to ME, turned up again today en route from Palestine to Group. I went for an afternoon swim with Squadron Leader Leggate, the Doc and Cro, and we had an amusing time because the Squadron Leader made an extra effort and reached the concrete marker on the edge of the Canal proper. Then, either exhausted or pulling our legs, he refused to swim back and demanded a boat. Eventually we decided that he meant it so we launched a canoe from the jetty — being viewed with great suspicion by the navy. We made the voyage back successfully and reported to the navy on the way back to the gharry — the naval lieutenant enjoyed the joke. The Squadron Leader apparently *was* serious.

At briefing at night we had a visit by two people from the Middle East Target Section. When we took them back to the mess there were great doings in the bar where the Group Captain was celebrating his fourth stripe. He's a jolly nice chap. Quietly, but very firmly he refused to let the ME chaps go and they were badly delayed. I had an excuse because an aircraft came back so I had to go off to interview the crew and also because it's my duty night.

29th September 1942
I got some sleep because all the other crews were late back and then we worked hard getting the reports off to group. There were some thick heads and short tempers at breakfast and our Wing Commander tore someone a wizard strip — obviously giving vent to his morning-after feelings! Flying Officer Allen came over to our mess in the evening and there was a night fire alarm when one aircraft landing had a flare go off underneath it.

30th September 1942

It was a very busy morning with the clerks more clueless than usual and their mistakes in typing led to trouble with Group. In the afternoon I had a swim at the Point with Squadron Leader Leggate and Tony Crockford — after a most interesting lunchtime talk with Wing Commander Saville about aircraft in general. He had stories about New Guinea Airways, Short Brothers' Aircraft Factory, Lerwicks, Maintenance Units, etc. etc. He's a most amazing and experienced airman with a fund of information and many stories of exciting incidents.

I did my part of the evening briefing — then had dinner with the Wing Commander and went out to the flare path with him to see the take-off at 21.00 hours.

Soon after our arrival at the Chance light an aircraft of 40 Squadron shot off red Very lights and came round immediately after its take-off to make an emergency landing. After recent experiences there was a little natural excitement and people got ready to dodge behind the Chance light or trucks in case of a crash. The aircraft came in fast and nearly hit the ground with the port wing — bounced off the port wheel — then on the starboard wheel and hurtled down the runway bouncing about in a most frightening manner. At the end of the flarepath — just as it appeared it would go into the lake — the Wellington took off again. Gradually gaining height (thereby showing that the engines at least were OK) he circled again. Meanwhile the ambulance and fire tender arrived at the Chance Light and I found out that the aircraft was 'M for Mother' (Sergeant Perry). In it came again with everyone taking cover and praying hard — but Sergeant Perry made quite a reasonable landing this time.

It turned out that a fabric patch from the starboard wing had stripped off and removed the IFF aerial and the patch and aerial were wound round the elevator plane preventing the aircraft from climbing properly.

As a result of this incident our aircraft were late on target (Tobruk) and this fact may have accounted for the loss of our 'F for Freddie' — Sergeant Hunt (pilot), Pilot Officer Ramage (second pilot), Sergeant Gillis and the others — I know them all and Bunny Ramage is a personal friend.

1st October 1942

Two aircraft were seen to be shot down last night — one fifteen miles SE of the harbour. He dived down but was caught and followed by searchlights and light flak until it crashed just south of the harbour. This was probably our 'Freddie' and it is unlikely that anyone got out as it was on fire in the main wing as it went down. Bunny Ramage? Basil Blogg also had a 'shaky do' last night owing to low cloud and difficulty in pinpointing. He was in the air for 9 hours 32 mins which must be a record without over-load tanks, i.e. only 750 gallons.

Tony Crockford who was swimming with me yesterday, has gone into hospital for an urgent operation for appendicitis.

3rd October 1942: Fun

I spent an interesting and enjoyable morning sailing on the lake in a Snipe class yacht. There was a 'stand down' in the evening and I was invited to go with the Wing Commander, Bob Ginn, the Engineer Officer, and Charles Baker, the Adjutant of our squadron, to the HQ of 205 Group. We had a convivial evening and I met Cro and Rhodes from the convoy days. About 01.30 we got ready to depart after prawns and beer and I was judged to be in the best condition so the Wing Commander ordered me to drive. I thoroughly enjoyed myself driving the Humber shooting brake or staff car back to Kabrit along the road running beside the Suez Canal.

4th October, 1942: Tragedy

There was a dark shadow over the Intelligence section today. Poor Bryant, one of our clerks, has received news that his wife and child are killed and missing respectively after an air raid on Colchester. We seem to feel this sad, remote news from home as much as one of our many squadron tragedies.

7th October 1942

Work as usual in the morning and a swim in the afternoon. We then had a squadron 'stand down' and Squadron Leader Strutt invited me to go to HQ with him. 'Willy' (Flight Lieutenant Williams SIO) came too and some others. We saw *Pinocchio* which was good fun. Then we had dinner at the French Club, some table-tennis and came back 'home' in the darkness while I thought of D's birthday which is today.

8th October 1942

We heard this evening of the crash at METS of Sergeant Grofski (formerly Harry Beale's second pilot). He was killed and Flight

Sergeant MacDonald had a leg amputated when the starboard engine cut soon after take-off.

9th October 1942
Tonight's briefing was at 17.30 hours and our Wing Commander (Wing Commander Saville) is taking the Group Captain (Group Captain Harrison) with him on 'ops' tonight — a 'gen' crew indeed!

10th October 1942
I was up early for interrogations and it was a very good operation over the battle area with plenty of fires started by bombing. Unhappily, 'H for Harry' is missing, the crew including Pilot Officer Penman (first 'op'), Sergeant Govett (navigation NCO) and Flight Sergeant Peters (signals NCO) — very nice chaps all of them. Flak and a small fire was seen near Daba which may have been connected with the missing aircraft.

12th October 1942
Bryant has learned that his child is safe — found in a hospital among the raid casualties at Colchester.

13th October 1942
It was a very busy morning and evening at the office and we were requested to plot the exact positions of all vegetables (mines) dropped last night — what a joke!

15th October 1942: Contrasts
Up at 02.00 for interrogating and 'T for Tommy' is missing with Sergeant Baldwin (pilot) and Flight Sergeant Elliott, the Canadian navigator, who was formerly with Pilot Officer Harlton. A plane was seen in flames at 4,000 to 5,000 feet over target.

In contrast, and this fact occurred to me, I spent a happy morning reading *The Motorists Companion* — then had tea in a tent of aircrew sergeants of 40 Squadron and a sail with Sergeant Staib on the lake in the Snipe. I am often uneasily aware of the contrast in risks taken. For example, my friends Basil Blogg and Laurie Page are going on 'ops' tonight — and also Pilot Officer Morrison ('Morry') who poked his head into Intelligence en route to a gharry. He is taking the place of a sergeant who has 'gippy tummy' and other troubles — he's *had* it! or is 'operationally tired' and will be rested. 'Willy' came in to tell me that the AOC will be at interrogation. A late take-off means a daylight return tomorrow and may mean a clear night's sleep for me if no-one comes back early. Lack of sleep is an occupational hazard with IOs of night bomber squadrons but there is no risk to life as with my aircrew friends.

16th October 1942

The AOC was there and talked to the crews and asked questions. Unfortunately it was a poor 'op', so it was disappointing for all of us including the AOC. A gale came up in the afternoon but I didn't mind, because I had received another delightful parcel of books from D. including *The Golfer's Companion*, *A Dorset Guide*, some *Autocars* and three or four novels. An hour after receiving the parcel, three very happy fellows ('Willy', Bob Ginn and myself) were looking at the *Autocars* in my room and it was an enjoyable evening.

There was heavy rain tonight — the first serious rain since March — and again operations are cancelled because of the weather.

20th October 1942

After briefing and dinner I went out to the take-off — with Wing Commander Saville. The usual excitements occurred:— (i) an aircraft of 40 Squadron came back immediately after take-off, (ii) 'X X-Ray' of 40 Squadron swung right off the runway and then proceeded to taxi back alongside the runway as the first Wellington was coming in to land! Later 'X X-Ray' took off again — still off the runway! (iii) Basil Blogg of our squadron had a u/s artificial horizon and when changed the new one was also u/s. The Wing Commander called him various things and Basil reacted and offered to take it to higher authority. Quite a little do for a time with tempers roused! Our Wing Commander can be very fiery-tempered at times — and life is pretty tense anyway.

21st October 1942: Second Operational Flight

I was up early for interrogations and then had breakfast and went back to the office. Squadron Leader Strutt (our 'A' Flight Commander) told me he was without a second pilot for tonight's operation and asked me if I'd like to go with him. It's a useful opportunity of seeing a new target (the enemy fighter landing grounds at Fuka) so I accepted and spent the early afternoon learning to log engine details, pump oil to both engines, turn on the nacelle tanks and let the front gunner in and out of his turret.

Then I played tennis with Johnny, George and Stan Dodd and later assisted with the briefing on Fuka (LG16), finding the files useful for once. We had dinner and then got ready for take-off at 20.30 hours.

'Strutty' is a good pilot and 'D for Donald' made an excellent start and climbed steadily. Nothing of importance occurred en route and we pinpointed on Ras el Kanayis a prominent cape and set course in to the target. I was sent to the astrohatch while over the target and saw flares, photoflashes galore, many other Wimpys flashing past, one fire at least and bomb flashes on the ground and coloured light tracer coming up — cluelessly fortunately — particularly in view of our fourteen runs over the target dropping single bombs and taking several photographs. 'Strutty' was determined to aim each separate bomb and make the enemy despondent for as long as possible!

We came away after an hour or so and set course for home on the first leg. I found my time throughout was well occupied with taking readings for the log and listening to the intercom. and looking out. The navigator, Pilot Officer Tommy Lonsdale, was excellent and we had no difficulties — in fact the whole crew looks like becoming a very good bombing team — determined and precise.

The Group Captain (Group Captain J.A.P. Harrison) was at the interrogation and seemed pleasantly amused at my having been on a second 'op'. He evidently agrees that it is a good thing. I interrogated Basil Blogg's crew who were in just after us and then went off to breakfast with the Wing Commander, 'Strutty', Tommy Lonsdale and Basil for a good talk about the war situation from Pearl Harbour to Stalingrad.

By the way, Pilot Officer Morrison lent me his flying kit and I had Bob Ginn's helmet — and everybody was jolly nice and helpful as usual. The esprit de corps in 104 Squadron is warm and comforting indeed, with ground personnel and flying crews of all ranks combining as a team and respecting each other's work and effort.

23rd October 1942: The Battle of El Alamein Begins
It was a busy morning and a very busy evening with briefings on the Battle Area. The business is about to begin! I watched the crews off from the cliffs and as always it was a stirring sight. In the morning 'Boom' Trenchard paid us a visit but unfortunately I was too busy to attend his talk to the aircrews. Late in the

evening Laurie Page came in to tell us of a narrow escape he and his crew had just had. He had a tyre burst while doing about 80 mph down the runway. The Wellington spun round and was written off fairly completely. Bombs rolled about all over the place and it was a miracle that one didn't go off or the plane catch fire. One of the bomb detonators had a dent in it and by about a 1 in 5000 chance it didn't explode.

24th October 1942: Alamein Artillery Barrage

Tom Allen did the interrogations with me and we found that the crews were excited about the terrific artillery ground barrage to be seen all along the line from our side firing into enemy held territory. I slept in the afternoon, had a shower and did a good briefing in front of the Group Captain and the Wing Commander — at least it seemed to go well. The activity at the Alamein front is stimulating and we all feel optimistic about the Army's chances this time against Rommel. After all, we've seen the equipment and supplies rolling in at Suez and the Bitter Lake jetties and we know that there has been solid preparation for an advance.

25th October 1942: Battle Area Operations Continue

Work was completed at 06.00 and I had breakfast before going to bed. Later I visited the dentist and received the OK about my teeth — good for my age! Briefing was at 18.00 hours and after dinner I went out to the take-off to check that each navigator knew the exact target area of the battle field. I watched the take-off and saw Johnny Martin make a very good start on his first trip as captain. Later Doc, 'Willy' and I listened-in to a church service on the forces programme.

The flies have been devilish the last two days.

26th October 1942: Successful Double Sortie

We had the usual hectic morning but last night's operation was very successful. We received a personal message from the AOC congratulating all squadrons in the group. 71 aircraft were ordered, 71 operated, 71 returned. Sixteen double sorties were ordered, sixteen operated double sorties, and sixteen returned safely. An unbeatable record! What a relief when we operate without losses!

Briefing in the afternoon for our squadron (104) on a landing ground target with dispersals all round, while Allen's squadron (40) are on the battle area again.

27th October 1942: Squadron Leader Strutt in Trouble
Interrogations and summaries took from 01.00 to 05.00.
Squadron Leader Strutt and his crew put up a very good effort
last night. They were hit over the target (battle area again) and the
hydraulics went u/s but they bombed and then got the undercart
down by violent manoeuvres and hand operation and landed
safely, thank goodness! I welcomed them back and filled in the
bombing report and details of the incident. Bed during the
morning and then received news of a 104 Squadron 'stand down'
tonight. During the afternoon I was shown a German anti-
personnel 'butterfly bomb' in the possession of our Australian
Navigation Officer next door to my room — it's probably still
'live' and I wasn't keen to handle it or even see it!

Tonight Tom Allen kindly invited me over to 40 Squadron to
dinner where the Group Captain and Wing Commander were also
present as guests. Quite a jolly evening with a very fine dinner.
We came away at 00.15 in the Group Captain's car with the
Wing Commander and a stray dog which the Wing Commander
insisted on taking to sleep in his room! Also I met Squadron
Leader Leggate back from leave and had a yarn with him before
getting to bed. In view of the constant contacts one has in Intelligence with senior officers it's remarkably fortunate for me that
they are all so easy to get on with and free from using rank in
normal conversations. I doubt if one would find this in the Army
or Navy yet it seems common in the RAF as I know it.

28th October 1942
The morning interrogations and Opsum were as hectic as ever.
Flight Lieutenant Williams (SIO) is still in Cairo, where his wife
has presented him with a son. However, Aubyn James is here to
help Tom Allen and myself in Intelligence, so we shall cope.

The AOC came to our briefing in the evening and things went
reasonably well. After dinner I had a most interesting talk with
Pilot Officer Morrison, 'Morry', on the Irish problem. He comes
from Londonderry and is a shirt manufacturer by trade. He hadn't
realised I was a school master and was quite surprised. Is this a
compliment or an insult? He thinks Ireland will have to be a
unified country one day and he himself is not opposed to this.

29th October 1942
There was a very long interrogation period from 01.50 to 07.00
hrs before having breakfast and getting to bed. Our attacks on

targets located in the battle area by our pathfinder Albacores went on all night and must be playing havoc with the enemy's nerves! Briefing took place in the evening and we had a Red Alert after dinner, but no enemy aircraft appeared.

30th October 1942: Intensive Operations Continue
It was a very good 'op' last night and a good night generally for the RAF, but Johnny Martin in our 'P for Peter' is missing. A tell-tale fire with Very lights seen at 01.30 in the target area. There was no flak reported and only a story of a possible Ju88 to account for the loss of another close friend of mine and his crew. Some good photographs were taken with several showing blast shelters for MT indicating the effectiveness of bombing. During the very busy morning Group Captain Harrison came in and was interested in everything. It really is good luck having such a charming man in charge of our wing — no 'side' — yet he keeps a good hand on the reins.

After dinner I had an interesting talk with Tommy Howes DFC, our Australian 104 Squadron Navigation Officer and Bombing Leader, about Australia and the prospects out there. He was the chap who might have blown us up with the butterfly bomb he tried to defuse! Tommy and Wing Commander Saville are two strong advocates for their country and its future and I find their arguments interesting and persuasive. After this war I may well consider emigration with my family. The Empire Air Training Scheme and the Commonwealth representatives in our squadrons have made countries like Australia, Canada, New Zealand and South Africa real and attractive to me for the first time.

1st November 1942: Still on Battle Area
We were up early for interrogation and the enemy in the battle area have had another uncomfortable night. A good fire and a smaller one in the target area were started by our 'S for Sugar', Sergeant Cairns and Sergeant Crenon, navigator.

3rd November 1942: Enemy Cracking at El Alamein
It was a busy day of briefings at all sorts of times, and exciting news from the front — and from the Adjutant (the squadron is to move to Malta).

I went to the flarepath tonight to see our squadron aircraft take-off to attack enemy vehicles in the Daba area and along the coastal road to Fuka. Everyone is feeling excited and the crews

are keen to carry on the good work. We shall have ideal targets
for our bombs if this is a real retreat.

4th November 1942: Rommel in Retreat
It's true! The front is fluid and the enemy are withdrawing from
Egypt along the coastal road and through the Sollum Pass etc.
Whizz oh! We are tonight bombing enemy transport along the
roads near the frontier.

And tomorrow, 104 Squadron, or part of it, is off to Malta to
bomb Rommel's supply routes from Italy to Tunis, Tripoli and
Benghazi. Things are certainly moving fast and in our favour.

*

The Battle of El Alamein was the climax of the months of RAF
bombing operations from the Canal permanent stations and the
squadrons and wings of 205 Group were now able to resume their
work as mobile units. In addition Malta was again to be used
strategically as an active base at Rommel's rear and astride his
lines of communications and supply from Italy to North Africa.
The History of the Second World War, Vol. IV '*The Mediterranean and the Middle East*'[1] comments as follows: 'Reflections
on the Battle of Alamein':

> Coningham's handling of the Desert Air Force and its attached
> American squadrons drew a generous tribute from General
> Montgomery, which covered also the indispensable contribution
> by the RAF medium night-bombers and the skilled pathfinders
> of the Fleet Air Arm.

General Alexander telegraphed to Mr Churchill . . . 'Work of RAF,
Dominion Air Forces, and USA Air Corps was beyond praise and
our air superiority had a great moral effect on the soldiers of both
sides.'

And according to Rommel as quoted in Brigadier Desmond
Young's *Rommel*[2] :

> British air superiority threw to the winds all our operational and
> tactical rules. The strength of the Anglo-American Air Force
> was, in all the battles to come, the deciding factor.

[1] Major-General I.S.O. Playfair, HMSO
[2] Collins, 1969.

CHAPTER FIVE

Malta GC Base

The strategic position of the island base of Malta was a constant worry to Rommel in 1942. Throughout the long retreat from Alamein to Tunis, the Afrika Korps and their Italian allies knew that behind them, their supply routes and ports were under constant threat from the Royal Air Force and Royal Navy units operating from Malta. On the other hand, the island and its people were frequently and heavily attacked by enemy bombers and were sometimes near starvation when convoys could not get through the Mediterranean. Malta and its people deserved their George Cross!

Number 205 Group squadrons were frequent visitors to the Luqa airfield, Malta, and 104 Squadron crews had been stationed there from October 1941 to January 1942, in May 1942 and now returned in November 1942.

*

5th November 1942: Kabrit, Egypt. 104 Squadron Detachment to Malta
I went out to the airfield dispersals and watched my friends loading up their aircraft. Unhappily, I am not required as there is a resident Intelligence section on Malta and so I stay behind. The afternoon take-off was quite an event, with the Group Captain and a small crowd of us to wave them off. When I shook hands with Wing Commander Saville I told him I took a poor view of him for not taking me! Laurie Page in 'D for Donald' took a long run right to the end of the runway. He has left his tennis racket behind for me to use but it looks as if tennis days are over for a while.

Others who went included 'Shag' Mercer, Charles Dallas, Sergeant Craig and Pilot Officer Morrison, Squadron Leader Leggate, Jack Parker, Sergeant Harris, Sergeant Corten and the rest of the Australians in Mather's old crew, Sergeant Sparksman etc. Squad-

ron Leader Leggate left his bush shirt and trousers for me to
look after and his letters to burn. I must admit that I'm feeling
rather miserable and forlorn at being left behind. The unity and
friendship links within the squadron are temporarily broken.

6th November 1942

The place is rather lonely but we shall be moving off soon. Squadron Leader Strutt, who remains here in command, has been
awarded an immediate DFC — good work! He deserves it because
he and the whole crew are a very determined and accurate bombing team.

7th November 1942: Leaving Kabrit

The war news continues good. The advance party of the squadron
left Kabrit today and made its way comfortably in convoy with
Bob Ginn ahead on his motor-cycle as marshal. We camped just off
the desert road from Suez to Cairo for the night.

8th November 1942: Allied Landings in Malta

It was too cold to sleep properly last night and then the flies were
very bad in the early morning. We are now at Landing Ground
N 237 along the Cairo—Alexandria road.

There is grand news today of US troops having landed in North
Africa in Algeria. Our Eighth Army advance continues, so all's well
in the war situation.

Unhappy news today was that our 'D for Donald' crashed and
blew up in taking off for an operation from Malta. I wonder who
was on board and do so hope it wasn't Laurie Page but as I know
and like all the chaps in the squadron it means more friends lost
anyway.

9th—11th November 1942 inclusive: Signals from Malta

The remainder of the squadron joined us by road convoy from
Kabrit. Advance party was then ordered off to our old ALG106
just beyond El Alamein and the main party is to follow in due
course. Another signal — this time from Malta — requested one
Wellington to join the squadron section in Malta taking spares and
to include Flying Officer Chappell in the crew. I felt very pleased
but worried about my kit. This had to be unpacked and the barest
essentials put into a single kit bag for the flight. I dashed into
Cairo to collect stationery, typewriter, maps, etc. among other
stores required. When I arrived back after all the flap I found the

main party about to set off but all our aircraft ordered to remain and operate where we are. The special trip to Malta is off and I am to stay put!

Other news from Malta is that the crew killed in the crash of 'D for Donald' included Sergeant Craig (NZ) captain, Pilot Officer Morrison second pilot, Sergeant Earney and Sergeant Holmes. 'Morry' who had such sensible views on the Irish question and was such a boisterous good fellow, killed!

12th November 1942: Egypt to Malta
The special trip is on again. Tony Crockford is captain and has a scratch crew including Sergeant Rogers as navigator. Six fitters are going with me as passengers in 'L for London'. We went to briefing and then collected flying gear for the afternoon take-off to our old advanced landing ground LG106 which is to be used for refuelling.

We duly took off and went over the battle area seeing many tracks, old defence lines, bomb craters, shell craters and one terribly blasted area of churned up sand where the artillery barrage had wiped out a square mile or so of enemy positions. Many vehicle wrecks were lying about and I noted one cluster of Hun crosses. LG106 was bleak but there was a meal waiting and Larry Wells, my Canadian friend from the early desert days, was there in charge of the place. At first there was a complete mess-up about arrangements for signalling but eventually we located Wing signals. We read over the instructions and discussed dinghy drill. (Lights flickering on and off denote distress and get ready for emergency landing in the sea.)

We took off again into a very black night and the Met forecast was poor with 5/10th low cloud and considerable high clouds in long streaks or rolls. I had the astrohatch position but my helmet was lent to Tony whose flying kit was in the desert and could not be located in time. This meant that I was not in touch on the inter-com with the pilot or other crew members. The first two hours were spent in alternately looking out and sitting down on boxes and kit bags. Then I tried to get some sleep but was wakened each twenty minutes or so by the wireless operator clambering past to launch flame floats from the flare chute. These are used to check wind drift for navigation purposes and the rear gunner estimates the angle of drift as the flame floats ignite and are left behind on the sea below. Over the low cloud, or when we went through cloud, there were severe bumps and a few air pockets —

one very bad one indeed which shook all of us and the plane. In between bumps we had a snack of biscuits and some tins of fruit.

Friday, 13th November 1942
Just after the worst bumpy period the emergency signal was given by the flickering on and off of the interior lights. The six fitters scrambled towards the astrohatch and one of them and myself lifted out the plastic dome and put it on the luggage. The air rushing by increased the noise level and we braced ourselves against the bulkheads or piles of luggage, held on tightly and prepared for trouble.

By signs I indicated that two of the fitters would go out first and second, and myself third. I looked closely at the dinghy release switch and made a mental note that I must operate this whatever happened when we hit the water. We seemed to be wallowing about a good deal and losing height slowly. However, the engines were running apparently perfectly and I concluded that it must be a part of the air frame or controls, probably the tail unit — that was damaged by the severe buffeting we had experienced.

Several times the warning lights flickered to remind us of the emergency and we braced ourselves afresh.

We had about an hour to go to ETA so I concluded that we should have a fair chance of being picked up in daylight. However, the speed of our travel puzzled me as I could feel no flaps going on to steady us for landing on the sea. Then after another half hour one of the fitters gesticulated and showed me a search light shining steadily and vertically from below on to the clouds — visible through the open hatch. Good enough! We should certainly be OK provided the kite made a reasonable crash-landing on the sea.

We seemed to go lower and circle slightly -- more light flickerings — it was about to happen, either a belly landing on land or the same on the sea. There was an obvious hold off and sinking — repeated — then a slight bump and more bumps — we were down to a perfect and normal landing on Luqa airfield. We all did thumbs up and clambered out, very relieved!

We learned that the inter-com was u/s, the wireless u/s and a short circuit of some sort in the electrical system had caused the flickering lights in the fuselage but the crew up forward were quite unaware of our anxiety. The rear gunner, however, shared our feelings — he too, had been expecting the worst since the first light warnings.

All's well that ends well!

There were details to be filled in on forms, after a long wait at the airfield and the unpacking of kit and freight. And so to a mess, billets and then a shift of billets because we met the Wing Commander and Squadron Leader Leggate who had both been on 'ops'. Everyone was jolly nice as usual. I was utterly tired out and almost asleep on my feet but could appreciate part of the ride to our new billets at Sliema some miles away.

I slept from 09.30 to 12.30 and then got up to lunch. Shaved and had a shower — then took a walk with the Squadron Leader along the sea front. It was interesting and beautiful in spite of the dullness of the day after our Egyptian bright sunshine. The Mess is very pleasant with shortages obvious but meals are better served than we have been used to recently.

Later at Intelligence I listened to the interrogation of a Beaufighter pilot (Flight Lieutenant Schmidt DFC) who had shot down two Ju52s and damaged two others. In his turn his port engine caught fire and he had to make a belly landing back at Luqa base. So this is Malta — where things happen!

14th November 1942: Test Flight Over Malta

I saw more of the island, our new home, from a bus to Luqa and then from the air as I went on an air test with Wing Commander Saville and Charles Dallas and some native fitters in our 'L for London' which had been fitted with a new main port wing. Another aircraft had taxied into the wing causing severe damage so it had to be replaced. Fortunately the new wing proved OK in fifteen minutes of test flying by the Wing Commander, including some almost vertical turns. From the air there were superb views of Valetta Harbour, the bays, cliffs and islands — and of the main island with its dense population, many towns, villlages and churches.

I felt very unhappy internally all day with 'gippy tummy' or 'Malta Dog' or whatever you like to call this diarrhoea and sickness.

In the evening I met the famous Squadron Leader Warburton DFC and two bars, of PRU fame, and spent the night of the 14th/15th working in the Luqa Intelligence office — phone ringing, different people in and out -- these IOs certainly work hard here and the methods used are sometimes different from our 205

Group practices. Luqa Intelligence handles quite a number of different types of aircraft on various operations — shipping strikes, night fighters, PRU Spitfires, Met flights, minelaying, bombers and torpedo bombers etc. etc. Some naval aircraft also operate from here.

15th November 1942

At 08.00 hours I finished duty and went back in a bus to the billets with Laurie Page and others. I slept all the morning and wakened at 14.00 hours to go to Luqa to work in the Intelligence section. Heavy rain caused cancellation of 'ops' for tonight.

Squadron leader Warburton, who went out today to photograph the results of our last night's bombing, did not return. Intelligence are worried about him.

16th November 1942: *Food Shortage*

More rain today and no operations because of weather. I cleared up the attack of the 14th/15th and got to know more of the local Intelligence people who are a very nice crowd. With the Wing Commander and Squadron Leader I went back to the billets and then to an evening out with them to the flicks — *These Glamour Girls*. The film was not bad, and two 'glamour girls' tried to attract us afterwards who were quite young girls, only 15 to 18 years of age.

We went on to 'The Chocolate Box' and 'Charlie's Bar' and had more drinks than ever before in my life — owing to the CO's 'Another one for the road', repeated about seven or eight times. We talked with two English girls married to civilians on the island and learned the truth of the food situation. They get one tin of bully and one tin of sardines per fortnight and live mainly on bread. This explains the nasty blotches on many legs and arms of civilians. We walked back to the mess with them and gave them a tin of bully, a tin of sardines and a tin of the Squadron Leader's cigarettes. And so to a late meal and bed.

17th–19th November 1942

On the night of the 17th/18th two Naval Albacores went out with an accompanying plane and sank a large enemy tanker. There were great explosions and the oil on the water caught fire. On the same night a Beaufighter pilot shot down a Ju88 and damaged another.

Our squadron bombers attacked a former French aerodrome now used by the Germans, for two nights, but in poor weather conditions. On the night of the 19th/20th we attacked airfields at Catania, Gerbini and Cormiso to give indirect support for a convoy nearing Malta from Alexandria. 'E for Edward' (Flight Lieutenant Mercer), was missing after Catania and believed seen shot down. 'Shag' Mercer is another fine chap gone — and a good crew with him.

20th November 1942: Convoy Arrives
This morning while completing the summaries at about 07.00 hours one could sense an unusual bustle of life and excitement outside and in the harbour area — the convoy has arrived! This convoy 'Stoneage' had all four merchant vessels unharmed — the first to get to Malta safely for many months. On the way back to the mess we saw the merchant ships and naval escorts in the port. I was so sleepy and tired that I fell asleep listening to the news at 09.00. After sleeping all the morning I was wakened at 15.00 by the Wing Commander to have a meal with him on the balcony overlooking the garden of the Sliema hotel which we occupy for billets and Mess. He talked freely and easily of his brother's station in a well-watered valley in NSW — of his father's cement works at Portland and the land they had bought near Bathurst. Then turning from his family and Australia, he discussed some of his own basic ideas in education, knowing of my background and interest in schools and schooling.

Among his suggestions were (i) that every boy and girl should be able to write a conversational and interesting letter as a vital means of communication and a social asset. (I think he realised from censorship experience that few men write good letters to their wives and families), (ii) that all children should be taught the use of the typewriter which is now so useful in commerce and even for letter writing, and (iii) that sex education should be part of the curriculum and that boys and girls should be educated in mixed schools. These are sound ideas. I can enjoy talking with Wing Commander Saville on any topic, and it seems to be mutual. He often likes to discuss squadron problems and perhaps this eases some of the tremendous pressures and tensions of operational command. We went up to Luqa together at 17.00 and I tried to sort matters out and make things ready for Squadron Leader Leggate who has most kindly offered to do my job tonight. What a squadron!

Then the Wing Commander drove the bus back as the driver had
cut off the top of his finger. He drove it very well and we told him
he should remuster as a driver.

And so to a quiet evening and early night for *me* — but at the
last minute the Wing Commander went off on 'ops' to pilot a
Wellington with a 4,000lb bomb which was requested at the last
minute by blasted HQ! He ought to be having a good night's rest
but typically does the job himself, knowing that all the crews are
as tired as he is.

21st and 22nd November 1942: Wing Commander Warburton

They have been days of sleeping until 15.00 hours — then working
all evening and nights from 17.00 hours to 07.00 hours next
morning. It's very wearing, this business of double and treble
sorties, and the preparation of consolidated reports and Opreps
takes a hell of a time after the interrogations are over.

On the 22nd I saw Squadron Leader, now Wing Commander,
Warburton DFC, as perky as ever and about to return to his PRU
work by going off at 07.30 in his Spitfire to photograph Bizerta,
Tunis and Tripoli. He had scared us all by not coming back on the
15th from a similar trip and now I heard the story. He had been
shot up over Bizerta and made a forced landing at Bone aerodrome
further west in our territory. Then 'Warby' made his way to
Gibraltar, collected a delivery Spitfire and on the way back to
Malta shot down a Ju88. What a man! He joked about his batman
whom he found on return had already made off with all his
clothes — but now said that he'd 'get it back from the laundry'.
Sounds as though thieving is the same here as in Egypt! On the
night of the 22nd/23rd the rest of 104 Squadron arrived from
Egypt with three sacks of mail. The 'tour expired' people have
been sent home and new crews have taken their places. Old
'Benny' (Pilot Officer Benitz) is back with us and Pilot Officer
Kemp, Squadron Leader Strutt DFC, Pilot Officer Tommy
Lonsdale and Flying Officer Tommy Howes DFC are all among
the arrivals. 'Strutty' has his DFC ribbon up. It's high time that
the Wing Commander had a decoration after all he has done with
the squadron.

23rd November 1942

I slept until 15.00, got up for tea and there was news of a 'stand
down'. Thank God! — I feel 'op tired' or 'clapped out' as they say
in the squadron.

Letters and some photos from home did much to comfort and refresh today, and D. still loves me apparently in spite of my absence of over a year. In some ways it seems an eternity but I'm sure that fifteen minutes together and all would be as though we had never been parted. Duncan looks much like I did as a child and as for Elizabeth, I can't tell at the moment — it's hard to realise that I have a daughter. Let's hope I see them soon before they lose all their funny little ways.

24th November 1942: Valetta
Two squadron aircrew chaps and myself spent a pleasant morning looking around Valetta after going across by ferry and climbing laboriously with perspiration due to battle dress and woollen underwear, up the steep steps and incline to the main street. Plenty of bomb damage is visible. It seems an interesting place with its narrow streets and tall houses and business premises. There is a fine view of the Grand Harbour, deep and with sheltered creeks overlooked by battlements. We went down the lift to the quayside road and suddenly the air raid sirens sounded and a few puffs of heavy A/A appeared high overhead.

Spitfires were up immediately and there was some cannon fire up above. For a few moments we felt a bit of panic, being caught in the open in one of the world's hottest places for bombs. The feeling soon passed and we found a shelter and watched from the doorway. No bombs were dropped and we were able to walk to the steps and up to the town again — and back by the ferry to Sliema. And so to work in the afternoon in the crowded squadron buses. There is good news from the Russian front — and we've taken Agedabia in Libya.

25th November 1942: Malta to Egypt (With Wing Commander Saville in 'B For Beer')
I worked all night and came back to breakfast tired and sleepy. At 15.30 I got up and had some bully beef with tea as I'd missed lunch. It was a good job I had the bully for at 17.15 the Wing Commander dashed in to say he was leaving for Egypt immediately and I was to go with him. We picked up a few clothes and dashed off in a car to Luqa. There we met Sergeant Setterfield and crew and got a very short and hurried briefing on 'met', beacons en route, etc. I couldn't get a parachute or a Mae West. Wellington 1c 'B for Beer' (40 Squadron) was still in a pen and hadn't been touched for a fortnight. In addition it had been

condemned as 'ropey' and unsuitable for operations by Squadron Leader Booth (40 Squadron) owing to excessive oil consumption.

However, nothing like that stops our Wing Commander! He had extra cans of oil put in, then started the engines and taxied out. And so off into the night — and what a night! I felt none too confident about the trip and had anyone else been piloting I should have been really nervous. We met heavy cumulus and cumulo-nimbus clouds, an obvious warm front, when an hour out. The CO called me up front to look at it and it was a lovely sight with the moon peeping over the tops and lighting up the cloud hills and valleys. We climbed up and up towards the dark mass and very ominous it looked to me. However, the Wing Commander found a cloud valley to go through the front and then swept over or through what followed. I went back to doze and look out occasionally at the clouds now in layers of stratus with rain showers from broken cumulus.

About three hours out from Malta we hit some bumps and lost height in a series of drops through sleet and hail which rattled on the astrodome and fabric of the surging aircraft. After fifteen minutes or so it cleared and we were out of trouble. The navigator took the opportunity to have flame floats dropped for wind drift. At five hours out the sea was covered by a dark mist of stratus and the moon was obscured by alto-stratus — one felt somewhat isolated and lost in mid air.

At six hours the navigator was obviously puzzled at the non-appearance of the coast. The cloud increased and I felt far from comfortable. Oil was being pumped regularly by hand pump into the engines and the main tank of 14 gallons was dry. We put in another 16 gallons from cans — a messy business.

In a clear patch I saw some half a dozen vessels below steaming rapidly west and leaving long white wakes behind them. I thought we must obviously be north of track and wanted to suggest going due south to make a land fall. However, the Wing Commander had the same idea and we turned south, off course.

After a false hope I really did see the coastline, dark in comparison with the sea and visible through breaks in the cloud. Once over the coast the cloud cleared except for some mist and rain showers. I recognised Matruh, or thought I did, then Ras el Kenayis — but later the real Ras el Kenayis came up definitely and I saw a beacon. At this point the engines, or one engine, ran very roughly and the aircraft shook with the vibration. Oil was quickly pumped through again and very gradually the vibration lessened.

I was now wondering if there would be a flare path out for us — we had seen no lights other than the beacon. Happily I soon saw a flare path and recognised it was ours and was extremely thankful! The crew were very relieved, too, as they had begun to expect some dinghy hours on their last flight — they have finished their tour of 'ops' and are probably going back to UK. Not only was the flare path out for us but we had a welcoming party of the Group Captain, Squadron Leader Carter, and Flight Lieutenant Kusiar come out to meet us. It was very pleasant and cheering to be welcomed in such a way and we enjoyed a good chat and had beer, cheese, bread and butter, biscuits and pickles which revived us considerably before we went to bed.

The reason for this hurried flight back to Egypt in a discarded Wellington with two worn out engines was that the Wing Commander was dissatisfied with our bomber strength on Malta. He wished to arrange for another squadron and the 238 Wing HQ staff to join 104 Squadron at Luqa.

26th November 1942: LG106 (at Sidi Abd El Rahman near El Alamein, Egypt
We breakfasted at 09.00 hours and enjoyed it immensely and felt on holiday and pleased with life. The Adjutant told me that my Flight Lieutenant rank has come through with his own and Stan Dodds. It was really good meeting the other squadron chaps again and only the latrine problem was difficult! The camp is rather primitive in this respect.

In the afternoon we toured the local battlefield and viewed enemy tanks and trucks destroyed by fire and high explosive — some probably from our bombing. I felt that our bombing had evidently done very well because of the numerous slit trenches constructed — including small ones alongside each vehicle. The afternoon made me feel melancholy at the futility of war. I picked up a *Panzer Gruppe* diary, an Italian propaganda booklet, two enemy identity cards and a ship recognition pamphlet. At tea we found that the squadron is moving back to reform, refit or something. I am moving off at midnight in the ambulance with Doc.

27th November 1942: LG106 to LG237 (40 Kilometres from Cairo)
We journeyed for some three hours seeing occasional small German cemeteries by the roadside and burned out vehicles and tanks. The Germans seem to bury their dead at or near the spot

where they were killed while our people seem to be transferred to big war cemeteries at central points e.g. Alamein. We stopped for tea and the night at a staging point where we slept fitfully on the front seats until 05.00 when breakfast was prepared of tea, beans, bacon, biscuits etc. Doc shared my mug and I shared his plate.

And so off through the desert to the new landing ground, with little seen except minefields, and idle wogs by the roadside. One thing annoyed us — the leading truck driver pulled up at a NAAFI because he thought he'd like some tea. Everyone stopped and hared off with mugs to get a drink. Wireless Officer Betts and the Doc and I tried to get them back but eventually half an hour was lost. Doc and I think the RAF could well imitate the army in having a bit more discipline. The flies are ghastly at LG237 — and this is the end of November.

28th–30th November 1942
Arriving on the 27th we pitched camp, eating with the airmen and sleeping in a tent with Doc, Bob Ginn and Leslie Coulter. Next day we had to move again and repitch the camp. Basil Blogg went off to Helwan on the 27th en route for England. I'm very glad and so was he! He promised to drop a line to D. when he gets home. In the afternoon I went into Cairo with three others — Cairo is now within easy distance. We stayed at The National and I went to the flicks with Bob after spending a pleasant fifteen minutes in Jacques buying D. some dainties and thinking rather tenderly and longingly of her.

Next day we visited the officers' shop and then went back to camp and the flies.

On the 29th evening I couldn't get my wireless set to work just when the Wing Commander wanted to hear Churchill's speech — 'Wing Co' had a few amusing comments on my incompetence. On the 30th we waited all the morning for the Wing Commander to go to Cairo. Eventually we got off after lunch of toast and beans, Harry and Arnold Beale were in the mess. We then went shopping with mess funds — first to the NAAFI where we bought jams, canned meat and fruits etc. for the mess and some individual items for Sergeant Lynch and crew. We cleaned up at Wellington House and made for Jacques where the Wing Commander astonished the girls by purchasing £50 worth of ladies' nightdresses, pyjamas, slips, knickers and stockings. We all clustered round and helped select the pretties and then went off buying sweets, shoes and a handbag in the arcades and narrow streets of the city.

We had dinner at the Bar Restaurant and spent the evening at Groppi's. There was an enjoyable altercation between the Wing Commander and the Military Police at the gate of the barracks over checking-out procedures. Then back to camp and more fun with the Group Captain and Wing Commander trying to compose a signal calculated to satisfy 205 Group! Wing Commander Saville has been successful in his mission and 238 Wing and 40 Squadron will be joining 104 Squadron in Malta to form a more formidable bombing force.

1st December 1942: Return to Malta by sea

I am to travel with the Wing HQ party by sea while Wing Commander Saville and most of the squadron personnel will fly back to the island.

Our transport was 45 minutes late in arriving and we left at 06.45 stopping at Half Way House before going on to Alexandria and a long wait at the Embarkation Office. No notice was taken of the Group Captain's rank — he is too nice to be fierce and the Squadron Leader Embarkation seemed cocky and incompetent.

Eventually billets were found for the night. The others went into town but the Adjutant (Flight Lieutenant Baker) and I stayed in and visited the mess with its notice 'Senior Officers only, invited'. We invited ourselves in, saw the PMC and got a wizard meal as a reward for our perseverance — tomato soup, veal, potatoes, onions, cauliflower, plus an unknown sweet with sauce, bananas and coffee. It was equal to Heliopolis mess and much cheaper.

2nd December 1942: HMS Welshman

We all went to breakfast in the mess. There were no incidents and we enjoyed it but extra rolls brought in were stale — deliberate? Lunch was later arranged at the mess for all of us by the camp commandant — but we never had it. We were urgently told to get 40 lbs of personal kit out — the rest of luggage to go separately. In doing this we missed our lunch and were put in big diesel trucks, now thinking we were probably going by air to Malta. But the trucks took us to the docks and there alongside a quay was HMS *Welshman*, big and impressive at first sight. We saluted the quarterdeck as we went on board and were very well received. I was placed in the Senior Engineer's cabin (Lieutenant Mackenzie) after he came to the wardroom and took me along personally. He told me that at sea the officers seldom slept in their cabins, preferring to lie down in clothes at their stations ready for instant action.

I went on deck to see the port disappear after good views of destroyers, cruisers and a battleship in the harbour. Out past a wreck and as we gathered speed I noted how very alert the gun crews were — scanning the sky constantly. A good dinner, a read of some geographical magazines and then to bed to sleep soundly in spite of movement and slight vibration.

3rd December 1942: 40 Knots

It was a day of great interest — we joined a convoy and sailed past some coastal places known before only as targets. HMS *Welshman* and some destroyers guarded the convoy of merchant ships and fighters patrolled overhead all day.

Two Red Alerts during the day gave a clue to the dangers the Navy has to meet — and so did a visit to the engine room and boiler room. Later we increased speed to something about the maximum of 40 knots and left the convoy behind as we went to the wardroom for drinks and dinner. Going on deck in the dark and to the stern I looked out over the boiling narrow white wake stretching out miles behind us and reflected how this could be seen from the air by enemy aircraft. This ship and its fine company of men has run the gauntlet many times between Alexandria and Malta and so far has survived attacks by aircraft and submarines mainly because of its high speed. She is a fleet minelayer but has been used to supply the beleaguered island with essentials when convoys have failed to get through.

(Unhappily HMS *Welshman* was torpedoed on 1st February 1943 by a German U-boat some forty miles east of Tobruk while between Malta and Alexandria. She sank with heavy loss of life.)

4th December 1942: The Grand Harbour

I felt the slowing down at dawn and on getting up saw land. After breakfast I went on deck as we entered the magnificent harbour with its off-shoot creeks. One could see evidence of bomb damage on shore and in the harbour (wrecks). We made alongside amidst handclapping and cheers by the populace and I saw the Governor, Lord Gort, among the people on the quay waving and smiling. We went on shore and to Air Headquarters — and almost immediately there was an air raid warning. There was a letter from D. waiting at the mess and then I got the bus up to the airfield to work — I'm on duty tonight.

5th December 1942: Another Convoy

Interrogations and summary were finished at 07.30 and I returned to the mess by bus. Another convoy is in — the one we left on the 3rd. Again one could sense the excitement and happiness of the people and there was hooting of sirens from the dockyard area and some distant cheering. I spent the day in bed until 16.00 and then went up to Luqa with the Wing Commander to do another night's duty — this time with Aubyn James to help me.

6th December 1942: Celebration

Early morning breakfast at the Luqa mess with the Wing Commander in very good mood — then back with him to Sliema and so to bed. In the afternoon I went up to work and did the briefing for Aubyn James's squadron (40). At 17.00 I went off with the Wing Commander and 'Strutty' but not back to the mess as I had expected. We called at the British Institute, a fine well-equipped building with a bar and a library. We had some rum at the bar and talked to a little Maltese—English girl of 17½ years — a pleasant and attractive lass. She took us to Monica's Bar and then went home, 'because Mama is strict', like so many wise Maltese parents (as our aircrews are finding out).

We went back to the institute and eventually got the Wing Commander to take us 'home' to dinner. I wrote letters and went to bed but the Wingco and the Adjutant went to Charlie's bar and returned about 23.30 in somewhat boisterous good spirits. An argument with the mess secretary over the closing of our bar woke me up and there was a terrific but amusing din going on downstairs. Old Wingco was inarticulate by this time but very forceful. Later I had a visit from the Wing Commander, Squadron Leader Leggate and the Adjutant all very merry and practically out. What a night! It was very funny actually — and no one was nasty or violent — just very merry — and they deserve and need these breaks to relax.

[In retrospect it appears that our Wing Commander, Flight Commander and the Adjutant were celebrating because of likely prior knowledge of the decoration made public on 8.12.42.]

7th December 1942: A Bad Crash at Luqa

I spent a lazy and enjoyable morning shaving and bathing in cold water and listening to Charles' account of last night. Then I went to briefing in the afternoon and was on duty at night. When the squadron aircraft returned from the first sorties I went out to the flarepath to collect the navigator's logs and interrogate the crews. While alongside the runway talking to one of our crews I witnessed a particularly spectacular and terrible crash. A replacement Wellington from Egypt came in to land and hit the ground on the wrong side of the Chance light. It bounced 50 feet into the air with the engines going all out in an effort to take-off again — then stalled and fell into and partly went through an aircraft pen near the eastern end of the runway. Immediately fire started and the plane became a roaring furnace giving off dense black smoke. It seemed impossible that there could be any survivors but I could see men running towards the plane and a hose playing on the burning mass. Apparently the aircraft broke its back and some of the crew and passengers were thrown out. Others were dragged out and later I heard that seven were injured, two were OK and four killed. Other aircraft coming in to land were in difficulties from the smoke but fortunately no one else pranged.

8th December 1942
[The Operational Record of 104 Squadron gives 8.12.42 as the date on which Wing Commander D.T. Saville received the award of the DFC for courage and devotion to duty. This thoroughly deserved decoration gave a lot of satisfaction to those who like myself worked under his inspiring leadership.]

In the evening I went out with Dick Kemp, Charles Dallas, Ted Stewart and Carmichael to see *The First of the Few* — the life of R.J. Mitchell the designer of the Spitfire. It was excellent. We went over by steam ferry and back by 'dicer' — the gondola efforts of the Maltese rowed by one or two men facing forwards and from the forward end. We just missed one boat and had to grab the owner of another who was skulking under the dark shadow of the ferry staging. It was teeming with rain and blowing somewhat, so I suppose the boatman didn't wish to go across the harbour to Sliema. Anyway he took us after we threatened to throw him in.

12th December 1942
War news is of patrol activity at El Agheila in preparation for an assault. On this front we have slight air superiority but in Tunisia the First Army seems to be enduring a nasty hammering from the Luftwaffe.

13th December 1942: A Good Night
A good night for the squadrons — we set an enemy tanker on fire.

14th December 1942

I began work at 07.00 hours and did 26½ hours without sleep. Another good night for the squadron at Tunis — La Goulette.

17th December 1942: A Bad Night

I was on duty at night and it was a bad night indeed. Flight Lieutenant Charles Dallas and crew (Pilot Officer Silver, Flying Officer Coulter, Sergeant Lines, Sergeant Booth, Sergeant Stanley) in our 'F for Freddie' are missing. They are one of our best crews and really good chaps, all of them. Three aircraft were sent out to search from Malta but no dinghy was sighted. There were night fighters on the prowl and 'A for Apple' (Sergeant Webb) was shot up and his wireless operator wounded. 'R for Robert' (Tony Crockford) was also attacked by a fighter and came back dripping petrol from two big holes in the wing. His gunner was slightly wounded and the hydraulics and the turret were u/s. I went out to the dispersal area with Tony to see the damage. Worst of all — a Halifax with a Polish crew and a total of 16 men on board, including among the passengers Flight Lieutenant Len Vaughan DFC of 40 Squadron, crashed at Luqa on landing after being recalled. They were all tour-expired men returning to England, and Len, a tail gunner of great experience and a real character in the mess, had survived 100 operations — and now was tragically killed on his way home. There is consternation and gloom in the mess over this cruel blow from fate. [This fine officer was awarded the DSO on 21st December 1942]

18th December 1942: Air Raid on Luqa

Luqa was dive-bombed tonight by some thirty or more enemy aircraft. Not all bombed the target area — some jettisoned in the sea — but in spite of this we lost seven aircraft destroyed and three damaged. The Wellingtons, back from a first sortie and refuelling for a second sortie, were caught in the open alongside the runway and not dispersed. One enemy plane was shot down which was not good enough. Luckily for me I was not on duty but heard and saw the raid from Sliema.

The amiable Flying Officer 'Splodge' Moore RAAF told me of his experience in this raid. He was the navigator of Ken Loveless' crew. Their Wellington was bombed up for the second sortie and just about to take-off, when they received a signal advising: '30 plus bandits have been picked up on the radar screen, on course for Tunisia — if a change of course takes place in the direction of Malta you will be signalled immediately. Meantime engines are to be switched off.'

The rear gunner commented on the inter-com., 'They're a panicky lot of twits, the kites are only transports on their way to Tunisia.'

The next moment they got an immediate signal: 'Bandits heading for Malta.' At the same time bombs started bursting everywhere. The crew ran for the nearest cover, ending up in a disused quarry about 100 yards away, where one of the crew in his anxiety broke his collarbone. Ironically the rear gunner had trouble in getting out of the rear turret, and had to use the manual operating device to do so — it was an object lesson to him not to open his mouth so soon in future. Splodge's comment was that to him the experience was 'as good as a dose of salts'.

There is no news of Charles Dallas and crew.

[In February 1943 we received news that Charles and at least some of his crew were prisoners of war. Thank goodness.]

19th December 1942
The damage was soon cleared away — Malta is used to this! At night I was off duty again and went to the flicks with Flight Lieutenant Davies. Most of the others were at a dance and returned home singing the 'Wog Anthem' and 'Up your pipe, King Farouk'.

20th and 21st December 1942: Changes in Command
Usual routine except for changes in command. The new wing commander for our squadron, Wing Commander G.H.N. Gibson DFC, has arrived to take the place of Wing Commander D.T. Saville DFC. And Squadron Leader J.F. Newman DFC is taking over 'B' Flight, vice Squadron Leader Leggate. About this time Wing Commander Morton took over 40 Squadron from Wing Commander Ridgeway. Wing Commander Saville has commanded 104 Squadron since 4th August so has had five months of intensive operations and has operated himself on many missions, usually those which were most hazardous. He deserves a long rest but is not the sort of chap to stay away long from a squadron.

*

Wing Commander Donald Teale Saville DSO DFC — of Sydney, Australia, born Portland NSW 22nd December 1903, was killed in action 25th July 1943.

In No 104 Wellington Bomber Squadron, Wing Commander Saville earned the reputation of being a supremely confident and fearless man, dedicated to the war effort, alert and daring but as a commanding officer, understanding and humane. He was well liked personally by those who knew him and highly respected by everyone under his command. Off-duty he had remarkable ability to relax and a splendid sense of humour.

Under his leadership the squadron crews attacked targets with determination and spirit, reaching a peak of efficiency in the varied and difficult operations from Malta. With the Wing Commander setting an example the aircrews rose above the additional strains of operating from bomb-ravaged facilities at Luqa airfield, amidst improvisations and shortages of all kinds, and under constant threat of retaliatory attacks by enemy bombers.

He assumed command of No 218 (Gold Coast) Stirling Bomber Squadron at RAF Station Downham Market, Norfolk, on 28th March 1943 — and (typically) went on operations the first night as second pilot with Squadron Leader Beck in 'O for Orange', the target being St Nazaire. Subsequently he operated as captain pilot on nine occasions with the squadron — the last time being the night of 24th/25th July 1943 when the target was Hamburg and the Wing Commander was in command of Stirling 'P for Peter'.

Twenty crews were detailed and briefed, one jettisoned and returned early, one brought bombs back, seventeen crews bombed the target and returned safely, one aircraft, 'P for Peter', was missing and reported shot down by a night fighter over the target. Wing Commander Saville was awarded the DSO under *London Gazette* authority 27th July 1943. In *Air War Against Germany and Italy 1939–1943* by John Herington, one of the official volumes in the series *Australia in the War of 1939–1945*, there are three references to him.

Like many squadron commanders, Saville chose to set an example by going on the most dangerous operations. He stated (privately) that he would never send a crew on any operation where he was not prepared to go himself. His crews knew this instinctively. He believed that risks had to be taken to win the war and that it was the job of a bomber squadron to hit the enemy hard and often. 'Don' Saville DSO DFC should be remembered as a great Australian.

*

25th December 1942: Christmas Day
I went up to the aerodrome to collect some aerial wire and give
the clerks some cigarettes and books. Flying Officer Brown of
Signals came back and helped me with the radio set. Then I
listened in to the King's speech with Wing Commander Ridgeway
of 40 Squadron, Pilot Officers Whitmell and Dobbin, and it was a
jolly good effort this year. It was enjoyable trying out the pipe
bought yesterday from the Malta pipe factory. Later I dashed off
to a church service with Aubyn James at 15.30 but it was a
mistake so we went for a walk instead.

As we went out the old Wingco and the Adjutant waved and
shouted already very happily celebrating. I found it rather hard to
take seeing the many happy families in the streets and spent a
quiet evening in the mess reading and listening-in.

26th December 1942
Work all day as usual and the squadrons are operating again.
Tom Allen helped at night and things went smoothly. A Liberator
flight sergeant aircrew produced some chocolate and biscuits
which we enjoyed as rare treats.

27th December 1942 to 4th January 1943
Nothing valuable to report apart from a useful visit to Air Head
Quarters Malta, to see Squadron Leader McNaught, the Senior
Intelligence Officer on the 30th. Flying Officer Ham Fuller RAAF
and crew joined 104 Squadron on 1st January 1943.

5th January 1943: Command Performance
I enjoyed a good evening with six others at *Command Performance* at the Valetta Theatre given by the men and women of the
Malta Garrison. Squadron Leader Strutt had arranged a box for us
and the old Vauxhall staff car carried us there and back sitting on
each other. 'Strutty' suggested it was time I did another 'op' with
him and I agreed to go tomorrow if it could be arranged.

6th January 1943
This afternoon AHQ Malta refused permission for me as an IO to
go on the operation to Sousse, although our new Wing Commander (Wing Commander Gibson) had readily agreed. I was not
on Intelligence duty but went up to Luqa and borrowed Strutty's
bike for a ride through Krendi to the coast at the Blue Grotto with
steep cliffs about 200 feet high and blue water and breaking seas

underneath. There I sat and smoked my pipe and watched the sun go down over Filfla Island — a small island off the coast which is sometimes used as a holding point for our returning aircraft to circle around. I rode back through Zurrieq with its narrow smelly streets and then along narrow lanes with stone walls, quarries with bottoms green with grass or shoots of young corn, terraced hillsides with small fields enclosed by stone walls. The frequent stone shelters in the fields and along the roadside are wise precautions against sudden air raids. Watching the take-off of the Wellingtons for operations against Tunis and Sousse I reflected that I might have been on 'F for Freddie' with Squadron Leader Strutt, Tommy Lonsdale and the others. They are flare dropping tonight for other bombers at Sousse. After dinner at the Luqa Mess and an enjoyable time listening-in, I heard that Tony Crockford was returning early so waited for him to come in. He had a duff engine, yet being Tony he brought back the 4,000 lb bomb and did not jettison. We went back to Sliema on the bus together, chatting cheerfully and little thought of what was happening at Sousse.

7th January 1943: Squadron-Leader Strutt and Crew Missing
Squadron Leader Strutt and his crew are not back from last night's operation and I soon learned to my sorrow that a plane had been seen hit over Sousse. An explosion occurred at 7,000 feet and then an aircraft fire with Very lights and small explosions from it was seen on the ground three to five miles SSW of the target area. Perhaps some of the crew got out — Sergeant O'Keefe might have done so as rear gunner. It's a rotten blow for the squadron — they were a 'gen' crew — keen and competent. I spent the day clearing up the office and working hard — just as well to do so on such a day. It is also a sobering thought that only a chance decision by AHQ prevented me from going in 'F for Freddie' — the second 'F for Freddie' lost in three weeks. In the evening after briefing for an attack on Castel Benito airfield near Tripoli I had an interesting talk with one of the PRU pilots who knows RAF station Benson near Oxford which I had visited during training. There would be a crowd in the mess at breakfast — no one at lunch and all at various points high over Europe in Spitfires or Mosquitoes then by 17.30 hours all would be back in England — with their photographs to be studied for intelligence information. This type of reconnaissance is an important source of intelligence, produces many of our bombing targets and provides a check on the success

or failure of particular missions through the comparison of 'before' and 'after' photographs. Here in Malta, of course, we have our own PRU Spitfires for these duties.

8th January 1943
I was on duty at night with Aubyn James and as usual went out to the flarepath to interrogate and collect first sortie reports in an old bus. We were surrounded by planes being bombed up from long bomb-trolley trains and refuelling parties hard at work with bowsers. It still gives me a queer sensation when I think about the possibilities of an accident or a sudden dive-bombing attack like 18th December last as there are no shelters close to the flarepath. Tonight the second sortie was cancelled because a gale sprang up and there was heavy rain.

9th January 1943
Back at 10.30 from Luqa I watched Tommy Lonsdale's kit being cleared up and his name is now crossed off the door of the room which he shared with Tony Crockford. In the afternoon I went up to the airfield for briefing and afterwards explained a new method of attacking a target as developed by Messrs Peet, Beattie, McRae and Chappell. Squadron Leader Newman listened sympathetically and so did the Group Captain himself but I doubt if anything ever came of it.

For a change I came back to Sliema by bicycle through Qormi, the outskirts of Hamrun and Birkirkara. It was a jolly interesting trip through built-up area most of the way. Birkirkara seems a decent place with better dressed people and a railway used to run there and out to Rabat, the famous lace centre, from Valetta. Now no rails are left but the route can be seen.

10th January 1943
On duty all day. The failure of the power supply in the evening led to an amusing scene in the Luqa Operations Room with the Group Captain, Wing Commander Morton of 40 Squadron and Squadron Leader Newman all trying to work a pressure lamp. Having nearly blown myself up in the desert on several occasions with pressure lamps in the Intelligence tent, I stood on one side and watched the proceedings with enjoyment. Then the Station Commander got on to the power house by phone and some chump at the other end couldn't understand what he was saying. 'This is the Group-Captain — the Station Commander! No! not the guardroom!

Lt. T. E. W. Howes DFC inside his 'above age' tent

Flying Officer H. M. Fuller usefully employed outside his tent

The officers of 104 Squadron at Gardabia May 1943. Wing Commander C. J. Mount DSO DFC seated centre flanked by Squadron Leader T. R. Fox and Squadron Leader L. A. Parry

Some were lucky; an example of the damage a Wellington could sustain and still return to base

Others were less fortunate: a Halifax of squadron explodes when bombing-up at Gard

A Wellington taking off at Kairouan crashes at the end of the runway owing to a burst tyre. Fire causes the explosion of the bomb load

Who is that at the other end? Get me Mr Crisp — is he there?'
and so on with repetitions.

15th January 1943: Tripoli
The night of 14th/15th was very successful when eight aircraft of
104 plus eight aircraft of 40 Squadron attacked Tripoli docks and
shipping and one aircraft of 104 attacked Sousse — all seventeen
planes attacked primary targets — all seventeen planes returned.
The AOC sent a special message of congratulation to the aircrews
and groundcrews on this achievement and our Group Captain
Harrison of 238 Wing added his message of congratulation. The
lone aircraft at Sousse was Squadron Leader Newman with the
BBC correspondents who recorded a running commentary on the
heavy flak.

*

WING COMMANDER SAVILLE'S LAST OPERATION WITH 104 SQUADRON
On the night of January 14th/15th, Flying Officer H.M. Fuller and
his crew operated against Tripoli docks in 'Q Queenie' 104 and
were taken out to their aircraft by Flight Lieutenant Ted Stewart
and Wing Commander Saville. Our former CO who relinquished to
Wing Commander Gibson on 19.12.42 had not yet left Malta and
apparently was having a last look at a 104 Squadron take-off.
However, the truck first stopped at the Wellington next to
'Q Queenie', and the Wing Commander, in his blue uniform and
not attired in any way for flying, got out to talk to an inexperienced
crew whom he must have known needed encouragement. 'Ham'
Fuller said afterwards that it was quite apparent that the Wing
Commander sensed some nervousness existed with the pilot so,
then and there, he very diplomatically climbed the ladder and
took over, being careful not to upset the crew in any way.

With the Wing Commander on board the crew later took off for
a successful operation and returned safely to Luqa.

Perhaps this effective but irregular and 'off the cuff' incident
illustrates something of the Saville-type leadership. It was a
personal leadership which inspired 104 Squadron crews to perform
courageously from Kabrit and Malta during months of intense
operational pressure.

*

16th January 1943
Today I heard an account of Squadron Leader Newman's recent
flight to Sousse with Denis Johnson of the BBC and another
engineer chap. As a main plane change of the Wellington was
necessary afterwards it was evidently a good trip from the experience point of view. It was lucky for them that they didn't
share Squadron Leader Strutt's bad fortune over that well-defended
target. The heavy flak is accurate at Sousse and night fighters
operate as well.

We had two visitors at the briefing tonight for Tripoli docks, a
Mr Batten of *Time and Life* (an American war correspondent) and
an Air—Sea—Rescue flight lieutenant.

17th January 1943: 'Shaky Do' at Tripoli 16th/17th January
It was a successful raid, and all the aircraft got back, but the crew
of 'G for George' had a 'shaky do'. In spite of their ordeal the
crew were calm and collected and in good spirits at interrogation.
The crew were: Flying Officer 'Ham' Fuller (captain and pilot),
Flying Officer 'Wally' Clarke (navigator, bomb aimer), Sergeant
'Phil' Collins (second pilot) Sergeant 'Jock' Grant (wireless
op.), Sergeant Paul Cameron (rear gunner), Sgt Berry (front gunner).

On the run up to the target at 9,000 feet 'G for George' was
suddenly illuminated by searchlights accompanied by a barrage of
accurate heavy flak. The run up was completed and the bombs
dropped in the target area, after which severe evasive action
was taken. This resulted in large strips of fabric being torn from
the fuselage, which seriously affected the flying qualities of the
kite.

The aircraft suddenly rolled onto its port side in a steep dive,
still held by searchlights, and it was only with the greatest difficulty and some manual help from the second pilot that the
captain was able to straighten up and pull out of the dive at about
500 feet. Severe vibration resulted from the damage done to the
fuselage making it difficult to maintain control and moreover it
was found that there were two 'rodded' hang-ups in the bomb bay
which could not be dislodged. However the pilot managed to get
the Wellington back to Malta and land safely — a fine piece of
flying. The incident was subsequently referred to in the pilot's
citation for the DFC.

Two other crews had seen 'G for George' in trouble over the
target area and had reported to Intelligence that they thought the
bomber had crashed.

When the extent of the damage was examined the pilot remarked, 'It did feel a bit chilly on the way back; now I know where the draught was coming from.'

18th January 1943
It was a quiet day working at the office getting things in order for what I think is coming — a move.

19th January 1943
On duty all day. Good news from Tripoli where an evacuation by the enemy is imminent as the harbour has been blocked or partly so. We ourselves as a wing and two squadrons are definitely moving back to Egypt — and torpedo bombers will take our place to deal with shipping.

20th January 1943
I finished work at 03.00 hours and all is bustle and preparation today.

21st January 1943
Message to 238 Wing from AHQ Malta dated 21.1.43. '*AOC sends farewell message to 238 Wing and wishes to thank them and 40 and 104 Squadrons for their fine bombing efforts during the past two and a half months. Malta is proud to have had the Wellington Bomber Squadrons join their team and hopes to have them back later in the year. Meanwhile we all wish you the best of luck*'. [The AOC of Malta was Air Vice Marshal Sir Keith Park.]

I was to have left in 'K for King' tonight but it has engine trouble — a valve has decided to slip into a cylinder. I bought D. a brooch and a squadron crest in silver and 'diced' back across the harbour with a wizard moon shining in the entrance.

A pleasant evening after dinner was spent with some very kind Maltese people opposite our billets. We drank 'Imbit' the native white wine and learned something of Malta conditions in peace and war.

— The dockyard is the main source of employment in peace time.
— Potatoes are important because three crops a year can be gathered.
— Orange groves are important in the interior beyond B'kara.
— Many people are poor and the Maltese eat a lot of bread and pasta.

— There is much trade with Sicily and imports of vegetables and fruits from there.
— People here are friendly towards Italians in normal times — they are thought to be a pleasant people — unwarlike. Mussolini and his régime are held responsible for Italian behaviour in the war.
— Emigration from Malta will have to be encouraged after the war — the island is already overcrowded mainly because all the people are Catholic and have large families.

22nd January 1943
Again we called on our kind friends and took them tins of corned beef and sardines. They gave me a beautiful Maltese lace doily which D. will love.

23rd January 1943: Malta to Egypt (by transport Hudson aircraft)
At 04.00 we left Luqa in bright moonlight in a Hudson which was very crowded. My weight was 152 lbs and with greatcoat and haversack, 172 lbs. We could see the stone walls and fields and general patchwork as we took off and climbed into thin stratus and then travelled eastwards 1,000 feet above the clouds at about 7,000 feet. Two and a half hours later the coast became dimly visible just after a glorious orange dawn had broken over the cloud tops. Later we saw the Jebel rugged and high with green valleys, shrubs and grass and some tilled areas. Going lower and to the south we reached the desert with winding wadis and tracks of tanks and vehicles but no sign of moving transport. We landed at a desert landing ground and were hospitably treated by the ruling wing commander — a breakfast of eggs was luxury.

Then up again and a most interesting two and a half hours via Tobruk, Bardia, Sollum and Halfaya Passes, the battle area and over Wadi Natrun with its red and green lakes and soda factory — to a circuit and perfect landing close to the Cairo Alexandria road. OK Egypt again! Malta has been a wonderful experience but I had begun to feel a sense of claustrophobia on the island which is too small and overpopulated for comfort.

*

Two amusing stories appeared in the local press while we were in Malta.
One was about the rear gunner of a Cant who baled out over

Malta without putting up any opposition when a Spitfire got on the Cant's tail. When taken into custody he was quizzed as to why he had not fired his guns at the Spitfire, it was a bad show. He meekly replied in halting English, 'Ah, Spitfire he come, Guiseppe he go.'

The other was about a Ju88 pilot whose kite was badly damaged over Malta by a Hurricane, but he courageously kept it airborne until all the crew managed to bale out. He was the last out at a low level in consequence of which he broke his pelvis.

He was greatly respected for his courageous action so the Hurricane pilot went to see him in hospital, introducing himself as the Hurricane pilot who had shot him down. But the Ju88 pilot was furious and adamant that it was a Spitfire that had shot him down!

After some argument the Hurricane pilot said it did not really matter what kind of kite had shot him down and that he had come to congratulate the Ju88 pilot for ensuring that all his crew had baled out safely before he jumped, as a result of which he had landed up in hospital – it was a 'good show', old chap! The Ju88 pilot refused to be comforted and said – 'Ju88 – for the pilot it is very difficult to get out.'

CHAPTER SIX

Victory in North Africa

The return of the Wellington Squadrons (40 and 104) from Malta to Egypt coincided with the fall of Tripoli. The African campaign was by no means over and until the final defeat of the Afrika Korps, 205 Group squadrons gave active support to the Eighth Army in the battle areas, bombed enemy held ports in Tunisia and airfields and ports in Sicily and Italy. These operations were flown almost entirely from Libyan airfields, constructed in the Gardabia area (south west of Misurata), and by Squadrons 37, 40, 70, 104 and 462 RAAF Halifax Squadron, controlled by 231 and 236 Wings. Squadrons 108 and 148 had left 205 Group in December 1942 but two other Wellington Squadrons 142 and 150 from Britain were now operating as a separate force with the First Army in Algeria and based at Blida.

LG237 — 40 kilometres from Cairo on the Cairo–Alexandria road: the diary entries from 24th January to 3rd February 1943 are mainly concerned with an enjoyable period of leave in Alexandria where we stayed at the Hotel Cecil and enjoyed all the food and delicacies missed in Malta and regained the weight and condition lost during the very active period of operations from the island fortress. In Cairo I had the job of re-equipping the 104 Squadron Intelligence Section with navigation maps, target maps, photographs, Intelligence files, stationery etc. from the Survey Department caves near Helwan and the Middle East Intelligence Unit. All the former squadron Intelligence materials had been left on Malta.

While we were at LG237, Flying Officer McRae (an Australian in 104 Squadron) and his crew, did a 'food drop' to some Australian troops beleaguered in a mountainous area in Crete. They had signalled their plight and asked for assistance. This was a tricky and delicate night mission, not only because of the navigation over mountainous terrain to the drop area, but also because of the timing which was of the utmost importance so far as the security of the troops was concerned.

The operation was carried out successfully and the troops signalled their thanks. Flying Officer McRae was later awarded a DFC.

*

5th February 1943

It was a warm sunny day at LG237 and flies like the warmth. P/O Moore called out to 'Ham' Fuller, another Australian, 'Ham, come over here and give the flies a break!' A Squadron Leader friend of mine who had been shopping prior to repatriation to UK told me that he had bought a complete outfit of gifts for his wife — 'from shoes to titty-hammocks'. It was evidently a day for *bons mots*.

I watched some very 'ropey' landings in circuits and bumps by a 104 Squadron Wellington and afterwards commented on these in the mess to Squadron Leader Mount. I said that the third landing was quite good but the others scared me. He said that he also had been scared as he was on board checking a new crew. He was glad I'd noticed the third landing as *he* had done that but *not* the others!

6th February 1943: LG237 to Soluch — 4 Hours 15 Minutes Flying Time

I made the trip to the new landing ground in 'U for Uncle' with Wing Commander Gibson and Squadron Leader Newman. The Intelligence section has to be there with the aircraft in case we are called upon to operate immediately. It was the usual desert stooge but we saw Sollum and the passes excellently, the best view I've had. Also we saw the remains of Fort Capuzzo, Bardia and Sollum barracks, and looked down at Tobruk in daylight and El Adem — what a place! 'U for Uncle' flew over the desert south of the Jebel to the railway between Benina and Benghazi and turned south to our new landing ground Soluch which looked exactly as portrayed on the target maps issued to each of the squadron navigators.

Tent erecting was a heavy business and after this we had a meal and a well earned sleep.

7th February 1943

The day was spent getting organised. We queued for meals with the airmen and NCOs as always happens in a new camp in the desert. Breakfast consisted of porridge, bacon and sausage — Tiffin of bully, cheese, biscuits and jam — Dinner of bully, beans, potatoes and jam puff. There was *Shai* (tea) with each meal — very sweet but heavily tainted with chlorine. We organised a table for ourselves and enjoyed our food. During the day I looked at the village, the water point, the station, and war wreckage including disabled tanks.

8th February 1943: Operations Again

I went over to Wing today and met AB Read and Archer and the old brigade of clerks at Intelligence. The squadron briefing for Palermo (Sicily) had to be done from the back of a truck with the Group Captain in attendance and I was reminded of the alternative target only by the Wing Commander's passing reference to it. It must have been a kind and gentle hint. Reynolds, my clerk, came back today and Squadron Leader Mount very nicely evacuated his tent so that Reynolds and I could use it for Intelligence.

9th February 1943

The 'op' was ruined by cloud over the target but one of our squadron (Flying Officer Panting) located and bombed.

10th February 1943: Benghazi Visit

There was heavy rain last night and today the earth looks a darker brown. I had a most interesting trip into Benghazi with the Wing Commander in his jeep. It was a bumpy fifteen miles to the main road and en route we could smell the desert flowers including white ones not seen around the camp. There were a few fields of barley, a flock or two of sheep and an odd herd of camels. Then we followed the coastal road — 'the silver thread stringing the oasis pearls' — a good road except where damaged by demolition or bombing. The country was green and improved as we went on with some gum trees along the roadside and later aerodromes on each side with evidence of Jerry's recent occupation. We passed the cemetery and went over the narrow gauge railway to pick up Squadron Leader Mount who had gone over in a Hurricane borrowed from someone. (Our flight commander was a fighter pilot in the Battle of Britain and also commanded a fighter-squadron in the desert before coming on to Wellingtons.) The earth was now red like Devonshire and with a green grass cover which was pleasant after the desert monotony of sand and camel thorn.

We reached the town across salt lagoons and found the native quarter not as badly damaged as I had expected. Nearer the port area the damage increased — as it should do. We looked at the cathedral, the ships in port and the railway station which itself appeared little damaged. There was evidence of repair work and adaptation where buildings were partly damaged. Coming back along the main road we moved well at 40—45 mph and then had a terrible hour or more bumping along the track. We were too late for a meal so we had biscuits and marmalade and went to bed.

11th February 1943
The main squadron convoy arrived today and departed again moving further westwards. Very violent winds last night made me think that the tent would take off. The conditions continue primitive at this camp with no mess and no sanitary arrangements. I've now organised my own latrine from three petrol tins and manage very comfortably.

12th February 1943: Soluch to Gardabia in 'U for Uncle' — 3 hours 40 minutes
We were up early to strike tents and get our kit aboard and distribute the Intelligence material among several aircraft. It was a tiring job transporting the heavy boxes around. Wing Commander Gibson took off smoothly and we were soon over the El Agheila area with signs of prepared positions — then pure desert again on almost to Misurata. White sand beaches marked the coast all the way. We saw the Marble Arch erected in honour of Mussolini who once passed along the entire stretch of road from the Tunisian frontier to the Egyptian frontier. An aerodrome stands alongside the *Arae Philaenorum* and at intervals along the road were white block houses or police points as I presumed. We saw one town or village — Sirte — with white flat-topped houses in rectangular pattern. The mined areas along the road could be seen marked by wire and white strips. The demolition of bridges in all places where the road crossed wadis was noticeable but the road merely made a detour to avoid the break.

After Marble Arch we ran into a sandstorm which developed into rainstorms with violent gusty winds and nasty bumps for flying. We went out to sea and found smoother air conditions but below us the sea was whipped into white-topped waves. When things improved we could see the effects of Italian colonisation along the coastal road — rectangular plots in the desert with twin white houses and a circular water cistern in between them. It looked a creditable effort at making use of the desert but obviously would be hard work for the farmers in such a dry sandy area.

Our Gardabia landing ground was merely a brown runway scraped clear of grass and scrub, and the Wing Commander made an excellent landing in spite of the high gusty wind. There is a wide grassy plain around here with only gentle undulations and it is very suitable for airfield construction. Hungry and somewhat cold we struggled to put up tents in the wind and rain. There is a definite routine or drill for tent erecting and at last I know it, but in a gale it's a grim and difficult business.

Later we walked a mile or more for a meal and then back to listen to the wireless and talk together in the tent. I think we earned our colonial and field allowance today. It was good to meet Flight Lieutenant Larry Wells again — our Canadian Flying Control Officer — the first time since at LG106 prior to going to Malta. He is in charge of the advance party.

13th to 15th February 1943
Cool wet weather and no operations.

16th February, 1943: Mines
The briefing was at 15.00 hours with the Group Captain (Group Captain Russell) beside me, but happily things went well (I thought!). We then pulled down the tent, piled it and our bed kits on to a gharry and departed to the new site a few miles away. We had dinner in a squadron queue. It was good to see the Mess going up today, and tomorrow it will be in operation. *And*, we shall also have proper sanitary arrangements.

After the meal I visited various tents to get my location. Bob Ginn had an RE captain with him and talk was of mines and minefields.
1. The captain saw two donkeys grazing near El Alamein — then *woomph! woomph!* — no donkeys grazing.
2. Stan Dodd and our squadron convoy parked at 100 yards or so from an army camp where a tank trailer was drawing an armoured car behind it. A mine was touched off, the armoured car went up and two men were killed.
3. A camel known as 'George' grazed in a minefield near one of our units and sentries when relieving used to ask first 'How's George — still OK?' He survived for a long time and seemed to

have a charmed life. Then one day — *woomph!* — and only the hind leg of a camel remained.

The stories fitted in with my own very healthy fear of mines and minefields.

17th to 19th February 1943
Operations cancelled due to Met reports and local strong winds and dust storms.

20th February 1943
We briefed in primitive fashion in the open with a notice board propped against the tent for an operation against Palermo where two good fires were started in the harbour area, one probably by our 'H for Harry' (Sergeant Carey, Pilot Officer Vinden). The Italian radio news admitted that we had raided Palermo long before the BBC news stated that Middle East Wellingtons had attacked the port causing fires and explosions on the night of 20th/21st February.

22nd February 1943
The rear convoy arrived today — things may improve now and I can hope for a larger tent for Intelligence.

Operations tonight (Palermo docks and shipping again) and everyone seems to be going — the Group Captain (Group Captain Russell), the Wing Commander (Wing Commander Gibson) and Squadron Leader Newman. The Group Captain is going with Denis Panting in 'U for Uncle'. I went out with the Wing Commander to his aircraft and brought back his jeep. It's a nice little job with good steering and plenty of power — a 15.9 hp engine developing 60 bhp.

23rd February 1943
Last night's visit to Palermo was reasonably successful with two fires and a Wellington fire I fear — but not one of ours. The Group Captain with Denis, and the Wing Commander with his crew, had good trips. Two fine photos were obtained of the harbour and town with a smoke screen over the harbour. Squadron Leader Newman landed back at Malta with some trouble. I drove over to Wing and Group with our results in Squadron Leader Mount's 15 cwt Dodge truck which has a difficult gear change. Work again in the evening with an enemy airfield close to the battle area as our target which is a good sign that the Army may soon move forward against the Mareth Line defences.

24th February, 1943: Photo Trouble

Interrogations began at 04.00 hours. It was a poor operation for observed results but was probably a nerve-racking period for Jerry. In the morning I had a row with the Group Photo Officer who expects photos in one and a half hours from the last aircraft down or at latest 08.30 or the reason why! He pointed out at great length to me that he had been a warrant officer and risen from an AC2 — he was not a jumped-up officer!

I hope my replies were suitable — that man has something coming to him. He also said that a General Duties (Flying) Officer with a keen interest in photography was usually in charge. Well, if I know anything there will be another one before long. I drove the Dodge again and found the secret was not so much acceleration as I had been giving in neutral while double de-clutching.

Tonight the squadron Intelligence tent was used for briefing for the first time. We are again attacking enemy airfields in the Gabes area behind the Mareth defences.

26th February 1943

At interrogation this morning at 04.00 hours all our crews were OK and all went well with the Group Captain and Squadron Leader Newman present. Reynolds tactfully gave them a cup of tea each which they enjoyed. Afterwards I was my own despatch rider using the new Matchless motor cycle that the squadron transport people have made available for me. Today I was briefing for the fifth day in succession — or is it six? I watched the take-off tonight and then we had a happy visit to the mess by Flying Officer ('Doc') Craig and Flying Officer ('Brum') Birmingham old friends from Kabrit and Shallufa — they both now fly Halifaxes with 462 Squadron. It's rather a joke bringing Halifaxes to the Middle East with Merlin engines when our 104 Wellingtons with Merlins so often have trouble due to overheating. It is generally agreed that the Wellington IIIs and Xs with Hercules engines are best out here.

28th February 1943: A 'Brass' Briefing

I worked in the morning and did the briefing in the afternoon. Wing Commander G.H.N. Gibson DFC is leaving us to go into hospital in Cairo as he has not recovered from jaundice. A quiet, pleasant and gentlemanly man, he has never looked fit since he joined us in Malta. Squadron Leader C.J. Mount DFC becomes the new wing commander of 104 Squadron. He's a grand chap and it will be interesting to see how he likes commanding a Wellington bomber squadron after a Hurricane fighter squadron.

And now the briefing — the AOC-in-C present (Air Chief Marshal Sir Sholto Douglas); Air Vice Marshal Sir Hugh P. Lloyd, his deputy; Air Commodore Gayford commanding 205 Group; Group Captain Russell commanding 236 Wing; and at least three wing commanders including our Wing Commander Mount taking his first briefing, Squadron Leader Newman and all the aircrews — quite a galaxy. My mouth was somewhat dry but the target was Palermo which helped as it is reasonably interesting — with Messina as the alternative. My effort was I think, fair, without being in any way brilliant. I had thought of referring to Palermo as another Tobruk and of Messina as the Dover of Sicily but I remembered only the first comparison. Anyway we all staggered through the briefing and the great men departed — but not without an amusing incident. The AOC-in-C was grim and rather Goering-like, without Tedder's charm and easy manner. He asked Squadron Leader Newman if our crews were an experienced lot.

'Oh yes, sir', said the Squadron Leader. 'How long have you been with the squadron?' said Sir Sholto to Sergeant Carey, one of our newest arrivals. 'Since January, sir', was the reply. 'And where were you before you joined the squadron?' 'At an OTU (Operational Training Unit), sir', was the damning reply.

Then the AOC-in-C asked Lloyd Parry, an Australian and the most senior pilot operating, 'How long have you been with the squadron?' 'Since December, sir!' said Lloyd — but had the sense to add that previously he had operated with 148 Squadron.

Our new Wing Commander and Squadron Leader Newman had a good laugh over the incident afterwards — it was really just too bad.

1st March 1943: Misurata

I was up at 02.00 to a cold night and in came their lordships and duly listened to my interrogations and asked questions themselves. However, I must say that they didn't interrupt in any way but insisted that I carry on as usual. Well — we have all sorts of situations to meet in the RAF.

In the afternoon I went into Misurata with Squadron Leader Newman, the Doc, Ted Stewart and others — about fifteen miles of terrible track. We had some fun with some wogs en route who wanted to sell us 'eggies' and some filthy wine. We were impressed by the orderly arrangement of homesteads, the layout of orchards and fields, the rows of palm trees, olive trees and the water supply raised by bullocks from shallow wells over a pulley. From the skin buckets the water gushed into a tank for irrigation purposes. There are plenty of trees around and crops of barley, beans, peas, spinach, grass etc. We saw cows for the first time that I can remember since Durban.

The houses — a single floor flat roofed type — all had *'Ente Colonizzazione Libia'* on the wall at the front. There were carpets of purple wild flowers (wild stock with a fragrant perfume) here and there, and yellow gorse bushes and other yellow flowers (ranunculus) — due to the recent rains. The town of Misurata has two distinct quarters — the Italian quarter with pleasant clean white houses, municipal block, cinema, Fiat service depot and some fine villas — and the native area, rambling and rather like an Egyptian town, but a little neater and cleaner.

We went to the market place and haggled for onions, peas and spinach for the mess. Ted Stewart bought half a sheep for £2 10s 0d — a little fly blown in the quarters but apparently this will be OK when cooked — I hope so! Some beggars came around but they were less persistent and a little cleaner than the Egyptian variety. The Italian police were still operating (with revolvers in pouches) and working with them were a number of 'Red Caps' and RAF police. Little war damage was seen in Misurata. And so 'home' to Gardabia and our tented camps.

Lloyd Parry is our new flight commander — so, with three decent blokes in charge, Mount, Newman and Parry — the squadron should continue its good form. One other posting — Reynolds is leaving soon to go on his air gunners' course and will transfer to flying duties. He's been an excellent clerk and we've got on well together.

2nd March 1943
After a busy day of rumours and preparation we eventually operated on the battle area. An amusing letter from home told me that Duncan wants to know who is *Elizabeth's* Daddy? He knows that *his* Daddy is in the Desert!

3rd March 1943: A Comedy of Errors
Last night's operation on the battle area was upset by the 40 Squadron flare-dropper getting lost. He went past the target area — turned north then out to sea — finally dropping flares forty

minutes late. Returning he landed at 70 Squadron by mistake. He then took off again and landed at our airfield by mistake. The crew then gave up the struggle and came into our squadron tent for interrogation. It was a crew I knew well from Malta so we had a good leg pull, gave them breakfast and sent them home in a gharry. Meantime, one of our crews landed at 40 Squadron, so we did an exchange.

Tonight we had a late briefing for battle area targets and a very late take-off. I got my wireless set to go again for the first time since Malta. It is quite a thrill to listen to the BBC Home News in the desert so far from Britain, and know that our families are hearing the same bulletin at the same moment.

4th March 1943

At lunch time there was a fire and thick black smoke from the direction of 40 Squadron who have had wretched luck and serviceability lately. The Wing Commander suggested that it looked as if poor 40 Squadron had become thoroughly brassed off and were burning their planes. (We heard later that it was two trucks laden with petrol.)

Operations were scrubbed this evening but it was a quiet evening in the mess as there is no drink in the bar — George Edwards, the life and soul of the party or mess, is still not back from Tripoli where he is trying to get chianti and our drink ration. Later, George turned up as we were going to bed. Unfortunately the Jerry cans used for wine had previously contained petrol not water as was thought by George.

5th March 1943: High Octane Chianti

Ops were cancelled today so it was a very merry evening in the mess. The chianti flavoured with petrol had few buyers. Lloyd drank some and was not the same afterwards. Ted Stewart mixed his with rum and sugar and was a sick man next day. Thank goodness I didn't touch it. Beattie, George and Henry Langton were all celebrating promotion as well as a stand down. George and I got rather amused and couldn't stop laughing. Splodge Moore looked like Charles Laughton and propped up the central tent pole all the evening. We drank to 'Pedagogy'! (Splodge is another schoolmaster and now the very capable navigator of Ken Loveless's crew). Ham Fuller removed part of Splodge's garments but he didn't mind — he was in no condition to remonstrate.

7th March 1943: Promotion

Operations were again cancelled due to weather, but news from the battle front is good. Eighth Army have destroyed fifty enemy tanks at Medenine. I went over to Group HQ and learned of several impending changes in Intelligence. De Saumariez ('SOS') is leaving Group and A.B. Read is to take his place. I am to take over A.B.'s post at 236 Wing as SIO. It's going to be a very sad blow leaving the squadron but Squadron Leader Streater, the GIO, pointed out that Wing is a flight lieutenant vacancy and there are plenty of others who would like it — he advises never refusing a promotion.

8th March 1943

Operations were cancelled again and I got down seriously to the work of clearing up the Intelligence section with Reynolds. In the evening I played bridge with Ted Stewart against George and Lloyd. I gave Uncle Ted several nasty headaches with my amateurish play — he's an expert at cards. He was good tempered and explained my mistakes more in sorrow than in anger — and thanks to my partner — we won.

9th March 1943: More Changes in Command

Our 'B' Flight Commander, Squadron Leader J.E. Newman DFC, is to become Wing Commander of 70 Squadron, an excellent appointment in every way. Squadron Leader Trumper, formerly with A.B. Read's 108 Squadron, is to be our second new flight commander. Wing Commander Beare, once CO of 104 Squadron, is to be Group Captain in charge of 231 Wing and Group Captain MacNair is to take over our 236 Wing vice Group Captain Russell.

What with Bob Ginn moving off as Engineer Officer to a Repair and Salvage Unit and myself going to 236 Wing as SIO — there are considerable changes in the squadron and wing.

There was a strong wind today and then a sudden sandstorm at 18.00 hrs — very hot and unpleasant with hundreds of winged insects invading the mess and all tents, dive bombing the occupants and all lights. Operations were cancelled due to the weather. Chianti has been christened 'Benito's Blood'. At a squadron mess meeting, George Edwards was made Mess Secretary and Ted Stewart very appropriately appointed Bar Officer, in spite of all his efforts to avoid office.

10th March 1943
It was an unpleasant grey windy day and operations were again cancelled for Met reasons. I worked at citations for Ted, Beattie and Sergeant Muggeridge. In the evening we had an open air cinema show at Wing which was quite good. There were two news films, a cartoon, a NZ travel film of Rotorua, and a film *Midnight* featuring Claudette Colbert. When we came back I had a long talk with Denis Panting and Wally Clarke before bed.

12th March 1943
In the evening Flight Sergeant Rogers came in to say cheerio. He has been a grand navigator and a nice chap to have in the squadron — first with Basil Blogg as his captain after Charles Stotesbury was killed, and then the last 32 operations with Ted Stewart — an excellent captain, and Flight said so.

13th March 1943: Test Flight
Today I enjoyed 40 minutes of flying in 'J for Johnny' with Squadron Leader Lloyd Parry. We found a bomb loose on the runway before take-off. Lloyd did a climbing turn off the runway to show his good spirits — then more soberly climbed to about 2,500 feet and let me take the stick for a while. I didn't try anything but to keep her straight and level. She started to climb and I had to push forward to keep the nose down — it was one of the ground crew moving back to the tail. I adjusted trim — a spiked wheel at left hand of the pilot and then the Wellington flew better. Trim was so good that Lloyd flew her hands off and she remained dead steady. We came in after a good look at Misurata and the Garibaldi Colonisation district, making a good landing in a slight cross wind. Then we taxied over to the duty pilot to arrange the removal of the bomb. This must have been a hang-up which came off the other night on return from 'ops' and it's lucky that it didn't go off!

14th March 1943: Leaving the Squadron
Second Lieutenant Geoffrey Holmes SAAF, arrived today to take over as Intelligence Officer for 104 Squadron. It's pretty sad for me to think of leaving the squadron. I played bridge in the evening with the Wing Commander against Ted and Lloyd and won this time after a bad start due to my two letters today from D. and my mind not being fully on the game. The Wing Commander says

he thinks my wife is *too* affectionate judging by my atrocious luck at cards!

This is my last night with the squadron — tomorrow I become a 'Wing type' and the prospect of leaving all my friends is depressing. I've been IO of 104 Squadron for over a year and worked under five different commanders — and got on well with each one of them.

*

In the Royal Air Force the squadron is the operational unit with the aircraft, pilots and other aircrew members who do the actual flying and the fighter or bomber missions against the enemy. The ground personnel of the squadron maintain and service the aircraft and provide for the needs of the flying men and themselves.

The bomber squadron in wartime may number about 500 men to maintain and operate a normal establishment of 16 to 24 aircraft. Because of its compact size and its direct involvement in the actual fighting the squadron members usually develop a strong sense of comradeship and pride in their unit. A bomber squadron is divided into two flights each with a squadron leader in charge and the commanding officer of the squadron is a wing commander in rank.

A wing is a small headquarters unit which exists to control or serve two or three squadrons. Many of the officers are General Duties (Flying) now engaged in specialist non-flying duties such as Operations, Intelligence, Armament, Navigation, Engineering, Transport, Administration, etc. The average age of the officers is usually greater than on the squadron and the officers' mess environment is somewhat different. There are no aircraft — and flying and operations are a little further away.

A wing is commanded by a group captain who can exert a strong personal influence upon this relatively small unit and upon the two or three squadrons for which it is responsible.

No 236 Wing at Gardabia served No 104 Wellington Bomber Squadron and No 462 Halifax Bomber Squadron. In its turn 236 Wing was responsible to the Group Headquarters of No 205 Group RAF.

*

15th March 1943: 236 Wing
And so to become a 'Wing type', as the squadron chaps say! I went over on the bike to see the lie of the land and meet the Adjutant (Flight Lieutenant Partington) and the new Commanding

Officer, Group Captain D.I.P. MacNair. After tea, Squadron Leader Lloyd Parry drove me over with my goods and chattels.

17th March 1943: Wing Intelligence
The Group Captain talked with me this morning about Intelligence and he asked me what I thought my job was. After my explanation, he gave me detailed instructions how an IO should do his work, lavishly illustrated by reference to the IO of the Liberator squadron which he formerly commanded. Not a good start!

18th March 1943: The Mareth Line
I did the briefing for 104 Squadron in the sergeants' mess under difficulties (the Intelligence tent was u/s) and with the AOC and the Group Captain present. The Eighth Army attack on the Mareth Line has started and we are helping by bombing enemy troops and landing fields in the battle area. At 462 Halifax Squadron we listened to A.B. Read's briefing and met some of the squadron chaps. Warrant Officer Vertican, formerly at Kabrit in 148 Squadron, introduced me to one or two others like Squadron Leader Buskell (Flight Commander) and Flight Lieutenant Mansell (Navigation Officer).

Afterwards, the Group Captain told me that the 104 Squadron briefing was very inadequate and that his idea is to have a much more elaborate set-up over here at Wing. (The squadrons won't like that as they are used to having their own briefing tents.) I went over to my old squadron and drowned my sorrows and played bridge. Lloyd drove me back in a much happier frame of mind.

20th March 1943: Diversion to 236 Wing
Operations were cancelled for our wing last night but no sooner had I fallen asleep than the telephone rang to tell me that aircraft from 37, 40 and 70 Squadrons would be landing at our flarepath because all other airfields were u/s with the torrential rain. I went outside, found the ground covered with sheets of water, and after slushing through to 'ops', learned the worst. It was 01.00 hours and there were bags of Wellington crews to cope with. 'Ops' roused Lieutenant Holmes and together we coped! The bombers had been assisted by flaredropping Albacores of the Fleet Air Arm to drop bombs on guns and troops from Mareth towards Gabes. One captain-pilot had been badly caught in flak and

remembering the bearing to the coast he told the second pilot to turn (the compass grid) to 40°. The second pilot misunderstood and immediately put on 40° of flap and the poor aircraft staggered on — the captain being too busy with evasive action to notice the trim, or absence of it, until they were out to sea. One Wellington was missing — a 40 Squadron crew whom I knew well in Malta. We completed work at 06.00 hours.

The Group Captain has changed his mind about the Wing Intelligence tent, owing to persuasion from Wing Commanders Mount and Warner. I did the briefing today for 462 Squadron (where Flying Officer Clulow is the IO) and drew a special map of the Mareth-Katena area to help location by crews, and wondered if the Group Captain noticed it! We are again bombing battle area targets in support of the Army's attack to ensure the enemy has no respite. Now for a little sleep myself as interrogations start at 03.00 hours!

21st March 1943: Record Operation
Interrogations began at 03.15 hours and the AOC (Air Commodore Gayford) and the Group Captain (Group Captain MacNair) made the rounds of the crews. The AOC smiled pleasantly and said, 'Good Morning' and for once this part of Intelligence seemed to impress our Group Captain. A map was propped up at the end of each table and a 50,000 map and plotting chart spread on the table top. Interrogations went well and it was a good operation which broke the squadron record — eighteen aircraft were detailed — eighteen aircraft operated and all eighteen bombed the battle area targets located by Albacore flaredroppers. One Wellington crashed on the way back — Flying Officer Dobbin RCAF in 'A for Apple' — but he landed it safely in a salt lagoon near Ben Gardane. The crew did full ditching procedure and then found to their surprise and relief that the water was only three feet deep.

We had a quick breakfast and went back to collect the other squadron results and prepared the Opsum, finishing at 11.00 hours. Briefing today was for another night operation between the Mareth Line and Gabes and after briefing it was pleasant to go over to the 'gen' squadron mess to recover from a feeling of exhaustion. The Wing Commander offered me a drink and everyone was as nice as usual. Then back to Wing to check bombing reports and to listen to Churchill's speech which was constructive and encouraging but had no mention of victory until 1944 or 1945.

22nd March 1943: A Bad Night
On the 21st/22nd we learned from 'ops' at 04.00 hours that Flying Officer George Edwards ('R for Robert' 104 Squadron) who shared a tent with Lloyd Parry, Don Boyd-Stephenson and myself, had crash-landed west of Tripoli. He is injured, but Don and Dickie Fry and the rest of the crew are OK.

It was a bad night for the squadron − 'V' (Sergeant Taylor) crashed in the sea off Zarzis and the captain was killed (a very nice chap, as usual) − two of the crew are missing, believed trapped, and three are OK. Then Flight Lieutenant Beattie made a belly-landing at Castel Benito but the crew are safe. There were few real results observed but the weight of bombs and the time spent over the battle area must affect enemy morale. Damage to our three aircraft resulted from accurate flak − no reports of night fighters.

This morning my Wing Intelligence clerk excelled himself. There was a *woomph*! and he appeared at the tent flap to say, 'The petrol has gone up, sir!' He had thrown a match on to the sand in the tin to see if any petrol vapour remained. Then he poured petrol on the sand as nothing had happened − but the match was still burning and the petrol blew back singeing his eyebrows.

23rd March 1943: Crash Landing ('R for Robert')
Don came in to tell me about the crash landing near Tripoli. George is all right and did a wizard landing − perfect except that they met a slight dip which completely cracked up 'R for Robert' − one wing ripped off and one engine was left dangling. Don was shot through the door from the navigator's chair to the bomb aimer's position. However, thank heaven, they are all OK and only George is in hospital. It was a day of exacting work. Flying Officer Clulow called and was very pleasant. It looks as if Holmes, Clulow and myself will get on quite happily as an Intelligence team.

24th March 1943
A couple of Arabs with a large camel and a baby camel went by my tent so I chased them and got some snaps for Duncan and Elizabeth. We had the usual hectic rush around briefing times and before take-off. The Eighth Army has had setbacks at Mareth and south of El Hamma and needs our continued bombing support in the battle area.

26th March 1943
After the two squadron briefings for enemy transport concentrations in the Gabes area, the Group Captain complimented both Holmes and Clulow on their particular part of the briefings and gave me a little reflected glory! Afterwards he asked me to play bridge with him and took 2/- off me. He's a good player with a very amusing patter. I had an unpleasant ache from a gum boil and didn't feel the best but it's good to find our relationship improving.

28th March 1943: RAF in the News
Tonight we listened in the mess to the 9 p.m. Home News and hoped that our families were also listening, for the RAF was much to the fore. The news referred to the Berlin raid of last night and other RAF exploits. Then Sir Archibald Sinclair spoke of the founding of the Royal Air Force twenty five years ago on 1st April 1918.

The RAF March Past was played after the speech – reminding me strongly of the record which we bought and played so often in the days before my call up. It made me desperately want to get home to enjoy family life again.

29th March 1943: The Mareth Line Taken
Good news was received today about the Army – the Mareth Line is in our hands and the enemy are withdrawing north of Gabes. Rommel and Co are lucky to be protected tonight by the weather as our operations have been cancelled. The Mareth Line battle has been the worst since Alamein and must have meant serious Army casualties in spite of all the air support given by the Desert Air Force and 205 Group.

30th March 1943
Briefings as usual. Tonight, I had to give a talk in the airmen's mess on *'Recent Operations by the Western Desert Air Force'* and it was well attended by officers and other ranks. Topics dealt with included General Montgomery's message and its reason – the units of the Western Desert Air Force – a typical 24 hours' programme by fighters and bombers – 205 Group in particular – strategic and tactical bombing – examples of recent raids, quoting from opsums and bombing reports and prisoner of war reports on the effects of our bombing – examples of recent successful raids by the USAAF on Palermo and RAF operations from Malta. Then

I answered questions and passed around photographs, MEIU build-ups, target maps, etc. The talk was well received and the questions were interesting and on the ball!

31st March 1943: Spectacular Results

Last night's 'op' was one of our most successful ever for spectacular results. The target was Sfax/El Maou LG but we seem to have hit something else that burned and exploded with 25 fires counted. Our Flying Officer Dobbin (Canadian) started the first fire and attracted the others to the spot. 'W for William' 104 is missing — last message 'Port engine u/s'.

Later 'ops' were scrubbed owing to Met. The Group Captain was fed up as this is the second time he has planned to go and the 'op' has been cancelled.

1st April 1943: 25th Anniversary of the Royal Air Force

It turns out from PRU evidence that the fires (30th/31st) were at Nakta, SW of Sfax and NE of Mahares — probably an ammunition and fuel dump. The AOC (Air Commodore O.R. Gayford CBE DFC AFC) came into tea and wished us all a happy birthday — the 25th Anniversary of the founding of the RAF. We had a parade and a talk by our Group Captain and the March Past was played.

Later, operations were again cancelled and I went over to the squadron and spent a cheerful evening with Don and Dobbie and George. George is OK again and brought me home as the other two were 'well away'!

*

Tripoli — Andata e Ritorno

At 104 Squadron I was told an amusing story about leave in Tripoli for some well-known members of the officers' mess:

In high spirits and with great expectations, Ken Loveless, Tommy Howes and Splodge Moore, had set off for two days leave in Tripoli where a leading hotel had been requisitioned as an 'officers' club'. It was due to open on the morning of their arrival.

Everything would be laid on, the boys were told — service deluxe, ravioli, chianti and what have you — no wonder they were in good spirits!

Great courtesy was shown by the management who, having treated their German allies similarly for the past year or more, were now 'honoured' to have these Air Force types as their guests, for the interim period at least, since it was tactfully explained that Rommel and his boys would undoubtedly be returning. As clear testimony of this it was disclosed that Rommel himself had generously arranged for the entire staff to be paid three months' salary in advance and, despite the fact that there would be a 'brief' British occupation of Tripoli, the management had received an instruction that their high standard of efficiency had to be maintained — they (Rommel and his boys) would definitely be back.

The manager's story was told with such conviction that it was felt there might be some truth in it, in more ways than one, and momentarily the intrepid Air Force types were left pondering to themselves.

'But please sit down by the window where you can see the beautiful oleanders, and the signorinas pass by there too', said the manager.

At this point Splodge interrupted and said, 'You mean the sheilas' and then added 'and please don't let us die of thirst while we're here.'

The beer was soon on its way, waiter service included. But at that moment the horrifying just had to happen — the air raid siren went, and so did the beer, onto the floor, complete with an empty tray. And with an earsplitting yell and the alacrity and agility of the man on the flying trapeze, a corpulent waiter was seen to dive through the nearest window, shouting as though he was suffering from convulsions.

This alarming and astonishing behaviour, in an officers' club of all places, even shook to the core the imperturbable Ken Loveless who exclaimed, 'Well, that's the bloody bottom! — I've heard that these Ities are good vocalists but what did the poor chap want to do that for? I haven't heard a bomb drop yet.'

Tommy Howes commented, 'Why the hell did we have to pick on a bomb happy waiter?' When they called for more beer their astonishment turned to anguish. The entire staff had disappeared, and now that the air raid siren had stopped its wailing, there was nothing but a ghostly silence in the place.

In a burst of profound intellectual enthusiasm Splodge observed, 'These Ities are a likable lot but unfortunately they suffer from inflamed imaginations — I think the climate, the cheese and the chianti are just a bit too much for them!'

On their return to the squadron, everyone wanted to know what the de luxe officers' club was like. 'You'd be just as well

off in a Rechabites' coffee shop,' they were told. 'Not only was
there no beer, but the service was lousy!'

*

2nd April 1943

Operations were cancelled owing to weather conditions over
Tunisian targets. The Army is held up at the Wadi Akarit. In the
evening I played bridge with the Padre (Squadron Leader Robin-
son) against Squadron Leader Milner and Flight Lieutenant Carr.
The Padre has an amazing system of bidding — he won't be put off
once he thinks he has a bid. We went down heavily but had a very
amusing evening of lighthearted bridge which I prefer.

5th April 1943: Tripoli Visit — on Business!

Up at 01.45 to help Holmes with 104 Squadron interrogations
after an attack on enemy airfields. We finished about 03.30 and
had breakfast — then completed the Opsum, before going to bed
at 06.30.

The Adjutant today asked me to go to Tripoli for him to collect
Welfare requirements. The Group Captain gave permission and in
twenty minutes I was at 'J for Johnny' of 462 Squadron waiting
for Wing Commander Warner who was flying to Castel Benito.

The Halifax seemed a very ropey kite to me with severe clanking from the starboard inner engine. We taxied, swung into the
wind and took-off. The climb was very slow indeed and made me
wonder if the Wing Commander would return. However, we
staggered on and beneath us were plantations of small trees and
sometimes palms alternating with brown sandy patches and to
the south the rugged grey green Tarhuna Hills with contour-like
markings from the horizontal strata and deep gashes of winding
wadis. To the north were glimpses of blue sea and white sandy
beaches. Then, on track, came green trees lining a straight stretch
of road and a rectangular airfield with ruined hangars on one
side — Castel Benito. We made one circuit and went in to land
following a DC3 and a Hudson and followed ourselves by Beaufighters. A very large collection of wrecks and other aircraft were
crowded around the perimeter — probably some of the wrecks
resulting from 205 Group bombing.

The Americans are in possession of one half of the airfield and
RAF the other, including our 205 Group Recovery and Refuelling
Unit with my old friend Larry Wells. The CO of the unit, Flight
Lieutenant Wheatley, kindly offered to take me into Tripoli next

day so I spent a happy evening reminiscing and a very cold night on a stretcher in the sick bay.

6th April 1943
We left the 'drome area passing a big newly painted notice in blue and white — 'Royal Air Force Station, Castel Benito' which looked rather smart.

The road into Tripoli was narrow but well surfaced and we entered at the Benito Gate to find streets of pleasant white houses with many trees and shrubs — the Governor's Palace with a dome like an observatory and a seafront and promenade with the best hotel in RAF occupation. It was strange to see girls and women — some quite attractive, including a pretty blonde on a bicycle. Of course she made me think of home and D.

The welfare business was muddling but eventually I obtained three wireless sets — two of them requisitioned from civilians but paid for. And so back to Castel Benito for lunch where I was lucky enough to catch a Wellington III just as it was about to take off. The control officer gave them a red — they stopped — I got in plus my valuables — and landed at 40 Squadron. After a very pleasant reception from old friends (Aubyn James among them) and a drink in the mess (only 'blood' left), transport was arranged for me back to 236 Wing.

There I picked up the threads of the work and got ready for tonight's operation. Tim Clulow will kindly help Holmes so there will be no need for me to surface until 05.00 hours. We are on tactical targets as the enemy retreat from the Wadi Akarit positions.

At take-off tonight there was a nasty bump and fire up the road at the neighbouring squadron but happily all the crew got out safely after managing to jettison bombs from only 300 feet before pranging — whew!

7th April 1943 — Wing Commander Mount Crashes
The results came in for the Opsum about 05.30 hours. After a busy morning and lunch, I collected my formidable Zundapp 750cc motorcycle from MT. It was not easy to start and made me nearly late for briefing because of this. Clark and Mason had to push me to start the monster. Briefing took place for tactical targets similar to last night amidst constant phone calls. After tea at the squadron mess, Bob Ginn gave the bike a look over and he says it's in bad shape but he will do something if he can. The air-

men's mess have their new radio tonight and are very bucked with it. At midnight Corporal Harris rushed into Intelligence to say that Wing Commander Mount had crashed four miles away. For one awful moment I feared the worst, but happily, Micky and all his crew are safe, thank God! The Wimpy (with Merlin engines) failed to gain height after take-off in high temperature conditions and the Wing Commander settled down gently on a low hilltop without detonating the bombs or causing a fire. Fortunately the grassy undulating country around Gardabia is good for emergency landings.

8th April 1943: Soccer Match
It was difficult to assess the results of last night's operation as bombs were not seen to burst in several cases due to cloud over the target area but the enemy morale must be affected by the pressure of bombing day and night. The afternoon was a definite 'occasion' — *Officers* versus *Sergeants*, at football (soccer). The Group Captain played right back and the team was as follows:

Goalkeeper	The Adjutant (F/Lt Partington)				
Backs	Group Captain		Cipher Officer		
	G/C MacNair		F/O Kirkby		
Half Backs	Doc	Signals Officer	Accounts Officer		
	S/Ldr Gimson	P/O Drummond	F/Lt Simpson		
Forwards					
Transport Off.	Armament Off.	Navigation Off.	Engineer Off.		Intell. Off.
F/O Dickinson	P/O Harris	F/Lt Carr	S/Ldr Morrison		F/Lt Chappell

We lost 3–2 in spite of playing extra time with the wind in our favour and being awarded three penalties from which we scored only one goal (Pilot Officer Harris). The Adjutant brought down the house several times and was applauded every time he kicked or handled the ball. He is so large that he nearly filled the goal himself. In the second half the defence played stoutly with the Group Captain charging about manfully and the Doc knocking down all and sundry. Drummond and Kirkby were sound and 'Ackers' Simpson did a lot of work too. I managed to get our first goal from a pass by Squadron Leader Morrison but my knees felt weak and ready to collapse long before time. Willie Carr was very amusing at centre forward, never appearing to know whether to handle or kick the ball. He elbowed very well but the referee was on our side and so were most of the spectators, who apparently enjoyed the match immensely. We adjourned to the mess and clamoured

for tea. It was definitely a successful day but we have operations
tonight as usual — targets along the roads between Sfax and
Sousse.

9th April 1943: Bombs in the Sea

It was no use going to bed because 104 Squadron were due back
before midnight. The Padre and the Doc came over to interrogations
but the operation was spoilt by the weather with 8/10 low cloud. I
enjoyed a funny story by Squadron Leader Trumper and his crew
— a new crew he was taking on their first 'op'. Seeing the flak and
getting a glimpse of Sousse harbour through the cloud the Squadron
Leader recognised where he was and said over the intercom. 'In we
go!' The navigator-bomb aimer thought he said, 'Let them go!' —
so he did! Trumper was rather annoyed about the matter. He says
the bombs went in the sea but the new crew think they were on
land. Intelligence accepted the Squadron Leader's opinion!

The wing mess today was filled with poor old men hobbling
around as a result of yesterday's football. My right knee is stiff
and swollen.

There were violent winds and a sandstorm today and 'ops' were
cancelled.

10th April 1943: Sfax Captured

Wind and rain all day but operations are on tonight with tactical
targets. The port of Sfax has been captured by the Eighth Army.

12th April 1943: Hang-Up Accident

The ghastly crack of a near bomb burst wakened me and I knew at
once it must be the jettisoning of a hang-up, or (far worse), a
hang-up which had fallen off as an aircraft landed. It was in fact
three 500 lb bombs which the crew had tried to dislodge in the air
but which fell off when they landed and blew 'Z for Zebra'
(Sergeant Wilkins) to pieces. All the crew were killed except the
rear gunner who escaped with a broken leg and burns. I rushed
outside to see activity on the flarepath and a fire. It made me feel
suddenly miserable and shaken — we haven't had bombs bursting
near us for some time, not since Malta. This fact is a clear example
of Allied supremacy in the air in 1943. In 1942 prior to Alamein
our airfields were frequently attacked by Luftwaffe bombers. The
telephone rang and soon I was busily engaged in normal routine
work. It was a good 'op' and there were clear photographs of the
airfield at St Marie du Zit — our main target.

Tonight was chaotic because of target changes — once at the end of briefing and again at take-off. Most aircraft had already become airborne and had to be warned by signal. We are again attacking targets in the enemy's remaining bridgehead in Tunisia. The war is going well and Kairouan and Sousse have been captured.

13th April 1943
'T for Tommy' 104 Squadron (Sergeant McLennan, a very nice Australian, and Sergeant McConville, his navigator, both friends of mine) is missing from last night's operation.

Operating again tonight — fourth night in succession.

14th April 1943
Early this morning I went over to take the 104 Squadron interrogations and give Holmes a clear night. He is showing signs of wear from lack of sleep, and can't seem to sleep in the day time to make up. The poor chap also has teeth trouble. Usual two briefings in the afternoon and 'usual' targets!

17th April 1943: Presentiment
104 Intelligence called me at 02.00 with news of last night's operation on enemy landing fields remaining in the Bridgehead area — the seventh night in succession for our squadrons in preparation for the next and final attack by the Eighth Army to take Tunis.

The 'op' was successful but 'S for Sugar' (Flying Officer Panting, Pilot Officer Harland, Sergeant Watters, Sergeant Lewis and Flight Sergeant Twiss) is missing and believed seen shot down over the target. Denis Panting is our racing motorist pilot — the perfect film type — thin keen face, spare figure, quiet and confident — and one of our most experienced and determined bomber captains. I know the whole crew of course. Mike Harland, the second pilot, is an Australian who recently joined the squadron and this was his first operation. The navigator, wireless operator and gunner are usual members of Denis's crew and nice chaps.

Later I heard a little more from Flying Officer 'Ham' Fuller which gave added poignancy to the loss of 'S for Sugar'. Ham told me that he, Denis, Wally Clarke and Mike Harland were all very close friends at 26 OTU, Moreton in the Marsh, before coming overseas to join 104 Squadron. Mike came out much later than the others.

Before take-off Mike handed Ham a letter to forward to his parents just in case he were to go missing. Ham assured him that flying with Denis he had nothing to worry about, but Mike nevertheless remained a little troubled and unfortunately it now seems that his presentiment was all too true.

In the afternoon the Group Captain asked (ordered!) me to take Clulow and Holmes to see the 231 Wing Intelligence set-up. My feelings were ungracious, to say the least, as we are all three tired out and today is a 'stand down', but the visit turned out to be useful.

Number 231 Wing Intelligence is much improved but, best of all, we got news that one of their crews, 'G for George', had reported seeing some parachutes open from the plane shot down in flames last night — our 'S for Sugar'. We got a copy of the bombing report and brought this back to show Wing Commander Micky Mount and everyone in the 104 Squadron mess was very pleased.

Then I decided to have it out with the Group Captain over this matter of wing or squadron briefing tents and rang up and he agreed to see me. We had a long talk — forty minutes or more — and I learned that he has no personal dislike or distrust of me, so that's something. I can say the same.

20th April 1943: Halifax Explosion
11.20 hours — a hell of a bang! I looked out of my tent and saw the debris and explosion cloud as a Halifax went up with black smoke and flames from the wreckage where previously there had been several trolleys laden with bombs, and armourers putting the bombs in the bay of the aircraft. A fire tender and an ambulance (with Doc Gimson on board) rushed over to the fire and got within a hundred yards or so, but obviously nothing could be done and further explosions might be expected. It was very brave of the fire and ambulance people and they picked up three survivors. While they were there, up went more bombs with another ear-splitting crack and a plume of smoke over a thousand feet into the air. Pieces whizzed down all around my tent and beyond for more than half a mile from the scene.

12.30: There are still some small fires and a 500-yard prohibited area has been announced which must include my tent. The casualties are two NCOs and seven armourers killed and three missing, i.e. twelve killed and three injured men in sick bay — a ghastly business and a major disaster for the squadron.

The explosions were heard in Misurata fifteen miles away and human limb fragments were found scattered near my tent and the Officers' Mess. Discussion about the disaster led to the opinion by the Wing Armament Officer that it was probably due to a human error in misfitting a delayed action fuse to one of the bombs. These fuses are particularly dangerous in that they cannot be unscrewed if a mistake is made, e.g. if a screw thread becomes crossed.

24th April 1943: Food Economics
A.B. Read and Squadron Leader Streater came over to tea and I invited Holmes, Clulow and Donnelly (a new IO gaining experience in 104 Squadron and 236 Wing). We had a pleasant evening together and the Mess Secretary told us some tales of recent food transactions with the Misurata market. Two wogs gave fifteen eggs for a tea cup of sugar worth perhaps two pence, but would give only three eggs for a 1/− note of military currency. Also in the market twelve fish were offered for 50/− but by bartering four cups of tea and two cups of sugar worth about 3/− possibly − the mess got the twelve fish. The wogs aren't daft − this is probably an example of the true working of economic laws.

25th April 1943: Flak
Another very hot day so I cleaned out my tent and put all the bedding in the sun as usual. We had plenty of work in Intelligence reading summaries and collating a questionnaire which Group issued to be answered by all our aircrews. One of the Wing Commander's answers amused me:
 Question (from Group): 'What do you want to know about flak?'
 Answer (by Micky Mount): 'How to avoid it.'

26th April 1943: American Pattern Bombing
Very hot again. We had a discussion in the mess about USAAF bombing and I think I convinced the others that it is not mere line-shooting − photographs of the results are impressive. If a daylight formation of Fortresses and Liberators gets on target the bomb pattern is most effective and damaging. The difficulties are navigation of a formation and heavy losses from enemy flak and fighter opposition. [As if to make the point, US Liberators on 26th April heavily bombed Bari airfield destroying 100 enemy planes.]

27th April 1943
The Group Captain had a long talk with me after breakfast. Group
Captain MacNair has very interesting views on the past and future
of air warfare and the RAF in particular. He likes American
bombers and equipment (he commanded an RAF Liberator squadron) and believes that the Americans will form a separate Air
Force after the war.

1st May 1943: Khamsin Weather
It was a terribly hot day with a strong hot wind from the south
bringing up the dust. Violent gusts after lunch brought swirls of
choking dust into the wildly flapping tents.

No 'ops' again — we're actually fed up with the long stand down
which is mainly due to weather. Being of a lazy nature, I find
enough to do and am not bored like some people. But like everyone else, I'm desperately keen to get this North African business
cleared up and we are all worried about the likely army casualties
in the heavy fighting for hill tops and against well defended
positions near Tunis.

2nd May 1943: Awards
Today we heard that Ken Loveless of my old squadron and
Warrant Officer Vertican of Tim Clulow's squadron have been
awarded the DFC. They are both jolly good chaps who well
deserve the honour.

4th May 1943: Wellington Crash
Still hot and windy. This afternoon I had a grandstand view of a
Wellington crash-landing as my tent is rather close to the end of
the runway — too close sometimes! 'W for William' came in fast
and high, put the nose down and lost height rapidly on to the
runway but didn't level out — just ploughed straight in. Debris
was thrown up behind as the undercart collapsed and the shock
was taken by the bomb compartment while the plane slid noisily
to a standstill.

I rushed towards the crash hoping to help in rescue work but
found the distance greater than expected. Several trucks and two
ambulances got there before me and it was miraculous how
quickly people were on the scene — and also miraculous that
there was no fire. The crew were OK apart from the captain —
Henry Langton — with a cut head. Apparently the fore and
aft control went completely u/s coming in to land and he couldn't

A primitive briefing in the desert in front of the IO's tent

Flying Officer H. M Fuller and crew (104 Squadron) at Kairouan in August 1943 before take off to bomb targets at Naples

Armourers with a 4,000
"blockbuster" or "cookie"

Flt. Lt. L. Wells (RCAF) a
Wing Commander D.
Crossley DFC who as Com
manding Officer of 1
squadron initiated a tec
nique of low level attacks
bridges using 4,000 lb bom
fitted with 11 second del
fuses

Results of Allied air attack
on two bridges at Guilianova

level out. He came in fast with no flaps and wheels down. Examination showed that the pin had fallen out of the pin-joint of the elevator control, leaving the pilot without the use of this vital part of the tail unit.

5th May 1943: Preparations for Final Attack (Operation Strike)
A busy day for a change. The AOC was at both briefings to make important announcements that the final assault on the Bridgehead is about to start. An armoured division and infantry and artillery have been transferred from Eighth Army to the First Army and the main thrust towards Tunis will be from the south-west. The Enfidaville front has proved tough for any frontal assault. We are to give direct support by bombing transport routes and troops in the Bridgehead.

Then suddenly a wet mist came up between 22.30 and 23.00 hours preventing take-off. What luck the Hun has!

6th May 1943
Another busy day of briefing and actual operations this time with a good number of aircraft. Our job is to attack focal points on roads and railways and troop concentrations within the Bridgehead in direct support of the First Army's advance. An inversion of temperature caused some overheating troubles,

7th May 1943: Tunis and Bizerta Captured
Warrant Officer Vertican DFC (462 Squadron) and his crew are missing from last night's 'op', ('Verty' — who has only just got his DFC). Otherwise it was reasonably successful. Things are moving up forward with the Army. We now know that two of our armoured divisions have broken through along the road to Tunis. We held briefings in the evening after another hot sweaty afternoon and targets are the same as last night in a smaller area. Tonight in my tent there was a large scorpion crawling along the roof — inside and just over my bed — probably the one that I felt crawling on my leg last night and luckily threw out without getting stung! He won't menace anyone else! Later the phone rang from 205 Group passing on grand news from the Army.

The First Army is in Tunis and the Americans are in Bizerta!

8th May 1943: Sabotage
This evening Flight Lieutenant Henry Langton (the pilot in the recent crash of 'W William') was at 104 Squadron briefing with

head and nose bandaged, but quite cheerful. He told me that the control had gone completely at 2,000 feet with his second pilot in charge. He took over and managed to keep the head up by use of throttle — made a circuit OK — then on coming in, the nose sank as soon as the throttle was partly closed. He opened up immediately and got the nose up slightly before hitting the deck. A jolly fine effort! He is convinced it was *sabotage* — the Wellington had recently been repaired in Egypt and he has heard of another similar happening.

9th May 1943
Our 'G for George' (Flying Officer Vinden) was missing last night. An aircraft was seen shot down by enemy flak and reported by Wing Commander Warner of 462 Squadron who was on the 'op'. Enemy flak is still very accurate over the battle area and our aircraft have to fly low to see their targets.

10th May 1943.
News continues good from Tunisia — only the Eighth Army front and the Cape Bon Peninsula remain to be cleared and we have captured 60,000 prisoners already. There is a 'stand down' for our wing but the 40 Squadron boys are going over tonight to keep the enemy awake and miserable by bombing a section of road.

11th May 1943
The news is excellent. Bombing ceased today on the Tunisian front which means that resistance is practically at an end.

12th May 1943: Victory in North Africa
205 Group have received a signal from NATAF Headquarters 'No suitable targets — no operations' and another signal, 'No further operations in connection with this campaign.' So the long to and fro business in North Africa is over at last.

CHAPTER SEVEN

Prelude to Italy

The end of the North African Campaign gave a short respite of a few days of 'Stand Down' for the Wellington squadrons. Operations then recommenced with Sicily and the Italian Mediterranean island fortresses of Pantellaria and Lampedusa as main target areas. 205 Group Wellingtons became part of the North-West African Strategic Air Force commanded by Major-General James Doolittle USAAF.

Even if the Allies were not yet prepared to make a direct assault on Europe across the English Channel it was obvious that the successful Eighth and US Armies from North Africa were soon to attempt the invasion of Sicily and Italy. It became the task of the bombing force to soften up these areas in preparation for the planned landings by the armies.

Number 236 Wing now consisted of 40 and 104 Wellington Squadrons, old partners who had worked together previously in Egypt and Malta. 40 Squadron came to take the place of 462 RAAF Halifax Squadron which moved to Benghazi to operate with American heavy bomber squadrons. The Wing moved from Gardabia to Kairouan at the end of May 1943.

*

16th May 1943 (Sunday): Thanksgiving for Victory
The Wing today held a Thanksgiving Service for the victory in North Africa and later we listened in also to the Westminster Abbey Service of Thanksgiving from home. It is rather thrilling to think that our 205 Group Wings and Squadrons have contributed directly to this victory which is such a great encouragement to all in Britain after so many defeats, retreats and withdrawals in this war.

17th May 1943: Leptis Magna
Work has started again but during the respite from operations I went with Tim Clulow and 462 Squadron personnel to the ruins of the Roman city of Leptis Magna close to the modern Libyan town

of Homs. The ruins of the harbour, roads, forum, theatre and
some other buildings have been carefully excavated by Italian
scholars and prepared for inspection. We were all impressed by the
magnificence of the site, the remains of beautiful buildings and the
evidence of thorough planning of the ancient city.

19th May 1943: Warrant Officer Vertican DFC and Crew

Great news today from Tim Clulow that Warrant Officer Vertican
and all his crew have drifted ashore in their dinghy west of Homs
after 10½ days at sea. They are weak but OK and were helped by
the natives. This is wonderful news because all hope had been
given up. The Halifax was forced down by engine trouble on
6th May while en route from Gardabia to attack battle area targets
in the Tunisian bridgehead.

  Winston Churchill has made another interesting speech — this
time to Congress in Washington. He was well received and there
were some stirring passages. Winston emphasized that we would be
with the USA one hundred per cent against Japan. A long war is
still possible but at least we are now making some progress.

20th to 22nd May 1943

Unpleasant news from home is that Flying Officer John King who
operated so well with 104 Squadron as a navigator and got back to
Egypt from a crash-landing behind the enemy lines, is missing
again after a Bomber Command raid on Dortmund.

23rd May 1943: 462 Squadron Leaving 236 Wing

In the afternoon we had another cricket match. Don Crossley has
now joined 236 Wing as Operations Officer after his second tour
of operations as flight commander with 70 Squadron. He made a
useful 15 runs and our Intelligence clerk L.A.C. Clark made an
excellent 40 runs. In the end we were unfortunate to lose again to
231 Wing — this time 109 to 126. In the evening Tim Clulow and
Wing Commander Warner came into Intelligence to write letters
and tell me that 462 Squadron are leaving tomorrow to join other
heavy bomber squadrons at Benghazi. 40 Squadron will take their
place with us and the Wellington force will be 37 and 70 Squadrons with 231 Wing and 40 and 104 Squadrons with our 236 Wing.

24th May 1943

After a busy morning we played another cricket match and this
time managed to beat a Group XI by 100 to 45 runs. In the evening

there was an ENSA concert by Pickard's Chinese Syncopators — a good conjuror, a moderate comedian and singer, and two very charming girls — not very talented dancers but otherwise rather above the usual cut of artists. The two girls had the Group Captain's tent for two nights and caused a bit of trouble without knowing it because officers' quarters were well nigh unusable from their position within feminine eye range. The take-off at night was spoilt by dust because the only trace of wind was down the flare-path and the dust clouds caused several 'shaky do's'.

25th May 1943
I was up at 05.30 to interrogate. All crews are OK but 'N for Nuts' landed at Malta, and 'R for Robert' (Squadron Leader Fox) had difficulty in getting back here on one engine. Tommy Howes was his navigator — and, of course, it was our 'R for Robert' — R seems an unlucky letter in our squadron. The 'op' was a good one (Messina).

The rest of the day was spent packing Intelligence and personal goods for a move tomorrow.

26th May 1943: Gardabia to Kairouan
This time I'm fortunate to be travelling with the Wing party by road so that I'll see the countryside at close hand and the battle areas.

Today we passed alternating palm tree oases, Italian colonisation schemes, vineyards and desert patches, occasional fields of barley and small olive orchards. We reached Tripoli and the RAF hotel for the night. I noticed the delicious drinking water after our desert stuff with its heavy chlorination.

27th May 1943: Tripoli
I visited the officers' shop in the morning and then climbed up a tower to get a good view of the harbour and town. Tripoli looked beautiful — a blue sea and ships to seaward, a front pleasant with trees and gardens, a town of white houses, a fine cathedral with a dome like St Paul's and a square tower, several mosques etc. Most houses are flat topped and white but there are occasional pinks and blues to relieve the monotony.

Moving off to the west in the staff car we arrived at Group HQ which is in a pleasant position away from the road and traffic. We slept in the car.

28th May 1943

We shaved in cold water and after breakfast set off again passing more vineyards but the land was becoming barer and more like heathland with some occasional fields of barley and wheat. A long straight road led to Zuara which is a small port with fishing boats in the harbour. The road got worse and the land drier with salt marshes on the seaward side as we approached the frontier between Tripolitania and Tunisia. The milestones read 40 km *Confine*, 20 km *Confine* etc. (*Confine* = frontier) and eventually we reached the frontier post at Pisida. There were no imposing arches — only wire marked the boundary. Ben Gardane was the first Tunisian settlement — with sparse palm trees and olives in the desert surrounding the town. Some curious houses like loaves of bread stuck together took my interest. The traffic was now quite dense with military vehicles being towed back for repairs. We saw one six-wheeled vehicle towing a trailer eastwards with a tank plus three trucks. Another truck was pulling seven others behind it. The road here had been widened by the army to almost a hundred yards in the flat terrain of bush and camel thorn. We found a pleasant stopping point for the night in a wadi with some fig trees.

29th May 1943

Medenine is apparently a market centre with some large buildings and several mosques and more of the bread loaf houses, sometimes in two layers, one on the other. The brown hills looked like Egypt as we passed along a good winding road undulating between horizontal strata to Mareth.

There were round store huts with thatched roofs and black sheep in the fields towards the famed Mareth Line. Minefields were everywhere with their black triangles and red and white signs on wire or on posts alongside the road.

A 'cleared lane' was proved by the rows of mines along the side of the track where they had been stacked after clearing or dragged aside in a hurry. Small cemeteries and cairns of stones marked areas of severe fighting. The country here was undulating with tussocky grass, barley and scrub leading up to the brown Matmata Hills. We saw two natives and two donkeys taking a big risk in the heavily mined area. Nearer Mareth were anti-tank ditches and wire — and more minefields.

A wadi with water here and there, we thought, was probably the Wadi Zigzaou of Mareth attack frame. Here were marked tracks with names like 'Y', 'SUN', 'MOON TRACK' and piles of green cases of ammunition amidst the fig and olive trees and in the barley fields. Mareth was considerably damaged but no defences were visible until another anti-tank ditch appeared.

Then the trees ended and a notice said 'End of Malarious Area'. Gabes was a native town (with women washing clothes in running water in the wadi) but also had a railway station and airfield. Crossing over the wadi we came into a palm tree area — malarious but fertile with little water channels among the trees.

To the north we passed through another dry region with much dust blowing. The Wadi Akarit impressed us with all its bridges blown up and graves on each side of the road, shell holes, dugouts and observation posts — and mines everywhere. The wadi is deep and steep-sided — a hell of an obstacle! The track made a big detour and then took us across on an earth embankment. German slit trenches, posts and graves were seen on either side of the road.

We had lunch at La Skira on the flat plain to Mahares. The locality seems clear of war debris except for a few wrecked vehicles, tanks and the ever present minefields. The whole trip is proving immensely enjoyable as a break from normal routine and I feel like a privileged tourist. Tunisia is evidently a food producing country with olives, almonds and barley as important crops. Some of the olive groves are very large. Between Mahares and Sfax I noted a dozen vehicles and two or three tanks burned out — I wonder if it was part of our night effort of 30th/31st March.

I was asked to go ahead to report our convoy to the Army Town Major at Sfax. Sfax is the first European-like town since Tripoli and has many good houses and factories on the outskirts. There is a walled fortress-like native city. European shops are found in the modern section and warehouses around the port area which has been badly damaged by our bombing. Many French residents were about — mainly women — and the usual natives with red skullcaps and dirty shirts or nightdress affairs. We had trouble with the convoy getting out of the town but eventually we got on the El Djem road which we wanted. We passed through olive groves and more barley fields as we moved along a good but narrow road northwards.

We camped at a pleasant spot in view of the metre gauge railway and with a circle of natives watching our preparations for the night. A pleasant and amusing Free French Officer came into our camp to get some oil for his jeep. He belonged to a Bisley squadron so I asked him what he thought of them as aircraft because I well know their poor reputation. He looked at me carefully and then said slowly and with a slight smile: 'The RAF don't like the Bisley — and us, we don't like them, too!'

30th May 1943
I slept well in the open with a ground sheet slung to the handles of the car to keep off the dew. It was a fresh beautiful morning — and we were off before 07.00 hours.

El Djem — the Roman amphitheatre like the Roman Colosseum showed up ahead along an avenue of olive trees. The railway ran parallel with the road and on an embankment. El Djem itself seemed just a native town and overshadowed by the grandeur of the monument to Roman skill and architecture.

The country was open with deep gullies of erosion typical of a dry country with insufficient rain to wear down the sides into a normal valley. There were sheep and some camels around and natives wearing very wide brimmed straw plaited hats like Mexicans. Groubrine had sheep everywhere and at Bourdjine we saw some dairy cattle.

To the west of Msaken the country was more open and less fertile. The olives began to thin out and the land was mainly pastoral with sheep and camels. We passed a big blue salt lake with white edges to our left. The natives here use small high carts perched on two big wheels — drawn by a donkey or camel or horse. They are similar to those seen in Egypt — the design hasn't changed in 2,000 years or 2,000 miles!

Sidi el Hani was a pleasant looking village where the railway crosses the road. Kairouan — the Holy City (surpassed only by Mecca, Jerusalem and possibly one other city, it is said) showed up white ahead with mosques and buildings peering over the brown walls. Around the walls were pools of smelly water but presumably it is a river in the rainy season. The smells and filth are impressive! Servicemen refer to Kairouan as the Holy City with the unholy smell! The new landing ground 'Kairouan — Cheria', scraped from black earth, looks most uninviting and the weather is hot and sticky.

31st May 1943: Kairouan — Cheria LG
It was a hard day of putting up tents and settling in. At night an enemy bombing attack on the port of Sousse thirty miles away produced some striking A/A defence fireworks very clearly visible from Kairouan.

1st June 1943
We put in the seating accommodation for the Wing Intelligence
tent but it was a relief when we received a 'stand down' because
much remains to be done. The heat is very trying as it is hot and
moist here. In fact it is terribly humid and quite different from the
desert and insects of all kinds rise up from the cracked mud of
these plains which in winter are morasses or shallow salt lakes.
Fireworks again at Sousse tonight.

2nd June 1943
The Group Captain gave some of us a pleasant break in the after-
noon by taking a party to the sea at Sousse in his car. At night the
Sousse barrage was again in operation against enemy bombers. Our
aircrews are most impressed by the Allied anti-aircraft defences at
Sousse, and they should know!

3rd June 1943: A Windy Briefing
We had a busy day completing arrangements for briefing. The
first briefing in the new tent went off well thanks largely to
Aubyn James. There were some terrifying moments because the
lights fused prior to briefing and an electrician had to hold up one
light all the time to prevent the others going out. The remaining
floodlight was perilously suspended on a hook above Wing Commander Bagnall's head (CO of 40 Squadron) and the wind rocking
the tent threatened to cause the lamp to fall at any moment.
However, my prayers were answered, the lamp held up and the
Wing Commander survived without even realising the danger.

4th June 1943: The Adjutant (236 Wing)
Up at 03.30 for interrogations and then learned that 'P for Peter'
had pranged on take-off and was lying very near our tent. Good
job it didn't catch fire and the bombs go up. The pilot was Flying
Officer Horry, an experienced captain and a good chap. In the
afternoon I drove the Adjutant's 15 cwt Dodge truck for him and
learned en route to Sousse and the sea that Flight Lieutenant
Partington went to Arnold School, Blackpool, where I taught for
three years. He, of course, knows most of the staff I worked with
and spoke well of the Headmaster.

Our adjutant is quite a character in his own right, very large,
bluff and hearty. He entertains by singing and telling jokes in the
mess and is popular with airmen and aircrews as he is always
willing to help if he can. For example, he produced a concrete

cricket pitch for the recent spate of cricket matches at Gardabia.

There was Tunisian wine in the mess tonight — cheaper and better than Benito's Blood. When Willie Carr and I went to our tent later we saw a strong white light on the horizon. He thought it was the Chance light at another landing ground. At that moment the 'Chance light' exploded and gave off a red glow from which came showers of hot splinters. Smoke rose up to a great height and plumed out into the usual mushroom — we knew quite well what it was but the noise was a long time reaching us. Another explosion followed and we counted off the seconds until we heard it. Then again there was a third terrific explosion including Very lights going up in all directions. Later we had phone calls and changes in arrangements — an aircraft had caught fire at take-off at 231 Wing and then set off two other Wellingtons. All three were bombed up with full fuel tanks and were completely destroyed in the accident.

5th–8th June 1943: Air Attacks on Pantellaria

A letter from home says John King has survived again and is a POW in Germany — Good luck for him and grand news. Pantellaria, the Italian fortified island, is now being bombed by day and night. On the 8th, Lloyd Parry had two excellent photographs of Pantellaria's harbour and of a ship on fire while Paddy Thompson's 4,000 lb bomb burst in the town area. The results appeared to be good from a bombing point of view but one aircraft is missing, Pilot Officer McLaren — formerly Flight Sergeant McLaren, an ex-Mountie. He had just got his commission and I had recently congratulated him and talked with Sergeant Bobby, his very pleasant navigator.

9th June 1943: Rescue

Wing Commander Mount went out with a crew at first light this morning to search for the missing crew. Later we had news that Pilot Officer McLaren had been picked up alive by a naval vessel but the other crew members had died of exposure in the sea — the escape dinghy having failed to come out when they ditched.

10th June 1943: a Nightmare Night

After an important briefing for another big attack on Pantellaria — everything went wrong! The troubles occurred in this sort of order:

1. There was a thunderstorm and very heavy rain.

2. 231 Wing's landing ground was flooded and put out of action after nine of their aircraft had taken off — they were operating earlier than us.

3. Our take-off was held up while 231 Wing aircraft were diverted to our landing ground on their return.

4. Dispersal trucks were missing or late so one aircraft sat at the end of the runway for fifteen minutes causing delay in bringing the other 231 Wellingtons down.

5. An air raid alert was received and there was a heavy enemy raid on Sousse with the usual fireworks clearly visible.

6. I was told to interrogate the nine crews from 231 Wing. Four crews turned up for interrogation — the others shot off home in their trucks.

7. Our take-off was one hour late.

8. 104 Squadron got nine Wellingtons away out of fifteen scheduled. 40 Squadron got thirteen aircraft off.

9. The fourteenth Wellington was 'T Tommy' (a Canadian captain and crew with whom I flew home from Castel Benito to Gardabia). It was about 02.20 (11th June) when I heard the normal roar of engines drowned by the terrible confused noises of an aircraft sliding and crashing at the end of the runway — and seemingly right outside my tent. The debris was in several pieces roaring and flaming.

10. In a few minutes the bombs went up in four mighty crumps with the usual fireworks of bomb splinters, ammunition and Very lights flung high into the air — then the whirring pattering down and heavy bumps as pieces returned to earth all around us. With Squadron Leader Brian O'Connor of New Zealand, who shares the tent, I was sheltering behind luggage cases — we had no slit trench and felt very exposed. It was just a matter of luck whether debris hit the tent or not. The rear gunner was picked up in his turret with concussion — the others were killed.

11. Our landing ground was now out of action as we have only one runway.

12. Our aircraft were diverted to a neighbouring airfield.

13. It was found that the explosion of 'T' had damaged three of the visiting Wellingtons from 231 Wing.

14. Operations reported that four of our Wellingtons were not accounted for.

15. Our diverted crews were said to have been interrogated where they landed.

16. The crews arrived back — they had *not* been interrogated — so we organised it. Several crews reported encounters with single-engined fighters, probably FW190s, over the Pantellaria area. S/E fighters are unusual at night.

17. Two of our aircraft are still missing — 'X for X-ray' (Flying Officer George Edwards, Flying Officer Jack Adams, Flying Officer Dickie Fry and others) — and 'W for William' (Sergeant Eason and crew), who were on their last operation before completing their tour. What cruel luck! Don Boyd-Stephenson would also have been with George but he is serving a week's suspension by Squadron Leader Fox. Old Jack had only just got back from leave and George is doing the first 'op' for some time — in fact, since his crash. What a night!

11th June 1943

The landing ground today is something of a shambles. There have been scares that some unexploded bombs were about to go up or be blown up deliberately. The tents were put out of bounds several times but the bombs are still lying in the wreckage.

12th June 1943: Pantellaria Surrenders

Grand news — George Edwards, Jack Adams and Dickie Fry are all safe after landing on Pantellaria by parachute. 'X X—ray' was shot down by a night fighter. They saw the take-over by our troops when the island surrendered after non-stop bombing attacks. George says the Ities surrendered the island to him or some offered to do so! Henry Langton joked in the squadron mess that it was 'the sight of "Grandpappy Jack-a-Jack Adams" descending on them (the Ities) armed with his famous fly swat that completely demoralised them and forced them into surrendering!' [Jack Adams, an Australian slightly older than the rest of the aircrews, is a determined swatter of flies. He took the jokes in good part.]

Unhappily there is no news yet of 'W for William' nor of the other three crew members of 'X for X-ray' — probably they landed in the sea. At briefing tonight, the bombs we were warned about yesterday, went off without warning. Everyone dived for the floor in wonderful style.

21st June 1943: Salerno Marshalling Yards

I'm going on an 'op' tonight with Wing Commander Mount, having obtained the necessary permission. My objectives are (i) to do nickel dropping myself and see whether it is difficult (crews complain of the difficulties of dropping these bundles of pamphlets over enemy territory. It is part of the psychological warfare campaign against the Italians and we have to handle it as part of Intelligence duties) (ii) to watch bombing at a blitz period. I haven't done an 'op' since last October with Squadron Leader Strutt and Tommy Lonsdale to Fuqa landing grounds, so it's about time I went again.

Later (on return):
We set off in Wellington MKII 'Y for Yorker' 104 Squadron at 21.26 hours, being third off the ground. Darkness was already setting in as we climbed slowly out over the salt lake and set course after a wide circuit. It was a steady trip in good weather, pinpointing on islands where there seemed to be night-fighter possibilities as a search-light was behaving curiously and may have been indicating for fighters. Nothing was seen, however, and we went on to find 8/10 to 10/10 strato-cumulus at the target. The moon rose blood red behind where the Italian mainland must have been. I saw what I think was Capri and the Campanella Peninsula with flak bursts beyond around the Bay of Naples. At 01.02 hours flares appeared a few miles from us and we raced in towards them weaving slightly to avoid possible flak. Under the flares (dropped by Sergeant Carey 'G for George') was Salerno — unmistakable in the light of the excellently placed illumination. We went in over the coast and turned sharply to run in to target on a 320° heading. Corrections were given by the bomb aimer — then 'Bombs Gone' and later 'Flash Gone'. The Wing Commander turned and banked very sharply to port and the bomb bursts were clearly visible to me from the astro hatch. Aimed at the railway station and marshalling yards the bombs were very close to this and parallel to the coast. There was no flash from the bombs only big puffs of smoke as they hit where the railway runs close to the shore. Bombing was at 01.06 hours from 10,000 feet with good accuracy. I saw another Wimpy over the target and an unidentified aircraft stooging around with a white light on it. There were plenty of photo flashes going off all around us and beneath.

No definite flak was seen but several bumps were felt under the aircraft as if from near bursts. However the Wing Commander says they were probably the slip stream of other aircraft. The rear gunner seemed to think there was some flak but obviously the main defences are in the Naples area.

Before bombing, the Wing Commander left the second pilot in charge up front and helped me drop the leaflets after opening the bundles and arranging them on the bed, the step and the Elsan lid. They went out easily down the flarechute but I saw from the astrodome later that some were wrapped around the rear aerial. On the return journey we came down through the cloud layers at 7,000 feet. The navigator kindly offered me his silk and outer gloves and also some lumps of chocolate — all these I accepted gratefully.

We hit the coast exactly where we wanted to, then had some difficulty in finding our own flarepath and in getting down — because of RT failure. We landed at 04.13 — flying time 6 hours 47 minutes.

And so to bed after breakfast at the squadron officers' mess with the Wing Commander and the other chaps. All crews got back safely. My friends, Lloyd Parry, George Edwards, Henry Langton were all on the same target with us and I felt a sense of comradeship in having been to Salerno with them.

Crew of 'Y Yorker'; Wing Commander Mount (captain), Sergeant Hick (second pilot) Sergeants Pape, Taylor, McIntosh, and Snowden (rear gunner) and Flight Lieutenant Chappell (nickel dropper!).

24th June 1943: Kairouan — Hani West LG
We have moved to a new landing ground at Hani West with more chance of escaping the mud and the floods. Changing camp is always hard work but no one is sorry to leave the black soil of Cheria. However the flies and insects are the same and we are still only a few miles from Kairouan — the Holy Smell.

25th June 1943: Bari
Briefing today was for an oil refinery near Bari. The results later proved to be less satisfactory that we at first thought. Flying Officers Ham Fuller and Wally Clarke and crew in 'Y for Yorker' did the primary illumination dropping their flares after identifying the target area. They almost collided with the cable of a barrage balloon and were caught by a dozen searchlights and some scattered flak from Bari before getting to the right place. However, something went wrong with the secondary flare-dropper and the small refinery was not identified. Something else got a heavy bombing but not the refinery.

27th June 1943: Naples
I watched the take-off last night for an attack on Naples and was
up early for interrogation. 'V for Victor' is missing with Flying
Officer Paddy Thompson and crew. He always wanted to go to
Naples as a target. Others in his crew I know well are a sergeant
who has recently looked tired and ill and Sergeant Quaile and
Flight Sergeant Capewell — wizard New Zealander types.

28th June 1943
Tonight we briefed for targets on the toe of Italy where 104
Squadron is to do the flare dropping.

29th June 1943: Security Scare
I was up early for interrogations this morning and learned that
'R for Robert' (Sergeant Cochrane) is missing. How many Rs is
that who have been lost? We held briefing for the same targets
again this afternoon. The Wing Commander is going tonight and
will try this illuminator business. George Edwards is also operating
tonight and my friends from 'Y for Yorker' at Salerno (Sergeant
Hick and crew) are taking 'T for Tommy' with a 4,000 lb bomb.
I watched the take-off and then there was a security scare on the
camp about enemy paratroops having been dropped. If so, we
didn't find them! [The story was that a crack German parachute
unit had been assigned the job of sabotaging our aircraft. For a
week or so, aircrews were armed and did patrol duties. Then some
Gurkhas were brought in for this purpose.]

30th June 1943
During the night I was called by Operations to interrogate as there
was a diversion of aircraft to our landing ground. All 104 Squadron Wellingtons got back eventually, thank goodness, including
George Edwards who had navigation trouble with a new crew.
'That must be Bizerta', says the navigator. 'Don't be a bloody
fool,' says George. 'It's the Kerkenna Islands.' It was. [Bizerta
and Kerkenna Islands are about 200 miles apart!] However they
got back and being George he had a burst tyre on landing and then
a Very cartridge nearly set fire to the top of the fuselage. 'T for
Tommy' (Sergeant Hick) had to jettison the big bomb due to
engines overheating.

1st to 4th July 1943: Flares at Palermo
On 1st July a very successful operation on Palermo was carried out

with 104 Squadron doing the illuminating by 'B for Beer' (Flying Officer Ron Thirsk, Flight Lieutenant Tommy Howes navigator and crew) and 'Q for Queenie' (Flying Officer Ham Fuller, Flying Officer Wally Clarke (navigator) and crew). 'B' dropped flares over the town area and 'Q' over the port and docks. The target was brilliantly illuminated so that guncrews could actually be seen in action along the waterfront where crews counted ten batteries. During interrogation at Intelligence later, Wing Commander Bagnall of 40 Squadron, who had been on the 'op', came over to congratulate both crews dropping the flares.

During these days we had burning hot winds at Kairouan making life miserable. Two afternoon trips to swim with the Group Captain helped a lot — once to Monastir and once to Hergla. It was good fun playing 'horses and riders' in the surf — Group Captain MacNair is jolly good at it and difficult to upset. I'm usually his rider and am not good enough at holding my breath under water in the struggles.

5th July 1943: Squadron Frolics

Geoff Holmes came round to invite me to lunch with 104 Squadron (who have a 'stand down') and then to go swimming with them at Sousse. I did and enjoyed it immensely, with Ham Fuller, who has a talent for fun, amusing us with his clowning, and everybody as cheery as ever. 'Farmer' Whitmell has finished his tour of 'ops' and is going to South Africa on a Staff Navigation Course. The Wing Commander gave some interesting information at lunch time about changes in command which are in prospect. He enjoyed my story of the Canadian crew who were mystified by the many lights on the sea marking the route between Tunisia and Sicily. My suggestion of flame floats had never occurred to them — apparently they never used them themselves to check wind drift.

6th and 7th July 1943

Again it has been frightfully hot with burning and violent winds blowing at mid-day.

The night 'op' of the 5th/6th was difficult to assess. Sergeant Dench and crew in 'Y for Yorker' 40 Squadron were missing and an aircraft was seen shot down over the target.

8th July 1943: Leave in Tunis

Flying Officer Kirkby (cipher officer) and I were picked up by squadron transport going to Tunis and enjoyed the trip except for diversions off the road and the dust. We saw the hill fortress of Takrouna on our left where bitter fighting took place. We stopped at a vinery with great vats of wine and tasted Muscat — golden yellow in colour and very syrupy and sweet — even a few sips gave a pleasant warm sensation! Crossing the plains around Enfidaville we noted wrecked Bren gun carriers and graves marking desperate attempts to penetrate the thickly sown minefields. Fighting here was grimly concentrated between the mountains and the sea. On through the gap leading from Hammamet to Tunis via Grombalia — passing landing grounds and seeing Soliman with its white buildings in the distance to the north. At Hamman Lif the mountains are close to the shore with a very narrow plain that made it easy for defenders.

On past Megrine airfield with German relics including the fuselage of a huge Junkers 290 transport — and finally we reached the outskirts of Tunis with factories, cement, engineering, zinc ore refinery, limestone quarries — then railway yards with damaged sheds and locomotives — and some examples of modern diesels and steam locos. Over the bridge and into the city which is a pleasant place with American type block layout with two main arteries north—south, Avenue de Paris and Avenue de France, crossed at right angles by an east—west wide boulevard, running from the native city to the docks. Many trees and a central path give character to the Boulevard Jules Ferry. We found a hotel and went out to lunch with Squadron Leader Paddy Foote, our 236 Wing Administration Officer. In the afternoon we took the electric railway to La Marsa Plage — a most interesting trip on an embankment alongside the Ship Canal from Tunis to La Goulette — then on through Carthage and La Corniche — a high and rocky coast here — to La Marsa and its *Plage*. We bathed from the beach but found the rocks awkward for swimming.

Coming back via El Aouina, the airport of Tunis, with wrecked hangars and aircraft we had a helpful little Frenchman on the train who was eager to talk to us but none of us was a good linguist. I already have the impression that most people are wanting to be pleasant to us and are thoroughly glad to be rid of the Germans. At dinner with Paddy we all had far too much Muscat and *vin blanc* — or maybe not too much, for we were all three very happy and amused with life and forgot the war.

9th July 1943: Shopping

The morning was spent shopping in the delightful colonnades or arcades shading the shops — but there was little to buy. 'Kirk' bought a French–English Grammar and 'Aid to Conversation', and we both stared rather hungrily at the ladies' clothing in the shops at exorbitant prices but very French in style and delicacy. The women here are all dressed smartly and look clean and attractive — and they walk and carry themselves so well! Most people in the streets are European and there are not so many natives as in Cairo or Tripoli. At the officers' shop I bought a pair of black shoes and was promptly told the shop was for Army Officers not the RAF. We told the assistant what to do about it.

In the afternoon we walked miles along the Avenue de Paris to the Belvedere Park Swimming Pool. In the beautiful park with trees and slopes there was a fine tiled fresh water pool with elaborate diving boards. We swam and lazed around in the sun — then were driven back in a horse-drawn carriage in style to the hotel. In the evening we attended a South African ENSA show at the Garrison Theatre.

10th July 1943: Invasion of Sicily
This is an historical day because the invasion of Sicily by airborne troops and landing craft started last night. We went out to Carthage on the electric railway to see the Roman ruins — for apparently the Romans built over the Carthaginian city after they had destroyed it. Many fine mozaics could be seen on floors of rooms and the remains of heating systems and water conduits. We found the Roman theatre where Churchill addressed the First Army recently — a vast semicircle in the hills with a wide stage and seats in steps cut in the earth and grassed over — probably once they had been covered with stone blocks.

11th July 1943: Back to Work
We visited the railway station in the morning — narrow gauge old-fashioned rolling stock and tank engines with tall chimneys — and some modern diesel cars painted blue and white and looking very smart. They have been used for hospital trains. On the other side of the station were standard gauge tracks for through trains to Algiers. Then I obtained permission to look around the docks and check on our bombing results. The warehouses were severely damaged but only one ship wrecked — and that was done in a daylight raid by a British plane according to the French Gendarmes at the docks. We had an interesting conversation in their bad English, our worse French and sundry signs, nods and *Oui's* —

and parted on good terms. An unpleasant hitch-hiking journey took us back to Kairouan. We had three lifts and this included a nightmare drive in an ambulance driven by two inebriated Americans who constantly drank Muscat from a bottle as we went along. We were invited to share occasionally and did so gladly to deaden the sense of panic and danger!

We worked at night, getting back to the war at once. Sicily is going pretty well, thank goodness, and that is what really matters.

12th July 1943: Monte Corvino
In the four days we've been away the squadron has lost two crews on operations. Tonight I prepared the briefing for a raid on Monte Corvino aerodrome near Naples.

13th July 1943: Leave in Tunis — Aircrew Style
It was an excellent result last night with sixteen fires started and a hangar blown up. There was no opposition and all our aircraft returned safely. Palermo is tonight's target.

At the squadron mess some of the lads were highly amused at my account of what Kirkby and I did on leave in Tunis — they hardly believed us! Ham Fuller provided a nicely contrasting story of how he and his crew enjoyed themselves a few weeks ago. In more or less his own words, this is what happened.

Tunis — Aller et Retour
Tunis had just fallen and exciting stories were already getting around about the life-style there — French wines, French cuisine, even gay and friendly French girls. Some of them, it was said, dressed up like bankers' wives but made it quite plain that they had nothing to do with the banking business.

This naturally greatly aroused the curiosity of the boys and Ham Fuller's crew was one of the lucky ones. Not only did they win the draw for the first crew to go on leave but the rear gunner, Paul Cameron, was a Frenchman. Paul's irresistible charm would ensure acceptance in any strata of Tunisian society — they would undoubtedly be greeted as heroes and liberators. Moreover, there was another side to Paul. Despite his tender years he was, according to the accounts he rendered in the sergeants' mess, an accomplished and ardent lover whom no girl could resist.

Paul's lively imagination was already cooking up the possibilities and prospects. Wally Clarke would be introduced as the navigator,

'Pete' Peterson, a New Zealander, as the front gunner and Ham Fuller as the pilot and skipper, all great heroes who had braved the enemy flak guns countless times and had shot down so many enemy aircraft that they had lost count of them.

And as Paul also explained, with enthusiasm, the Free French were there, and where there were Free Frenchmen it was only logical to assume that there would also be 'free' French women.

There would be transport back from Tunis because the mess gharry had to pick up some stores, but the trip to the city would be a hitch-hike job. They were lucky again. While sitting in a restaurant at Enfidaville Paul exclaimed, 'It's the Free French!' and a large Citroen car pulled up and out got a Free French officer. He was alone. Paul spoke to him and he agreed to give the boys a lift to Tunis.

Pete jokingly said, 'You are a Free Frenchman, can you tell us where the "free" French women are?' The officer smiled delightfully and replied, 'You are a very naughty boy, I see. The "free" French women are here, there and everywhere, but no one can ever find them. But if you have the luck to find one, "*vous n'auriez rien à regretter*"!'

He then looked curiously at Ham's pilot wings where he saw the letters RAAF. These he spelt out, slowly and deliberately, 'Ar — ah — ah — ef.' 'Yes!' he exclaimed, 'To know you 'eet' is very interesting for me. You are Australia man.' He added, 'My sister is in Australia — in Potts Point, Sydney. She says Australia is a strange country, with very strange animals and very, very strange people. She also says in Potts Point the people are "rough as bags" and always talk of "bullsheet" — I do not understand these expressions, so I do not know what she means.'

Wally then said, 'If you shared a tent with Ham for a day or so you would soon know — he's the greatest apostle of "bull" ever known.'

The Frenchman frowned and looked puzzled. He then said, 'I still do not understand — you mean the Australia man here is an "apostle".'

'Yes,' replied Wally, 'of bull "sheet".'

'*Mon Dieu!*' exclaimed the Frenchman, 'my *logique*, where is eet — eet has gone. What is all this sheet business my sister wrote to me about?'

Paul then explained it to him in French.

'*Bon,*' said the Frenchman, 'it is now to me clear — I know what she means. In France we put it on our strawberries. *Alors, à l'auto, à Tunis,*' he cried, and waved his arms excitedly. So the boys got into the car and were driven in state to Tunis.

The scene was quite different from that imagined on the squadron. 'Heroes' and 'liberators' were to be seen by the thousand, representing every country of the Allied forces, all with fat wallets and inflated pay books.

'Paul's in for a shock,' said Pete, 'the place is like an agitated ant-hill — he's in for competition, even though he's a Frenchman.'

Ham remarked, 'There will be no socialite "blue orchid" parties here — we'll be bloody lucky to get a beer.'

Paul turned up at eight o'clock. 'It's Chez Calvin tonight,' he announced. 'The Free French officer told me about it — run by a Madame Carfax and her four daughters; just the job, come on you types, good drinking time's going up in smoke.'

To their surprise the place wasn't overcrowded, the reason for which did not become known to them until the following evening.

Introductions were made all round and, as Paul had imagined, all were accorded a hero's welcome. The bar got a bashing for an hour and then, to use an Australianism, it was a question of 'putting on the nose bag'.

'French cuisine,' said Paul, 'it's good.' The others agreed.

And so it was back to the bar for more beer and an amiable chat with Madame Carfax and her daughters. It was a cosy place if not elegant, and also relaxing. But suddenly without warning the scene changed. Madame Carfax leaned over the bar and boxed Paul's ears with such force that his eyes nearly shot out of their sockets. Then with tigress agility she upended his stool and dumped him on the floor. '*Diable incarne,*' he yelled. But the worst was yet to come. With the able assistance of her daughters, the ferocious onslaught was extended to Pete, Wally and Ham.

When they were at a safe distance from Chez Calvin, the aircrew dusted themselves down and gradually regained their composure.

Wally said, 'If Splodge Moore had been there, he would have described that as "the climax of embarrassment".'

Paul said, 'Those people are French and yet they are not French — there's something strange about them. All I did was to make a little approach to the youngest daughter — I thought it would be flattering to her — that's the usual response, but she went up and whispered something to Mama. There's definitely something strange.'

'That explains it,' said Wally. 'Just lay off the "noble" girls in future, especially when we're with you.'

They then came across a bistro called Chez Diable, and as it was only 2 a.m. and because of their unnerving experience, they ducked inside. It was crowded with Yanks and British Tommies. After about half an hour an argument started. Pete said, 'It won't be long now!' And sure enough a lively fight soon developed. Wally asked what the trouble was all about. 'Well,' said a Yank in a friendly, casual manner, 'one of our boys called one of yours a "Dunkirk harrier" and yours responded by calling ours "a Pearl Harbour evacuee".' He added, 'Funny, wasn't it?'

So it was *terminé* for the night and the boys returned to their digs.

Next evening Paul turned up in high spirits — he had slept all day and was in the party mood. 'Tonight we go to the Caveau des Innocents — lively entertainment,' he assured Wally, Pete and Ham. 'Madame Bizertee runs it — she's great fun, a broadminded type.'

Caveau des Innocents certainly had atmosphere. It was a subterranean den, inside the entrance of which was a plaster cast bust of Napoleon, plastered with lipstick and adorned with a Free French officer's cap — quite an *objet d'art*.

The air of gaiety was something that only the French could create, with servicemen of all nationalities and vivacious girls only too happy to show their appreciation for being 'liberated', drinking, laughing and teasing each other. Drinks were ordered and a cordial conversation struck up with the handsome Madame Bizertee.

'There will be entertainment soon,' she said, 'you have arrived *juste à pointe.'*

The orchestra struck up and a Maurice Chevalier type sang a cheeky song. It had the right touch to get things moving. And then the fun started. With the orchestra playing, the girls linked arms and romped around in a circle, whooping and laughing. Suddenly they proceeded to do catherine wheels. The applause was raucous and deafening. When it died down the clientele were invited to join in, much to the delight of everyone.

For Madame Bizertee it was a monumental success — and everyone loved it. Fat wallets were being depleted, but why worry? The war was far from over and all the servicemen wanted was fun — relief from tensions built up from shattering and unnatural experiences — and they were getting it by the basinful.

Then Pete saw the Free French officer who had given the boys a lift. He was delighted to join them.

Paul told him of the incident at Chez Calvin. He laughed and said, 'To you I must apologise. I forgot to tell you, they are of Huguenot stock, more Calvinistic than Calvin himself, only interested in making unconscionable profits from selling drinks and food to jaded servicemen, nothing else. I sent you there because eet is a respectable place.'

'But why,' said Paul, 'why did you send *us* there?' 'Because of the Australia man,' replied the Frenchman. 'Your English friend said he is an "apostle" — what could I do?'

Then Paul said jubilantly, 'Just the job, eh!' as a 'noble' young girl latched on to him. This one became 'radiant', and she was not remarkable for her modesty. And she certainly was 'just the job' as Paul discovered later on getting back to his digs — his wallet was missing.

The return journey was uneventful. Dog-tired they made their weary way to their tents. Splodge was there to greet them, his usual cheerful self, in a great state of merriment.

'Ah there, you lucky fellas,' he called out, 'I've got glad tidings for you — you're on tonight — it's a maximum effort, a low-level on Catania — the Commandos are moving in afterwards and want a little assistance from us.'

14th July 1943
Naples tonight.

15th July 1943
'S for Sugar' (Warrant Officer Sloeman) is missing and no news except that he had some engine trouble and was making for home. Briefing tonight is for a viaduct at Reggio on the toe of Italy.

16th July 1943: Good Bombing
At Reggio last night there was some excellent flare dropping by 'D for Donald' of 40 Squadron and Wing Commander Bagnall put a 4,000 lb bomb exactly where directed and got a photograph of it. Another aircraft got a confirming photo. Excellent bombing! Tonight we briefed for leaflet-dropping visits to Rome, Naples and Sicily.

18th July 1943: Change in Command at 236 Wing
Group Captain P.I. Harris D F C arrived today to take over 236 Wing. Group Captain MacNair is posted to Group as SASO. A 'stand down' tonight — a rarity in these days of intensive bombing.

By the way, mess talk is that the new Group Captain is a stern disciplinarian and we can all expect trouble!

19th July 1943
The briefing tonight was for Aquino airfield between Naples and Rome where PRU reports say that a considerable force of Ju88 bombers has arrived. We took great care in preparing hints for locating the airfield because of anticipated difficulties. Aircrews got the message that this was a chance to get *them* by surprise before they attacked *us*. [And for once it all paid off!]

20th July 1943: Aquino — a Brilliant Attack
Last night's attack on Aquino was one of the best we have ever done. Crews reported fires everywhere and about twenty appeared to be burning aircraft. The fires were seen up to sixty miles away on the run home and all our aircraft returned safely. I read through my Opsum with somewhat reserved feelings — worried lest I had exaggerated the success. When the photographs came in they well confirmed the statements made on the bombing reports. Excellent!

[Later, PRU photographs showed 36 aircraft destroyed or damaged on ground plus much damage to buildings and hangars.]

Briefing tonight for Crotone and Naples.

21st July 1943: Bale-Out
Last night's visit to Crotone was OK but Naples was more doubtful. At interrogation an extraordinary happening was reported last night in 'G for George' 104 Squadron (Sergeant Pulford). This aircraft came back from Naples minus the wireless operator. He was at the flare chute preparing to release a photo-flash when last heard on the inter-com. The main fuselage lighting came on and he — the wireless operator — put it out by smashing the bulb. Then 'G' was caught in searchlights and Sergeant Pulford took violent evasive action. The aircraft was shuddering on coming out of the dive when a bump was felt by the entire crew and the rear gunner reported a black shape going past his turret on the starboard side. The Captain thought the bump might be due to bundles of leaflets so told the wireless operator not to put out any more. No answer being received the navigator went back to investigate. To his horror he went right back to the tail and also looked on the bed but found no wireless operator. The astrodome was off and lying on the floor broken.

Apparently the wireless operator must have thought the plane was in an uncontrollable dive and he baled out — though why through the astrohatch which is known to be extremely dangerous because of the danger of hitting the tail? Ground examination of 'G for George' showed fabric torn on top of the fuselage and on the starboard tail elevator — and two dents on the starboard elevator. Inside, the aircraft was a shambles with flares and bundles of leaflets everywhere as a result of the evasive action. Another piece of evidence from the crew was that the wireless operator had been the only survivor of a severe crash in England when an aircraft hit a church steeple. This could well have something to do with the baling-out.

I did the squadron briefing tonight as it was 'my target' again — Salerno.

22nd July 1943
I was up early for interrogation and it's another hot day but we managed a swim, thank goodness. Another attack on Salerno marshalling yards is detailed for tonight. These raids are designed to disrupt communications and prevent supplies reaching the Germans in the south of Italy and Sicily. Geoff Holmes is back from rest camp and he did the briefing.

23rd July 1943
At interrogation we learned that 'L for London' (Flight Sergeant Holmes) is missing. They are all nice chaps as usual, including Flying Officer Eric Lees as navigator — one of the most pleasant and quiet chaps in the squadron. He used to be with Dobbie and also had a turn with 'Uncle Ted' Stewart. There was a faint message, not decipherable, and flares were seen fifty miles south of target. As they were flare dropping they may have had trouble and had to jettison.

24th July 1943: Violent Winds
The wind became gusty in the afternoon and at Kairouan we had a thunderstorm with rain and dust blowing everywhere. Briefing took place under great difficulties with the tents threatening to blow down at any moment. Willy Carr's tent blew down and on the way to the mess I checked mine. It, too, was flat and flapping madly. Brian and I, with the help of the clerks, got it up again by the time it was dark.

25th July 1943: El Djem

A 'stand down' at last. After interrogating and Opsum early this morning a small party of us from Wing had a fascinating day visiting the Roman Amphitheatre at El Djem about forty miles south from the airfield. It looks like the Colosseum and is an interesting ruin with tiers three or four storeys high and catacombs or prison cells or pens for animals underneath. The arena is broken open in the middle exposing the underground rooms but this must have been covered up originally making an area larger than a circus tent – about 50 yards diameter with two entrances at east and west and a number of smaller doors or openings for letting in wild beasts or gladiators. The place must have seen some terrible and bloody sights in Roman occupation days.

Today the Arabs have built a squalid little town around the fine Roman structure – using some of the stone broken from the ruined amphitheatre. Arabs were sleeping here and there among the ruins – along the corridors upstairs – and everywhere was filth because they obviously use the place also as a latrine. We decided that we needed a swim after the smell of El Djem so made our way across open country with olive groves and melon fields to the coast. Eventually we found a little cove and dived in off the rocks to enjoy the warm blue sea. On such brief occasions one can forget the war and rejoice in feeling healthy, happy and relaxed.

26th to 31st July 1943: Aircrews

Mussolini has resigned and Marshal Bagdolio has taken his place. There has been much debate in the mess as to what this will mean – will Italy give in? – or will the Germans fight on in Italy? The German spokesman on radio says it is now a military question – not a political one for them.

We had a bad night for the squadron on the 28th/29th when two aircraft were lost – out of nine operating on Naples (Capodichino aerodrome) – Sergeant Clark with Flying Officer Roberts (Robbie) in his crew, and Flight Sergeant Tennant and crew. One aircraft was seen on fire and went down in flames over the target. Good chaps all – and this double loss in one night made us all think.

I greatly admire the way in which my squadron friends stand up so quietly, cheerfully and bravely to the risks and terrors of their night operations. Some have signs of strain in premature greyness, a few have nervous twitches of some muscles particularly the eyes, some are tense at briefing, nearly all of us drink heavily and relax on 'Stand Down' nights, sometimes with boisterous activities of mess games to follow. Yet talk is always good in the mess — the usual all male subjects of sex, religion, education, politics and of course bombing operations and the war. We live an unnatural life away from our wives, lovers and families, yet we remain kind and considerate to each other. These young pilots, navigators, bomb aimers, wireless operators and gunners are loyal to each other, and at Intelligence they are pleasant, friendly and courteous to deal with. The air war has not made them rough or cruel — rather the effect has been to make them more serious and thoughtful.

1st August 1943
I watched the take-off tonight for Naples and had a chat with three of the crews — those of my friends George Edwards, Lloyd Parry and Henry Langton. We are starting an offensive again as the Italian Government have made no sign of giving in.

2nd to 5th August 1943
On 3rd August crews at Cantanzaro Marino bombing a bridge reported flares dropping above and amongst the attacking Wellingtons. Flares have been used in Germany over the mainstream of bombers so that they could then be attacked visually by fighters.

On the 5th, Catania in Sicily fell today to the Eighth Army, and Orel fell to the Russians. No news yet of Italy falling.

We had late briefing 22.45 for 40 Squadron and midnight for 104 Squadron. The target is Messina beaches, so it seems that the Germans are leaving Sicily. The whole area of the Straits of Messina is now strongly defended by many flak batteries and by night fighters.

6th August 1943: Messina Beaches
I was up at 05.15 for a long period of interrogations as we had a big number operating. It was fairly successful with Wing Commander Bagnall having a good show as usual — he hit and set on fire a landing craft on the beach. Group Captain Harris and Wing Commander Mount also went on this target. Some crews reported seeing naval ships (destroyers?) bombarding the beaches during bombing and finding the ships' gun flashes useful in finding the target area. Unhappily, Pilot Officer Challis DFM and crew in 'F for Freddie' and Sgt Boundy and crew in 'A Apple', are missing.

Some fires were seen which may have been aircraft burning on the ground. They are two good crews and Challis is a most pleasant and capable man who was formerly a flight sergeant and president of the sergeants' mess.

We all hope that Sicily finishes soon — I'm feeling very washed out with so much night duty and insufficient sleep. Happily the operations are mainly very successful and we can see the results. The war situation is excellent.

7th August 1943
Still the round continues. We are operating again on the evacuation beaches tonight.

8th August 1943
I managed a swim this afternoon after a busy morning clearing up work which has accumulated. Briefing at night for usual target area — the beaches north of Messina.

9th August 1943: Fatigue Effects
Up at 02.00 for interrogations and worked until 08.30. Two more squadron planes shot down in flames by enemy night fighters over the toe of Italy — both were sergeant crews fairly new to the squadron. The only hope of a rest is weather — rain is likely this month or early next month. Geoff Holmes (Intelligence 104 Squadron) is looking grey and tired and is short tempered. Ralph Dunning (Intelligence 40 Squadron) is tired and briefed lethargically tonight. I'm pretty tired and can't summon up interest in anything. I keep noticing psychological hints of tiredness during interrogation — my mind suddenly switches from the table and forms in the tent and the chaps sitting drinking tea and answering my questions, to my home at Hill Top or some lovely Dorset scene or to Matilda the old Austin Seven and a family picnic. It's queer and disconcerting but I can't control my mind switches.

What do the 24 hours hold?

02.00–08.30	Interrogation, reports and Opsum.
08.30–12.00 noon	Fitful sleep, sweating and dozing and bothered by flies.
12.00	Shave and lunch.
13.30–17.30	Perhaps a swimming trip to Sousse.
17.30–19.00	Work in the office.
19.00–19.30	Dinner.

19.30–20.45	Briefings.
21.00	Back to the mess for News from BBC — hoping that D. is listening and that our Wellingtons will be mentioned. They often are.
22.00	Bed and uneasy sleep until aroused by the Operations Duty Officer for the first crew landed — and interrogations again.

As I write this and prepare for bed one's thoughts turn naturally to those chaps who are now setting off down the flarepath. But tonight I'm too tired to appreciate that fact as much as I do normally.

10th August 1943
Up at 03.15 for the weary round again and bed at 08.30 after completing the Opsum. Up at 12.15 to shave and go swimming with the Group Captain. This was enjoyable and so back to evening briefings.

I have been appointed Camp Security Officer with effect from yesterday and haven't a clue what this means.

Today I received £29.9.9 or 5900 francs as compensation for my loss of kit at El Arish last year.

Briefings as usual tonight for the beaches at Messina.

12th August 1943: Night Fighters
I got up at the droning overhead of the first Wellington returning this morning. This time two of Ralph Dunning's 40 Squadron crews are missing and two aircraft were seen shot down in flames over the target. These wretched night fighters got two within five minutes of each other. Two parachutes were seen so perhaps some crew members are safe. They were good crews and well known to me for their previous performances, Warrant Officer Shepherd and Flight Sergeant Bartlett DFM. Apart from these losses the operation was successful. [236 Wing have lost six Wellingtons in three Messina operations — two on the 5th/6th, two on the 8th/9th and two on the 11th/12th.]

Entertainment in the afternoon — Bob Hope, Frances Langford, Harry Pepper and another chap. We had a great crowd at Wing this afternoon to watch this show on a hastily erected stage with the troops sitting on forms and on the ground or perched on trucks for grandstands. Fortunately the weather was good and

Bob was very good indeed — well up to his reputation for wise cracks, many of them topical and suited to his audience. He looked pale and tired but carried on gamely like a true comedian.

Frances Langford sang well and has a lovely figure so naturally she came over well. The other two were nothing exceptional. Afterwards the party came into the mess for tea. No wonder they looked tired for we learned that they gave a show this morning and are off to give another one tonight. We had our usual briefing tonight.

13th August 1943
On duty for 15½ hours out of the 24.

14th August 1943: Djebel Climbing — 'Healthing' With the G/C
A break from routine this afternoon by Group Captain Paul Harris inviting Squadron Leader Don Crossley, Flight Lieutenant Drummond (Signals Officer) and myself to accompany him on what he calls a 'Healthing Trip' into the mountain country west of Kairouan. We left the plains at Fondouk and went south west through rough grazing country which was brown and dry with a few poverty-stricken hovels here and there. Crossing some wide sandy waters, which must be a sight in the rainy season, we climbed into the hills to a lead mine and a village at the foot of the Djebel which here rises steeply to about 3,000 feet. We climbed up this to the summit — or rather the Group Captain, Crossley and Drummond did so, while I felt too worn out to go further and halted to enjoy the views from the upper slopes. It took twenty-five minutes to come down again to the car and there we had some good fun at shooting practice with our revolvers against the steep hillside. And so a fast ride over the bumpy roads back to camp and briefing — operations continue as always! [The Group Captain is keen on physical fitness and efficiency in general. He often visits aircrews in their tents to talk with them and they realise that he has a sincere interest in their welfare. Aircrews are frequently invited to go with the G/C on 'healthing expeditions'.]

15th August 1943: Intelligence Crisis
The usual early morning interrogations and summary of operation were followed by a period in bed with irritating flies for company. Tonight we reached an Intelligence crisis for Geoff said that he couldn't carry on. He has shown signs of the strain for some time so it was not a complete surprise. Squadron Leader Salmon (40

Squadron) kindly offered to help interrogate with Ralph Dunning and myself.

16th August 1943
Last night Sergeant Bamford and crew went missing — a very young and pleasant crew with whom I often had jokes about their aircraft 'D for Donald' which had been a rather eccentric kite.

17th August 1943: Shooting Trip
Work continues though we are all clapped out or very nearly so. I did the interrogations early this morning and went to bed until 09.00 when I had to visit the dentist. Later after another period in bed I heard that we have a 'stand down' — Thank God! In trying to make good use of it I had a swim after lunch and then came back for a quick meal before setting off on a shooting trip into the mountains with Wing Commander Bagnall and Squadron Leader Crossley. We drove across the flat brown plains to the hills and climbed up a winding pass with precipitous drops down into tree-lined wadis. This country was rich and green with plenty of trees and shrubby bushes and occasional cultivated fields — mainly scrub from grain crops.

When we saw some birds ahead I was commissioned to drive the car while Wing Commander Bagnall and Don Crossley stood up and fired from the open sunshine roof. They missed and we continued through country not unlike Scottish moorlands. Eventually the hunters shot a partridge and a large hawk or eagle who came fluttering down near the car and died looking at us with hatred in his cold baleful eyes. Several other 'probables' couldn't be found because minefields made retrieving dangerous. There were other relics of battle in damaged vehicles alongside the road and a tank in a gully.

It was now getting dusk and we made a mad dash back to camp with the Wing Commander at the wheel. There were several narrow shaves at bends and with native carts without lights.

Messina fell today! The Sicilian Campaign is over — and that's another milestone towards final victory.

CHAPTER EIGHT

Italy Invaded

The Wellington medium bombers were used intensively in this period to attack ports and facilities, airfields and communications on the mainland of Italy. Enemy night fighters were active over major targets and it became all too common to lose one or two aircraft nightly from each squadron on these operations. The Naples area was protected additionally by a heavy and light flak barrage.

Living conditions at the Kairouan airfields were unpleasant for aircrews and ground staff because of the hot moist conditions in summer and the accompanying swarms of insects of all types.

Sleeping was difficult and with periods of intense operational activity with few 'stand downs', signs of strain became more noticeable among aircrews and Intelligence staff. Swimming trips to Sousse on the coast were a great help to morale in spite of the long hot dusty ride to get there and the fact that we were all hot and sticky again before getting back to camp.

The occasional visit to Tunis or a brief trip into the Tunisian hills to shoot or enjoy the scenery, loom large in retrospect. The period of operations from Kairouan is regarded overall as a memory best forgotten by most RAF personnel who served there in 1943.

*

18th to 20th August 1943
Business as usual except for the night of the 19th/20th when Sergeant Field was missing and fog caused all 205 Group aircraft to land back at our field with much confusion for Operations Centre and many interrogations for Intelligence.

21st August 1943: Visit to 205 Group HQ
This was a busy day which required me to visit Group HQ to collect target information. As a result I had an enjoyable lunch with A.B. Read now Squadron Leader Read (Group Intelligence Officer), and Flight Lieutenant Aubyn James. They produced some *vin rosé* which was pleasant and potent so that afterwards

we all had quite a good view of life. Group Captain MacNair
(SASO) saw me and asked after 'Horses' at swimming and was in
a very friendly mood. Perhaps he also had had the *vin rosé* because
he made his exit by walking over a table-top. He told me that he
hasn't much time now for swimming and I can well believe that in
his new position.

I went to Group and returned — no mean feat — on our Wing's
clapped-out Norton motorcycle. It did quite well in spite of the
gearbox being semi-detached from the engine, and the gears hard
to distinguish from each other. I dashed through the smelly city in
fine style with much exhaust noise to confuse the natives and
warn them as there was no horn on the machine. It was a terribly
hot day and after my successful efforts in collecting information
the operation was cancelled because of the weather. Ham Fuller
left yesterday for Group. Brian O'Connor left today to become
Squadron Leader Operations at 231 Wing so I'm alone in the tent.

Some good news and bad news at Group today about crews.
Sergeant Atkins from Flight Sergeant Bartlett's crew baled out
over Sicily and got into the American lines with some thirty
Italians who decided to stay on in Sicily rather than escape to the
mainland. The bad news is that Wing Commander Peter Warner
of 462 Halifax Squadron is missing from a Sicilian raid some time
ago. We liked him a lot in 236 Wing.

22nd August 1943: A Volkswagen
Bob Ginn, the Squadron Engineer Officer, kindly mended the
Intelligence typewriter again this morning. He allowed me a run in
his German Volkswagen built up from two or three captured cars
and a new engine found in a crate. It seems an excellent little car
with the engine at the rear and a pressed steel body with a tubular
chassis welded as one unit. Torsion bars at front and rear provide
independent springing for each wheel. The 4-cylinder OHV air
cooled horizontally opposed engine is of about 8 hp and gives
38 mpg and speeds up to some 60 mph. I'd like one!

23rd August 1943
This evening I did the briefing for a nickel operation on a northern
target and was complimented by Wing Commander Bagnall, who is
not easy to please but when he *is*, he says so!

24th August 1943
Up early for interrogation of the leaflet droppers and bombers,

and it proved to have been a very successful night with 51 aircraft operating and all 51 safely back.

25th to 30th August 1943: Losses

During this period we made two successful raids on the harbour of Taranto. On the 25th/26th the crew with whom I went to Salerno on 21st June, Sergeant Hick and crew, were missing and believed shot down in flames off Taranto. On this occasion they were flying in a Wellington X, 'U for Uncle' one of the new aircraft with Hercules engines which are replacing the Mark II Wellingtons with Merlins so subject to overheating in the desert summer temperatures. This crew were good friends of mine and had become an experienced team in the intervening weeks. Our Wing has lost fourteen Wellingtons since 1st July, eight from 104 Squadron and six from 40 Squadron.

31st August 1943: Fishing

After the usual start to the day with interrogations and Opsum preparation I was invited by the Group Captain to accompany him on a 'fishing trip' to Sousse. He had been promised some hand grenades by the Anti-Aircraft people but these failed to turn up and we went off with only three home made bombs constructed by Flight Lieutenant Gregg, our Armaments Officer. Each contained about 1 lb of gun cotton and a piece of fuse. At Sousse we hired a boat and rowed out into deep water to try our luck. The Group Captain lit the fuse which spluttered and fizzed and then he gently tossed the bomb into the water by the bows of the boat when I had expected him to throw it well away from us. Worst of all – the tin refused to sink – it floated fizzing merrily alongside us! The Group Captain immediately dived overboard away from the bomb – the others of us crouched low in the boat hoping for the best. There was a violent bang, a gust of air over the boat from the blast, and the boat shuddered from end to end. Happily we had no holes in the boat or in us. One tiny fish was stunned by the explosion and floated to the surface.

The Group Captain was vastly amused and asked why we had not followed him overboard? He tried again, this time holding the bomb under water before lighting the fuse. This time the bomb went off under water and sent up mud and water in a foaming bubbling circle. One fish resulted which we dived overboard to retrieve but it was very small. The third bomb went off very well under the water but produced no fish. Somewhat relieved to find ourselves in one piece we rowed ashore and gave the boat back to its very anxious owner who had watched from the shore.

3rd to 6th September 1943: Landings on Toe of Italy by Eighth Army

Reggio was quickly captured and San Giovanni — a good start. During this period most of our bombing attacks were on railways and highways leading south towards the Naples and Salerno area — and on airfields.

On the 6th Flight Lieutenant L. arrived from Middle East HQ to take over from Geoff Holmes as IO of 104 Squadron. Also on this day Joe Reid, 'Colonel' Britton and others went with the Group Captain on another fishing party to which I was fortunate enough not to be asked! Apparently it was a hair-raising affair which started with a bumpy journey in the staff car to Sousse with the Group Captain driving, while they had at their feet a pile of bomb detonators tied together in threes and fitted with a fuse, and in the boot of the car a box of hand grenades. Each bump in the road brought a bump in the passengers' hearts. The explosives failed to kill any fish and afterwards the Group Captain remarked with some truth that he thought he could detect signs of alarm and despondency among his boat crew.

7th September 1943: Trip to Sicily

Flight Lieutenant L. rang up last night to say that he was going with the Wing Commander to Licata, Sicily — did I mind? I immediately rang up Wing Commander Mount and asked if I could go as well. 'Certainly, Chappie,' he said in his usual charming style. We made a good take-off at 08.00 hrs in 'Q for Queenie' and soon passed over the coastline and away into a hazy sky over the very blue sea. After one hour we passed Pantellaria, going within a few miles of this mountainous island wreathed in white cumulus clouds which sat firmly on the peaks. Presently the island of Sicily appeared as brown mountains with a faint white ring of surf at their base and clouds above the coast line. I was struck at once by the similarity to Palestine because of the dry looking hills and only a few shrubs as vegetation. We identified Port Empedocle, Agrigento and Licata where we landed at the airfield already crowded with aircraft mainly American transport planes.

Several jeeps came up to us as soon as we stopped off the runway and one stalwart US paratrooper said, 'Say, is this a

Lancaster?' We assured him that they were rather larger and more modern than our Wimpy, but the troops were still very interested in our turrets and bomb compartments which were opened for demonstration and inspection. While the Wing Commander went away on his business we conducted several parties over the plane and ourselves had a look at a jeep and trailer being unloaded from a DC3.

The railway ran alongside the airfield and I was fascinated by two big steam engines coupled together — a 2—8—0 and a 0—10—0 of standard gauge, which were cheerfully puffing in unison as they helped each other pull a long train of wagons loaded with heavy war equipment. As a change from the dreary landscape of the Kairouan area the visit to Licata was invigorating and we flew back to Africa in relaxed and happy mood. Wing Commander Mount must have felt the same for after Pantellaria he took 'Q for Queenie' down to a few feet above the water and I could see from the astrodome two merging lines of disturbance behind us as our propeller wash flattened the wave tops. We were very low, so low that we had to jump up sharply as we crossed the Tunisian coast and made for our airfield.

After briefing I wrote up my diary, while outside the daylight take-off proceeded normally with the regular roar and rumble of Wellingtons down the runway. Suddenly the pattern was shattered by an explosion announcing that someone had pranged and rushing outside the tent I could see the towering mushroom of black and brown smoke and the red fire of a burning aircraft at the end of the runway.

Miraculously, the crew — one of my old squadron — got out before the explosion although two of them had burns.

Another Wellington was very bravely taxied away from the crash by her captain, Flight Sergeant Simpson, and he was only a hundred yards away when the bombs went up. Later, to avoid delay, Wing Commander Mount set the example by taking off *over* the still burning debris and the other crews followed. After this I went over to the squadron mess to spend a pleasant evening and say cheerio to Geoffrey Holmes SAAF, Ham Fuller and Splodge Moore, both RAAF. Ham is flying them down to the Delta tomorrow.

This might be a good time to add a note about the Australians in our squadrons. There have been more Australians in the RAF Wellington squadrons than in the so-called Australian 462 Halifax Squadron, for some unknown reason.

Australians at Gardabia and Kairouan

The Australians were a practical lot who readily became attuned to desert conditions. The weird and wonderful creatures that crawled and flew in the desert held few fears for them and horned vipers, scorpions, giant spiders and the ubiquitous dung beetles, became objects of fun and provided a means of playing practical jokes on the others, a form of humour not always enjoyed by the recipients.

Splodge Moore, Tommy Howes, Archie Clarke, Ham Fuller and Jack Adams were among the ones well known to me in 104 Squadron. [Squadron Leader Lloyd Parry and Wing Commander Donald Saville have been mentioned earlier.]

Jack Adams, because he was slightly older than most aircrew, was popularly known as 'Grandpappy Jack-a-Jack'. From a mile away he could be distinguished because, having an absolute horror of flies, he was always armed with his famous fly swat, a dual purpose device since it could also be used as a fan. After much practice Jack eventually evolved a technique second to none in promptly disposing of his two-winged insect enemies. Initially he used to flourish his swat with great abandon and attempt to come down on his intended victims with a stupendous bang only to see the implacable desert flies lodge cheekily on another section of the bar or on a table.

Tommy Howes, a 'gen' man, pointed out that flies have a 360° vision and are, therefore, never likely to be caught napping. Jack then adopted what was known in the mess as the 'orchestra conductor's' upswing technique, a very slow and deliberate upwards and sideways movement of the swat, with pauses here and there, so as to leave the flies undisturbed, then finally a pause at the top followed by a sudden swift, smooth downwards crack aimed with unerring accuracy. This method rarely failed and had the added advantage of causing less consternation than his former bash and smash tactics. Also it always provided a subject for humorous comment when there was nothing much else to talk about in the mess.

The Australian contingent were quite good at throwing all sorts of diverse subjects into the ring for impromptu mess discussions. One evening they introduced the subject of 'bull' and after this intangible matter had been debated for some hours it was unanimously decided that 'bull' (i) makes the world go around, (ii) can be recognised in two forms as *either* a solid substance *or* something of a slippery nature — the former being preferable, and (iii) is vital to RAF personnel who have no possible way of getting rapid promotion without it!

The New Zealanders seemed to have much the same approach and outlook as the Australians — perhaps they were a little less boisterous, but on reflection I doubt it. Flying Officer 'Pete' Peterson (later awarded the DFC) was one easily remembered. He was a fine rugger player and was largely instrumental in cleaning up the 462 Squadron boys 13 points to nil at Gardabia.

Splodge Moore was a very good navigator with a gift for quaint phrases and descriptions which were the delight and envy of his Mess mates. In times of shock or stress his imitators would offer a typical Splodge comment — or say 'Splodge would have said . . .'. What was particularly likable and commendable about this comedian was his ability to make funny comments in dangerous situations.

Tommy Howes was Navigation Officer and Bombing Leader with 104 Squadron on his second tour of operations with Wimpys. Incredibly young he was a recognised 'gen man' on a variety of subjects and had the ability to teach and interest others in the serious games of navigation and bombing.

Ham Fuller was full of fun and high spirits, in and out of the mess. At Gardabia he achieved fame by blowing down the clothes line and washing of Group Captain Paul Harris DFC in a low-flying escapade which shook the Wing types considerably. Punishment was ordered and Ham was forced to drive the Wing Commander's jeep from Gardabia to Kairouan!

Ham and Tom were earnest students of operational flying techniques and keen to discuss theories and practical matters concerned with flying and survival. They believed that some of the crews coming from OTUs to squadrons had not received adequate training on the actual hazards of operational flying and how best to cope with them. In consequence some losses were due to inexperienced pilots being unable to recover from violent manoeuvres during evasive action from searchlights and flak. Their view was that more emphasis and flying instruction should be given to this aspect of operational training.

Flight Sergeant Archie Clarke DFM, who was later commissioned, was a most reliable pilot who completed an excellent tour of operations with 104 Squadron.

*

8th September 1943: Italy Surrenders

It was announced tonight just after our briefing and while aircraft were actually taking off for operations, that the Italian armed forces have surrendered and an armistice has been granted and signed today. To my astonishment our planes were not recalled — and to my further astonishment, we learned on the wireless tonight that the Armistice was granted on 3rd September, having been asked for about a fortnight ago! Political reasons? Or is this a military need to catch the Germans now in Italy? Today we held special briefings for both squadrons and our part is to cause diversion and attack communications while the army is starting the main invasion of Italy. The Russians announced the capture of Stalino today. The war news is excellent everywhere.

9th September 1943: Landings at Salerno

In support of the Allied landings at Salerno our squadrons were given communications targets around the area — target details arriving only minutes before briefing time at 15.00 hours. Normal preparation for briefing was impossible but our crews are well aware of the importance of their bombing to hamper enemy resistance to the landings. Operations in direct support of the Army and Navy are always popular.

10th September 1943: Squadron Commanders

I was wakened at 01.00 by phone call from 'Ops' and staggered out feeling terrible with sickness, gippy tummy and fatigue. A trip to the latrine helped but I kept coming out in a cold sweat. Aircraft were circling overhead and landing as I pulled myself together. Somehow I completed the interrogations and Opsum, left my enquiries to Ralph and got back to bed at 04.30. I couldn't face breakfast but roused myself at 11.00 to go swimming. This was enjoyable and did me good.

Today we had news of Taranto being occupied and of the Italian Fleet sailing out to surrender from other naval bases. On the squadron front I heard today that Squadron Leader Don Crossley is to take command of 104 Squadron. I'm certainly glad that good old Micky Mount is finishing and has a safe Inspector's job to go to after miraculously surviving tours on fighters and now one on bombers! He's a grand chap and has been thoroughly well liked by everyone as a warm friendly thoughtful and understanding leader. A former Battle of Britain Hurricane pilot who accounted for four of the enemy, Wing Commander Mount has a quiet style of command derived from a tremendous sense of humour and natural endowment of leadership qualities. All ranks know him as 'Wingco Micky Mount' and he is so admired and respected that no one would ever dream of presuming on his good nature — they respond to anything he asks of them. 104 has been a happy and very successful unit under his leadership.

Don Crossley has a different personality — more reserved and formal but nonetheless extremely efficient and competent. I've known him since Kabrit days early in 1942, first as a very determined young pilot in 148 Squadron (Pilot Officer Crossley), and lived with him, sharing a tent at LG106 when he was in charge of the airfield; worked with him when he was an Operations Officer at Wing; seen him at work as a very efficient flight commander in 70 Squadron, and now here he is as wing commander of my old squadron. Thinking back, I've worked under five 104 Squadron Commanders. Wing Commander Crossley is the sixth and he will be absolutely first class like the others.

12th September 1943

After a heavy day's work and two briefings I was watching the take-off when I saw two big spurts of dust just behind a Wellington as it became airborne. Something had fallen off the aircraft and immediately a car raced down the runway and two men jumped out and rolled a large bomb off to one side. Flying Control fired reds into the air to hold up take-off but another Wellington roared down the runway taking no notice. Things were confusing for a while but happily the men and the car were not hit and the bomb did not explode. The take-off continued. Then the next to last Wellington worried me as it appeared unable to gain height, and looked as if it would prang on the mess or the sick quarters on the small hill. It crept over the rise and disappeared still very low. Thank heaven, nothing happened.

13th September 1943: Army Support

What a day! We had changes of target and several briefings between 15.00 hours and 18.00 hours — and eventually a maximum effort was requested to bomb roads in the Pompeii area where a German armoured division was said to be located. We were informed that severe fighting is taking place north of Salerno and we can expect maximum efforts from now on.

14th September 1943
We briefed the squadrons on roads in the Battipaglia — Eboli area. Fortunately there were no last minute changes in the target today.

15th September 1943
We briefed on another road target tonight and again in the Pompeii area and another maximum effort. The famous and ancient ruins will be receiving some punishment I fear.

16th September 1943: Horrors!
This morning I fell into bed after another night of interrogations and doing the Opsum and then had an amusing dream which illustrates my present worn out state. I dreamt that D. and I were out together in the country and trying to find a spot for a little cosy petting after our long time apart. Each time we sat down and all appeared well — up popped the Group Captain and spoilt it all! [As a thorough gentleman, I'm sure that he wouldn't really act as in the dream!]

But tonight he disturbed the briefing of 40 Squadron which was given by Flight Lieutenant L. as he was on duty. The IO was warbling on in his rather quivering small voice and got things a little muddled. To everyone's horror, the Group Captain interrupted the briefing and said loudly, 'L. I think you are briefing on the wrong target!' Ye gods! — there was a hush of awe in the tent as we grouped around the board — Group Captain Harris, Wing Commander Bagnall, Squadron Leader Salmon, Squadron Leader Turner (Operations Officer), Flight Lieutenant L. (IO 104 Squadron), Pilot Officer Dunning (IO 40 Squadron), and myself (SIO) — and eventually the Group Captain recognised that L's sketch was meant to be the correct aerodrome target at Cisterna Littoria and the briefing continued. I'm afraid that at this point most of the aircrews had only a hazy idea of the target. Then, very luckily, new target maps, good ones, arrived from Group HQ and Ralph Dunning and I quickly gave them out. The situation was saved because any nitwit could locate the correct target by using the map now provided. After the briefing the Group Captain pointed out that the sketch map on the blackboard was not good, so I drew another one with suitable promptings from L.

He was a bit better with the second briefing, for 104 Squadron, but it must have been difficult to hear him at the back as he constantly addressed the board and hopped about using his ruler to pinpoint various things. He obviously hasn't been through a teacher training course on the use of a blackboard in giving a chalk and talk lesson! To my amusement and the Group Captain's annoyance (*he* tried to attract the IO's attention but couldn't do so) Flight Lieutenant L. used the 1/500,000 map on the board for briefing on location and didn't use my newly drawn map at all until the end when he used it momentarily to point out the neighbouring aerodromes not to be confused with the target landing ground! After the two rather hectic and hair raising briefings, the Group Captain completed the evening by asking me to do his scheduled talk to the airmen's mess on 'Targets and the War Situation'.

17th September 1943
It was my duty day and I spent a busy morning with photographs of the target and reports from the leaflet droppers etc. After our much criticised briefings, the raid last night on Cisterna Littoria was very successful with many fires started. The photographs taken with bombing were all plotted on the target area.

18th September 1943
Little to report except that I did both briefings myself and both squadrons went astray! The joke is certainly on me this time — but the weather was poor over the target.

19th September 1943
We had another amusing briefing today by Flight Lieutenant L., as nervous as ever, but I thought he was a little more understandable this time. I was torn a terrific 'strip' by the Group Captain with regard to my failure to understand his requirements in the Opsum. Woe is me — at the moment! Fortunately, the Group Captain is not unfair with his disfavours — he spreads them around us all and it may well be the Armament Officer or Navigation Officer who next incur his wrath! Last night's operation on a bridge was reasonably successful judging from the photographs. Sardinia is now free from Germans according to the news bulletin. *And*! the Group Captain has agreed to my application for *leave*. Thank heaven for this, because I really feel in need of leave and a change.

21st September 1943
Today was very hot and sticky and my duty day. Pilot Officer Winn was posted in today from Group to replace Flight Lieutenant L. for Intelligence duties. Unfortunately, Winn somehow also

started on the wrong foot with the Wing Commander and the Group Captain — and the latter threatened to stop my leave. Eventually he didn't do so, but told us to take eight days and visit Blida — the operational base of the western Wellington Wing. Flight Lieutenant 'Bishop' Gregg (Armament Officer at Wing) and Flight Lieutenant Jock Warden (Wing Adjutant) are to go on leave with me.

Then old L. (He's a most pleasant chap but too old to be suitable as a squadron IO) came in to say goodbye and he drew a map of the target for my briefing tonight on Bastia (Corsica) and ornamented it with a picture of a ship leaving the harbour with the Nazi flag flying and another drawing of Hitler's head. It was kind of him but after he had left I deemed it unwise to risk my leave again so I removed the drawings from the map in case the Group Captain was in no mood for such levity! My briefing went well, so now it's heigh-ho for Algiers and some ice cream and cream cakes — I hope!

22nd September, 1943: Le Cafard

Today things worked out very differently from my high hopes of yesterday. Firstly the Adjutant couldn't leave because Squadron Leader Partington, the Wing Administration Officer, is not yet back from leave. Then Flight Lieutenant Gregg was given a job to do which required his full attention for at least four hours. Additionally car trouble was experienced, so after getting up early I helped with interrogations instead of proceeding on leave. It proved to be one of those days that have to be experienced to be believed. At 07.00 hours it was cool and pleasant but by 09.00 hours I was beginning to sweat in my tent sorting out stuff to pack after doing the interrogations. At 12.00 hours it was very hot and sticky. At 13.00 hours it was blowing hard with sand and dust flying everywhere and visibility reduced to a few yards. The whole afternoon was a nightmare of swirling dust and sticky heat with the Intelligence tents swaying and groaning in the wind and visibility inside quite limited. Chairs were hot to sit upon and the desk's steel top too hot to touch. In spite of these conditions work had to be done for an early briefing and I tried to draw a sketch map to illustrate. Huge bundles of nickels (leaflets) arrived and had to be sorted into smaller bundles for each crew. Phone calls interrupted me every few minutes — Group, the Group Captain, Operations, both Wing Commanders, Operations again, the Group Captain, Operations, Group Captain etc. etc.

My language was becoming blue and my nerves somewhat strained.
I dashed for a cup of tea in the mess and dashed back again to the
dusty briefing tent to brief the first squadron at 16.30. Two
extra nickellers on two different targets were added to my troubles.
The second squadron came in for briefing and after this about
18.00 hours the heat got a little less and great storm clouds
came up over us with the threat of a complete break in the weather.
This is a horrible country and I can now understand *Le Cafard*!
I'm pretty near that state of exhaustion and madness myself after
today's hot winds and frustrations. I went out with Wing Commander Crossley to the flarepath and distributed rations and
watched the last minute flaps — a turret unserviceable here — a
magneto drop there — a half open bomb door which refused to
close properly on another Wellington. But all the defects were
put right and all the squadron aircraft detailed, duly took off — a
good squadron and an unflappable Wing Commander.

The landing ground became strangely quiet after the last aircraft
droned into the distance and we went back to the mess for dinner.
Tomorrow we shall try again to go on leave.

23rd to 30th September 1943
Leave to Tunis, Constantine and Bone.

1st to 10th October 1943: Bad News and Good News
Naples was captured on 1st October and from the state of the
railway yards and roads there is no doubt that our bombing helped
to hold up the movement of enemy supplies to southern Italy.
Since our return from leave the weather has continued either hot
and sticky or showery, and operations have been cancelled twice
due to bad weather here or along the route to target. On the night
of the 4th/5th Flight Lieutenant McDermott and crew went
missing in 'R for Robert'. A few nights earlier his aircraft had been
damaged by bomb splinters after bombing from about 250 feet
and the plane had to be sent to RSU for repair. Since joining the
squadron, he has captained two Wellingtons which received
damage and one Wellington which was written off completely
after daring low level attacks.

News arrived later that Mac and his crew were safe having been
picked up in their dinghy from a successful ditching and after they
had been hit over the target when they were bombing from 1,000
feet. Apparently they have a good story to tell and were well
treated by Italians in the Naples area who hated the Germans.

On the 8th/9th 40 Squadron lost their 'R for Robert' owing to hydraulics failure and a bomb hang-up. The crew could not lower the undercart to land normally and risk the hang-up falling off — nor could they belly-land because of the bomb. They circled the airfield firing reds and calling on RT but their own receiver was useless. Eventually they climbed and all the crew baled out safely but the aircraft dived straight down into someone's dispersal area and went up with a 'woomph' of flame. The armament people claimed, with a rather characteristic reaction, that there was probably no hang-up at all. There was, of course, and the Group Captain rang up the Armaments Officer in the middle of the night to ask him why the bomb had hung-up.

On the 9th Flight Lieutenant Harman joined us as Navigation Officer and Brian O'Connor and two others came over with him from 231 Wing and spent a pleasant evening with us. Unfortunately they were bearers of bad news that Flight Lieutenant 'Brum' Birmingham of 462 Squadron went missing a month ago and was believed shot down over an airfield target in southern Italy. 'Brum' has been a good friend of mine since early 1942 before the retreat when he was Pilot Officer Birmingham of 37 Squadron and known for his large emblem of Birmingham's coat of arms on his flying jacket and his crew members wore the same emblem.

The visitors also confirmed that Wing Commander Warner went missing over Sicily though some of his crew are safe. And someone said he had heard that Wing Commander Saville had finally 'bought it' over Europe. It's tragic news, if true, for he had done so much operational flying and we need men of his calibre to survive for duties in peacetime. On the local front we have happier news of honours and awards — Wing Commander Bagnell and Wing Commander Mount have each received the DSO and they both deserve it thoroughly. Wing Commander Mills of 205 Group has been awarded the OBE — a very nice chap and a first class officer. The MBE has been awarded to two of my friends, Flight Lieutenant Aubyn James of Group Intelligence and Flight Lieutenant Bob Ginn, our Engineer Officer. Bob took me over to Group to celebrate these awards at Aubyn's invitation — and we had a very good party.

11th to 20th October 1943: POWs
Work went on as usual during this period but instead of day to day entries in the diary only a few main events in chronological order are recorded:

1. We received news at Wing of Flight Sergeant Bartlett and crew – all except one crew member are safe. Sergeant Bamford has also been found in an Italian hospital so perhaps some others of his crew may also be alive.

2. I had some fun with Italian POWs recently while they were putting up wire fences and I had noticed that they were reading some of the Italian 'nickels' put in the latrine for use as bumph. They were very interested when I gave them copies of the Badoglio speech on the entry of Italy into the war against Germany and they stopped work and read the leaflets very seriously. Others without the leaflets came up and asked for copies for themselves. I explained what I was doing to their guards and had a talk with them about their prisoners. They told me that the Italians were fit and happy and very easy to control – the guards in fact treat POWs as schoolchildren. However the guards said that the German POWs are very different and not easy to handle. The young ones are mainly Nazis and still believe in Hitler and that German armies from Algiers and Oran will soon free them. When told of the continued German retreat in Russia they laugh in disbelief. The older Germans are more serious and seem tired of the war and want to get back home to their families.

3. Flying Officer R.L.W. Cheek of Ralph Dunning's squadron (40 Squadron) has been putting up some sensational shows of late. At Marigliana he seems to have done more damage than the rest of Group together. After bombing in five sticks which caused two fires, he went down below 500 feet and machine-gunned some twenty assorted aircraft. The crew claimed to have set six aircraft on fire and saw three of these blow up. At the end of the bombing and gunning there were nine or ten fires burning and it was indeed a very good night for visible results. Next night Cheek took a new crew and was one of only two Wellingtons to locate the target. Bad weather obscured the target for other crews but Cheek and his new boys went low to shoot up the target and cause an explosion and fire while at the same time being hit themselves by light flak.

They returned with holes in the fuselage and it must have been 'some introduction' for the new crew!

4. Somebody dropped two 40 lb bombs off while in circuit overhead before landing from last night's operation and they landed very close to our Repair and Salvage Unit. Frankie Ellis, the CO of the RSU, rang up in a terrible rage and took it as a personal attack on himself!

5. I took delivery of a new Indian motorcycle on 19th October. It is brand new — a 500 cc side valve V-twin with left hand throttle, right hand gear change and foot clutch. The long wheel base makes handling difficult on loose stuff but it rides well on the road.

21st October 1943: Giulianova Bridge

Tonight I did the briefing for an interesting target — the road bridge at Giulianova which also has an adjacent railway bridge. These bridges are important links in German communications along the eastern side of Italy between Pescara and Ancona — and so far all bombing attempts to destroy the bridges have been unsuccessful. We are using some suitable 500 lb bombs in sticks and some Wellingtons, including that piloted by Wing Commander Crossley, are carrying 4,000 lb bombs with 11-seconds delayed action fuses. The Wing Commander believes that the 11-second delay will allow bombing from a low altitude with these dangerous blast bombs which I know from the experience at Tobruk can give the aircraft a severe kick even at 8,000 feet. The theory is that you dive in, drop the bomb and are out of reach of the blast when it comes. But what if it goes off on impact? After the briefing I went out to the dispersals with the Wing Commander to give out rations and bring back his car after he and his crew had clambered up into their Wellington. I watched the take-off with my usual feelings, perhaps even more involved than usual. In a squadron there is a queer sense of drama and tension amongst the ground personnel while the night bombers are away on a mission — and this persists until the last aircraft is reported safely down and we know that no squadron crew is missing.

22nd October 1943: Bridge Bombing Success — Wing Commander Crossley

Interrogations started early this morning and it was really exciting for the raid seems to have been a brilliant success. The Wing Commander and his crew bombed from 600 feet and believe the bomb exploded alongside or under the road bridge at the northern end. It was probable that both road and rail bridges are severely damaged.

25th October 1943: A Day to Remember

After the usual interrogations and Opsum I heard that we have been given a 'stand down' for today and decided to use it by having a trip into the mountains on the Indian motorcycle. After lunch I burbled gently through Kairouan and out along the flat straight road to the distant hills. I had a wonderful sense of freedom and enjoyment as I listened to the engine's quiet note and went through the foothills and up into the wooded country of green pines and other trees. At one viewpoint I stopped to munch some chocolates and smoke my pipe. Then I got out the tool kit and adjusted the position of the seat and the mirror. The scenery was soothing, the air crisp and delightful –

I felt almost completely happy but remembered 'Colonel' Britton's comment that even at its best this life is mere existence, not real living. He means, of course, that we haven't our wives and families around us and our peacetime enjoyments of our own home or car or garden or the freedom to go and come as we wish when work is done.

The return journey took me past a little German cemetery near one of the passes through a ridge and obviously a scene of fighting. I looked at the neat white crosses with black letters – usually it is black crosses with white letters – and the names and details inscribed. The names and ages of those buried made me think of the squadron chaps of similar age now missing and probably without known graves. One German, Gerhard Dihme, born 16.10.09 and died 28.1.43, caused me to think more closely of my own situation and prospects of survival – he was of my age and he probably didn't expect to die in Tunisia in this unfortunate war. One of the crosses had fallen over so I put it up and fixed it with large stones and in a gloomy state of mind, restarted the bike.

At the outskirts of the town there was a nasty tinkle from the engine and it suddenly died – one of the valve springs had broken. I pushed for three quarters of a mile to a telephone and rang up for transport. Overhead heavy clouds were gathering and already there were lightning flashes and the rumble of thunder. After a long wait a truck arrived in the nick of time as the storm broke with a violent wind from the west which at the camp blew dust into tents and threatened to blow them down. Rain came down in sheets while lightning alternated between bright blue flashes from cloud to cloud and occasional more dangerous cracks of forked lightning. The mess was inundated and water rushed in broad streams across the floor while rain poured down from the joining areas between the marquees or EPIPs as these big square tents are called. We had some ENSA visitors including three women staying the night, presumably for shelter from the terrifying storm. The

Group Captain rose to the occasion splendidly. He called for the Doc, Squadron Leader Gimson.

G/C — 'Doc — I want to make a punch — please get me some rum — all you have — I shall want a lot.'

Doc — 'Sorry, sir — I can't use the medical supplies of rum — they are for emergencies.'

G/C — 'Doc — get the rum — this *is* an emergency!'

Doc — (*looking rather desperate*) 'Yes, sir.'

The Group Captain borrowed bowls from the kitchen and various bottles from the bar and the entire rum stock from medical comforts — and set to work happily mixing 'a punch'. He ordered supplies of boiling water from the kitchen and everybody in the mess had glasses of rum punch mixed with hot water. It was fierce but just what we needed. The hot liquid brought life and feeling back to our jaded bodies and we soon began to take a lighter view of the storm and the flooded tents — we were all standing in running water and sloshy mud inches deep. Conversation improved and eventually the noise and laughter in the mess competed strongly with the noises of the storm outside.

Afterwards I splashed quite happily and carelessly to my own tent to find it down for the third time in two months and all my bedding and baggage soaked. I laughed at this further set-back and Pilot Officer Bob Pountney, newly posted to 104 Squadron Intelligence, insisted that I share his tent which miraculously was only half down and we made do with wet blankets on two camp beds while the rain dripped constantly down on us. I remember being amused by the stream of rain drops and soon fell asleep in a pleasant stupor. Next morning I found not only my own tent down but the clerk's tent and the two Intelligence store tents also flattened by the storm.

26th October to 11th November 1943
[The diary does not have day to day reports for this period but makes some comments on some of the occurrences and events.]

1. The brave and daring but unlucky Flight Lieutenant McDermott and crew (104 Squadron) are again missing on only the second operation after their dinghy escape.

2. Flying Officer Dick Cheek of 40 Squadron has been awarded an immediate DSO as a result of his accurate bombing and low level machine-gunning attacks on enemy targets. Most of us think that all his crew members should also get awards for bravery for they have shared in the dangers and successful attacks. The usual

crew members are: Flying Officer R.L.W. Cheek (Captain-pilot), Flying Officer F.W. Mason (navigator), Sergeant V. Mais (bomb aimer-second pilot), Flight Sergeant H. Cook (wireless operator), Flying Officer R.L. Newton (rear gunner).

3. In intelligence the expected big change has occurred and we have reverted to Squadron Intelligence tents for briefing and interrogation. We pulled down two of the three large (EPIP) tents coupled together (which had so recently been moved 250 yards to a new site on the low hill overlooking the airfield) and left one for my office. The squadrons each took one tent to add to their own Intelligence sections.

4. 104 Squadron has had an unfortunate time with losses in October — four aircraft lost on operations and another one blew up on return causing one death and others burned.

5. The weather has continued to be very wet and windy but has only occasionally prevented operations.

With the rains the flat land has become marshy and low parts of main roads are often flooded and impassable. Enemy demolition of bridges is now causing trouble because we have to make big detours to get across wadis.

12th November 1943

Last night Flying Officer Cheek had another extraordinary bombing report after the attack on Pistoia and Prato. The crew bombed as detailed at Prato and machine-gunned a light gun. At Pistoia they shot up aircraft on the ground and dropped incendiaries on a train which was set on fire. Then they saw a truck on the nearby autostrada and strafed this. Cheek's guns fired 7,900 rounds of .303 ammunition on the mission. These adventures are extremely difficult to report in the Opsum because after all it is a general summary of the success or failure of a bombing operation, but this young man and his crew are setting a new style of night attack with their sheer audacity in going in at low levels to use the guns like a fighter bomber in daylight.

Flying Officer Pountney left Wing today to take over as Intelligence Officer of 104 Squadron while Pilot Officer Winn, who has been doing the job temporarily, has arranged to go on operations tonight with Wing Commander Crossley. I am keen for this type of experience by my Intelligence Officers — the aircrews take more notice of IOs who have been to a defended target and at least know something of what it is like to bomb amidst flak and what goes on in an aircraft on a mission.

13th November 1943: Bridge Bombing
Up early this morning for the fifth night in succession and this time it was a brilliant success at both targets according to the crews I interrogated. At Cecina the 4,000 lb bomb did not explode but the other aircraft hit the bridge and photographs show it to be two-thirds cut through and unusable for traffic.

Pontassieve was also a good raid and Wing Commander Crossley went low after doing some dive bombing so Winn really had a good trip with plenty of excitement. Flight Lieutenant Ronny Thirsk had the 4,000 lb bomb at Pontassieve and reported a near miss — very close to the bridge.

In the afternoon of the 13th I went over to Squadron Leader Wise at the other Wing and met my old 104 Squadron flight commander friend who is now Wing Commander Leggate with his own squadron. We had some Muscat wine in the wing mess together and I returned in a somewhat merry mood.

14th November 1943
At wing mess tonight the Group Captain was entertaining the Kaid and his wife and the Caliphs, but I enjoyed myself with the squadron chaps instead.

There is news of a move from Kairouan to a landing ground near Tunis.

17th November 1943: Brothels
Today was spent in taking down the tents and packing our Intelligence boxes on to 'P for Peter' ready for tomorrow which is moving day to a landing ground at Oudna just south of Tunis. We are all rather excited at the prospect of leaving Kairouan. The Holy Smell is as bad in winter as in summer only now we have mud and floods which can stop all flying operations.

This evening we came over to the Repair and Refuelling Party camp for a meal and night's accommodation because Hani West is almost bare and our mess has been packed on to transport vehicles. We were lucky — the 'Party' had a turkey laid on for dinner and this had been given to them as a result of a curious chain of circumstances.

Apparently the 'Party' have been good clients of a small and select ('very clean') brothel near Sfax, and Madame, her husband and the girls (four) have been regularly inspected and treated by the Doc. In gratitude Monsieur gave Doc a fine turkey and also invited the officers and NCOs to a house-warming at the new site

of the brothel in Sfax. Anyway the turkey was very good and we
toasted the new brothel and the girls. It was a mild relief to hear
of this so called 'select' establishment in Sfax because I've seen
the ghastly queues of soldiers and airmen in Sousse lined up for
their turn at the usual assembly line brothels.

18th November 1943: Oudna Airfield

We were up early today and eventually took-off in 'P for Peter'.
The port motor vibrated badly in running up but this was due to
oily plugs which soon cleared as Flying Officer Johnny Johnston
opened up the throttles. Squadron Leader Britton and I took a
last look at the Holy City of Kairouan which looked white and
clean from the distance and then we were soon out over the coast
and following the line of sandy beaches to Hammamet at a very
low altitude — perhaps fifty feet above sea level. Johnny took the
Wellington up to a more respectable height through the gap
between the rugged mountains and we could look along the coast
of the Cape Bon Peninsula and recognise Zambra Island out in the
wide blue waters of the Gulf of Tunis and the towns of Grombalia
and Soliman set in green countryside dotted with vine-yards.

We climbed over a ridge into the valley south of Tunis and
identified the new airfield at Oudna, close to the long line of
beautiful arches of a Roman aqueduct. While we circled over the
airfield we could appreciate the position of Tunis and the ship
canal to La Goulette and even see the Corniche district and
Carthage with the coastal mountains and the swing of the coast
towards Bizerta. After a careful inspection from the air Johnny
made a lengthy approach with plenty of fine pitch and 'P for
Peter' settled to a good safe landing — the sort I like! From then
on we had to cope with unpacking and tent erecting (an exhausting
job) and the 'Colonel' and I had to put up our tents without help.

19th November 1943: Jock's Birthday Party

Today was somewhat hectic because the main Intelligence tent
had to be erected but this task was eased by working in a more
pleasing environment than at Kairouan. Oudna is surrounded by
green farmland and with a river, Roman aqueduct and view of the
mountains to help one's spirits — and so far there is no smell!
Operations were cancelled, which was lucky because it was Flight
Lieutenant Jock Simpson's (our Accountant Officer) birthday and
he had invited many of us to dine with him in Tunis this evening
at the Majestic.

I went down in the Group Captain's car and we had a poor dinner but plenty of wine and amusement. There were old friends there from the other squadrons including Flight Lieutenant Pilley, formerly with Brum Birmingham's squadron. We had a good chat about old times at LGs 09 and 106 while things around us were getting merrier as the wine made people relax. Jock himself was violently happy in his rugger forward style and barged into people and sometimes upset their drinks with his bonhomie. Joe Reid, an Australian himself, stopped a fight at one point when Jock had accidentally knocked another Aussie's drink out of his hand. Our other Jock, Jock Drummond was celebrating a 'Mention' and was completely u/s and leaning against the wall of the dance hall. 'The Colonel', 'Bishop' and the AA Major formerly with us — all got hold of doubtful looking females and danced with vigour, hilarity and some abandon. I watched and admired their efforts. Unfortunately there were no drinks after 23.00 hours and the party finished at midnight when the drunks were collected and put in trucks. Dicky, the MT King, had safely immobilized his car to such an extent that neither he nor Squadron Leader Morrison, the Engineer Officer, could put it right, so we had to leave it. Jock Drummond had to be removed from the driving seat of his vehicle and another driver substituted. Squadron Leader Partington was urged out of his truck through the Group Captain's good offices — the latter having some interest in this as his own car was parked behind and hemmed in. The Group Captain's driver was sent to yet another truck as driver and I managed to get into the back seat of the staff car, now driven by our Commanding Officer. The back seat position, wedged in between Jock Simpson and Dicky, was not the best but I was relatively lucky because in the confusion, 'Colonel' Britton, Joe Reid and another officer were left behind and had to ring for the duty driver at Wing to rescue them.

20th November 1943: Visitors
It was a 'stand down' today and I was able to work on the maps and displays in the Intelligence section. This is a better camp site altogether and makes one feel happier and keener. A.B. Read rang up from Group to say he was flying over to visit 236 Wing with a Captain Kaughman of Psychological Warfare. I met them on the aerodrome and found Aubyn James and a pilot with them — they had flown over in a natty little Beechcraft biplane. The party toured the squadron and Wing Intelligence sections and had tea in

our mess before we took them back to the aircraft and watched them take off in the dusk. I thought what a fantastic world this is when people come to visit my section by special light aircraft. 'A.B.' had news of future movements and tonight we had the AOC (Air Commodore Simpson) and some American visitors in the mess — perhaps indicating closer co-operation of ourselves with the USAAF. I also had another visitor today — an American lieutenant (Intelligence) in the US Army Air Force who invited me over to his place to call on the 'heavy bombers' Intelligence section.

23rd November 1943: a Gale

The weather changed to a gale today and operations were cancelled. Our tents were threatened by the wind and much work was necessary tightening guy ropes and placing sand bags in position against walls. Ralph Dunning of 40 Squadron lost his big Intelligence tent which was ripped by the wind and I expect Bob Pountney's tent went as well because the conditions were really violent in the worst gusts.

24th November 1943: Leaflet Experiments

The wind was still very strong and gusty this morning but I went up to 6,000 feet in 'O for Orange' with Flight Sergeant Johnson and Flying Officer Jock Welsh of 104 Squadron to experiment with leaflet dropping and watch what happened from the bomb panel. We took a squadron leader of Operation Research and an American radio expert with us and the aircraft made a good take-off and soon reached the required height. We performed our experiments and came down again passing at one point through a snow storm of nickels which had spread out from the bundles. The landing was difficult in a strong crosswind of 25 to 30 mph. 'O for Orange' was caught by the wind and skidded off the runway and then back again — it was good piloting to get her straight again. It felt very queer inside the Wellington and I could feel the sideways motion and the tyres skidding. In the midst of the landing problems the squadron leader of Operation Research was suddenly violently sick but mainly over himself, thank goodness. After landing I had a talk with Jock Welsh and the captain, wireless operator and rear gunner about the leaflet experiment and the landing difficulties — little thinking of the tragic night operation which was to follow.

In the afternoon I took part in the briefing for an attack on a ball-bearing factory at Turin in northern Italy. This is a very long trip indeed from Oudna across the Mediterranean and over Sardinia and Corsica to the Ligurian Sea and then over the mountain range to the plains of Piedmont and the Turin complex of industries. This operation has been in the offing for some time and prevented only by the weather conditions either at base or along the route to target. Elmas in Sardinia is to be used for refuelling and emergency.

25th November 1943: A Disastrous Operation

I was roused by Operations at 01.00 hours and told that the aircraft are in all sorts of trouble; some have landed in Sardinia, others have baled out or have not reported — and apparently the weather has made a shambles of the whole operation. In the darkness with some aircraft circling and about to land, I made my way on the motorcycle to 40 Squadron Intelligence tent to help Ralph with his interrogations. My forebodings were unhappily realised and the night of our first raid on Turin will live long in the memory. Flight Sergeant Gosling and crew in 'H for Harry' baled out over Sardinia and so far there is no news of their safety. 'E for Edward' landed at Castel Vetrano. Wellingtons 'C' and 'M' of 40 Squadron are missing without news. Those crews who were interrogated were tired and quiet after a long worrying flight in cloud and turbulence. The winds experienced had been far stronger than expected. At 104 Squadron the reports were similar — the weather was very bad north of Corsica and two Wellingtons are missing, 'D for Donald' captained by the Wing Commander, Don Crossley, and 'V for Victor' captained by Flight Sergeant Johnson with Jock Welsh as his navigator — the crew that flew the plane for leaflet experiments yesterday.

The 236 Wing result in summary was:

30 Wellingtons operated (16 of 40 Squadron and 14 of 104 Squadron)
3   located Turin but not the target and returned to base safely
14 turned back unable to locate because of severe weather conditions and reached base safely
2   landed back elsewhere
2   crews baled out and their aircraft were lost but one crew was known to be safe

  5   aircraft failed to take off from Elmas due to refuelling
      troubles
  4   Wellingtons were missing without news — believed lost
 30   total

The 24th/25th November 1943 was the worst night for 205 Group
aircraft that I can recall (I believe it was finally 17 aircraft lost out
of 70 operating or 24%) and it was due entirely to the weather
conditions not to enemy action. In the weather experienced, navigation must have been extremely difficult and some of the missing
aircraft probably came down off track and hit mountains when
they expected to be over the sea. Among those lost in the other
wing was Flight Lieutenant Ray Taaffe of 37 Squadron, who was
formerly Flight Sergeant Taaffe of our squadron and an old friend
at briefing and interrogation. What can be said of the loss of Don
Crossley? I saw Bob Pountney and a sense of gloom pervaded
104 Squadron today. Wing Commander Crossley can ill be spared
for he was giving excellent leadership in the squadron and the
crews were responding to his methods.

Later:
We are still feeling the aftermath from Turin and were thankful
when operations tonight were cancelled because of weather.

26th November 1943
Briefing for a bridge target.

27th November 1943
We cleared up last night's operation and there was a 'stand down'
today. A new Intelligence Officer, Flying Officer Feliciant, arrived
from Group on attachment to our wing and we had some fun
together at dinner this evening in the mess. Some local chickens
have taken a fancy to our mess tents and caused quite a com-
motion at dinner by poking their heads through the air venti-
lation holes and squawking. I scored a direct hit with a piece of
bread and got temporary relief. Then they returned and one
dropped a large and splashy visiting card on to Feliciant's open
cigarette case as he was offering me a cigarette. It might have been
worse!

28th November 1943
Winn came over by the Beechcraft and Paddy and Larry Wells

came with me for a brief flip to try it out. It is upholstered inside like a good car and would be a wonderful little bus for a family. We made two circuits at about 100 mph and then came into a perfect landing. My Indian motorcycle was returned to me today in excellent condition by L.A.C. Holmes of Wing MT. He says he found a mass of soft oily soapy stuff in the bottom of the carburettor. Tonight I briefed for Ralph and will be doing the interrogations for him as the poor chap is having a tooth out which has an abscess underneath.

29th November 1943: American Bombing
Interrogations began last night at 22.30 and I finished work about 03.30 and went to bed. Today was a 'stand down' so I was able to visit the American Fortress Group HQ to which I was recently invited. The Intelligence and Operations people were extremely nice chaps who were as eager to hear of our planes and methods as we were to hear of theirs. It was a good morning to be at the HQ because their squadrons were forming up overhead for a big effort on enemy aerodromes in the Rome area.

The lengthy process of climbing and circling to get into battle formation for the massed flight to the target is an awe-inspiring spectacle. Daylight bombing raids in formations of over a hundred aircraft send shivers of apprehension down my bomb-conscious spine — firstly for the crews of these huge Fortresses and Liberators who present such clearly visible and compact targets for German flak and fighters — and secondly for the human beings underneath and near the target area when these formations release their streams of high explosive and incendiaries in a great carpet of destruction.

These bombing procedures are in striking contrast with our own night-bombing methods. I would think that the American daylight bombing produces more accurate attacks on a given target but that their losses must be extraordinarily high. How can they maintain morale in a squadron sometimes suffering ten per cent or greater losses on single missions? The complementary nature of our two air forces in providing a 24-hour service for bombing tactical and strategic targets is something which must have a vital effect on the outcome of this war.

In the afternoon I went off for a short ride on the Indian up a track leading to Zaghouan. It was pleasant country with mountains on each side and many relics of recent fighting. Because it is more unusual to find British graves I meditated a while at the cross put up to a sergeant killed in November 1942 and wondered how he could be there at that time unless of course he was an RAF man who had perhaps baled out or been killed in a crash. Around me were ammunition dumps of tank and anti-tank shells, some larger artillery shells (all German) and the wrecks of three German light tanks, derelict transport vehicles, and a Stuka. Many mortar shells were lying about at the sides of road and track as though collected and put there by natives when ploughing. I picked some white daisies and some blue crocuses or orchids and thought of more pleasant things than war.

30th November 1943: 104 Squadron Commander
Squadron Leader Harold Turner DFC who is our Wing Operations Officer, is to take over the command of 104 Squadron left vacant by the loss of Wing Commander Don Crossley on the Turin operation of 24th/25th November. Harold will do the job quietly and efficiently — he is in the mould of those leaders I've learned to recognise and admire.

1st to 8th December 1943: Africa to Europe
During this period we were made aware that a move was planned for the whole group of Wellingtons — this time we were to leave Africa and return to Europe. (The prospect is thrilling when I consider that I left the United Kingdom over two years ago to serve in the Middle East.)

We moved from Oudna on 5th December after spending the night in the open with all tents packed on to transport. I travelled quietly and pleasantly in the Group Captain's Chevrolet staff car with Squadron Leader Britton, Flying Officer Johnson and a driver. We went around Tunis and along narrow roads through rolling open country to Ferryville and the Bizerta Lake with its shipping. The long convoy of laden trucks parked near the Bizerta docks and for two days and nights we waited quietly for the navy in conditions which would have gladdened the eyes of a German reconnaissance pilot looking for an easy target. I must confess that as an Intelligence Officer I was well aware of our danger and scanned the skies anxiously for signs of an Me109 fighter bomber or a bomber formation — but happily for us we were unmolested.

*

The 205 Group medium bomber force which was to move to Foggia airfields in Italy now consisted of three wings and six squadrons of Wellingtons which had operated as a unit since coming together at Kairouan in May and June 1943:

231 Wing with 37 and 70 Squadrons
236 Wing with 40 and 104 Squadrons
330 Wing with 142 and 150 Squadrons

CHAPTER NINE

Bombing from Foggia

Between the spur jutting into the Adriatic Sea from the long leg of Italy and the mountain backbone of the Apennines is a wide fertile plain with Foggia as its nodal point. The Allies' control of the airfields around Foggia (from October 1943) enabled American and British bombers to strike deep into enemy territory from a new direction.

The flat area of grassland, grainland and olive groves became scarred with the runways and camp sites of the bomber wings which formed a dense concentration of air power. American Fortress and Liberator day bombers with their Thunderbolt, Mustang and Lightning fighter escorts and the British and Canadian Wellington night bombers worked in complementary harmony as a formidable strategic force under the operational control of Mediterranean Air Command.

At times of army crisis such as the landing and holding of the Anzio bridgehead and the attempts to capture the heights of Monte Cassino, the strategic bombers were switched to close support tactical targets. Their normal duties included the interdiction of transportation routes in northern Italy and attacks on marshalling yards and repair shops south of the Alps, in addition to their main strategic targets such as weapon factories and airfields in North Italy, Germany and Austria, the Rumanian oilfields, the mining of the River Danube and transport facilities in the Balkan capital cities.

In spite of Allied air supremacy, the land war in Italy became a prolonged and difficult struggle against a determined enemy clinging to strong natural defensive positions. The Allied armies were also hampered by transfers of some divisions and logistical support to Britain in preparation for the D-Day invasion of Europe – and additionally were, to some extent, competing for supplies with the Foggia strategic air forces. Significant dates in the slow progress on land in 1944 were the Anzio landings on 22nd January, the bombing of Monte Cassino on 15th February and 15th March, the opening of the spring offensive on 11th May and after much hard fighting, the capture of Rome on 4th June — two days before D-Day in Normandy.

At Foggia the Wellington wings and squadrons of 205 Group realised for the first time the strength of American air power and watched with interest and respect the great daylight formations forming up overhead and setting off to attack distant airfields and industrial targets. Similarly at night the American fliers watched our squadrons roar down the flarepaths and set off in a stream to attack targets under the cover of darkness but in conditions which required accurate individual navigation and the use of flares for location.

Number 236 Wing and its squadrons, 40 and 104, after a brief stop at Cerignola, became established at the former Italian Air Force base of Foggia-Gino Lisa, now known as Foggia Main. The aircrews made themselves as comfortable as possible in the classrooms of an elementary school in Foggia while the ground personnel and administration lived in tented camps adjacent to the airfield, one mile south of the town.

*

9th to 12th December 1943: Bizerta to Taranto by sea
We embarked on Landing Ship (Tank) No 361 on the morning of the 9th and noted with amusement its imposing ship's crest of Donald Duck wielding a tommy gun with a tank on his back and a shell passing between his legs. The inscription read — '*Nihil sed Optima Litora*' (Nothing but the best beaches!).

It was a pleasant cruise with views of the islands of Malta and Gozo and of the glorious snow-capped peak of Mount Etna in Sicily rising majestically in a perfect cone to nearly 11,000 feet. The coast of the toe of Italy looked green and attractive with mountains behind a coast of fine beaches and beautiful villas and larger buildings. Because of the need to keep to a swept channel through the minefields we followed a route very close to the coast and finally had the thrill of entering the magnificent harbour of Taranto on 12th December through the protective booms and so through watching crowds into the inner harbour and disembarkation on a pebble beach. It was intriguing to see the Italian housewives gossipping and their intimate garments hanging out to dry on the clothes-lines around the inner harbour. We felt almost envious of these Italians apparently living normal lives. We were quickly ashore with our vehicles and away along narrow roads between the olive groves. At night we slept in our camp beds under a tent top slung between the truck and an olive tree.

Our route on the 13th was along the edge of the Apennine
plateau with olive groves, wide fields of green young corn and neat
well-cultivated fields of vegetables. I travelled on my motorcycle and took my turn with two others to marshal the convoy
of vehicles at crossroads or turnings. On the evening of the 16th
we reached a pleasant olive grove which is to be the site of our
camp, and put up the living tents. The nearest town is Cerignola.

19th December 1943: Foggia
Today I visited Foggia with Squadron Leader Britton. The country
between Cerignola and Foggia is flat and fen-like with mountains
in the distance both to right and left. The town has been badly
damaged and the railway marshalling yards are full of burned out
rolling stock, twisted rails, bomb craters and the general chaos of
war. The railway sheds have been hit but some repairs are in progress and there were several locomotives in the yards, some of
them in steam.

20th December 1943
The day was taken up with preparatory work in the Intelligence
section.

21st December 1943
This morning I visited Barletta and was surprised at the amount of
goods in the shops. Before we came back to camp we had some
very good coffee in a cafe — which was said to be German coffee.
If this is the German substitute for coffee it's remarkably good. At
tea time today the Adjutant drew me on one side and showed me
a signal from Rear NAAF which contained a message from my
mother that ,my father was desperately ill and the doctor considered that my presence would aid his recovery.

The Adjutant could give me no hope of getting home on com-
passionate leave as this was reserved for a case of illness of one's
wife. I knew he was right and settled down to write letters to my
father and mother.

22nd December 1943
The Group Captain confirmed today that there was no hope of
getting home even if the matter was pursued further — and he
advised me to cable. The Group Signals Officer will do his best to
send off a message for me — 'Leave impossible. Keep Father
cheerful. Expect to see him next Christmas carving Turkey.

Writing. Roy.' It sounds rather lighthearted but I feel that in Pa's case he will need brightening up and if he determines to get well he can do it — he is only 66 years of age.

Letters arrived at tea time which showed that my father is in hospital for an operation for removal of gall bladder. D. wrote a particularly sweet letter about the matter which I appreciated.

24th December 1943: Bari

With Squadron Leader Britton I went to Bari to visit 205 Group Headquarters which we found temporarily situated in a fine building formerly belonging to the Regia Aeronautica. Squadron Leader A.B. Read was not available but I saw several American A2 Officers and got some maps which we require. Then 'Brit' and I looked around the town and front and saw the results of what is considered to be one of the most destructive bombing raids of the war in which a force of German Ju88s hit an ammunition ship in the crowded harbour on 2nd December and set off explosions and fires, sinking in all some 17 ships, shattering most of the windows in Bari and causing at least 1,000 casualties. We journeyed back in the gathering gloom to our damp tents and a somewhat liquid Christmas Eve.

25th December 1943: Christmas Day

Last Christmas I was in Malta — now it's Italy and Cerignola as the background for the usual festivities. We attended Church Service in the airmen's mess and then had the local mayor and his friends come to our mess. When they departed, in came our sergeants — then the officers went to the sergeants' mess for further drinks — then officers and sergeants moved to the airmen's mess and served the meal for the airmen. It was a wizard traditional Christmas dinner of tomato soup, followed by turkey, roast pork, potatoes boiled and roasted, greens, apple sauce — Christmas pudding and custard. We had a cold lunch and a walk before our own dinner at 18.00 hours. The evening was enlivened by Fred's efforts (Squadron Leader Partington) — he insisted on each officer singing a song or chorus and the entire mess burst into the 70 Squadron song sung to the tune of 'Clementine', and then went on to the other favourites which use the tunes of 'Lili Marlene' and 'Over the Rainbow'. [70 Squadron had the distinction of the longest period of service in the Middle East and seems to have had all the song-writers. But the other Wellington squadrons knew and used the songs.]

Seventy-Squadron
(To the tune of 'Clementine')

Down to Flights each ruddy morning,
Sitting waiting for a clue,
Same old notice on the flight board,
Maximum effort — guess where to?

Refrain: Seventy Squadron, Seventy Squadron,
        Though we say it with a sigh,
        We must do this bloody mail run
        Every night until we die.

Get your guns cleaned, do your dailies,[1]
Round it off with an air test,
Rumour has we're going Northwards,
But we know we're going West! [*Refrain*]

Take-off from the Western Desert,
Sixty, Fuka, or 0 nine,[2]
Same old aircraft, some old aircrew,
Same old target, same old time. [*Refrain*]

Navigator! have you lost us?
Come up here and have a look,
Someone's shot our starboard wing off!
We're all right chaps, that's Tobruk![3] [*Refrain*]

Oh to be in Piccadilly,
Selling matches by the score,
Then we would not have to do that
Bloody mail run any more. [*Refrain*]

1. Pre-flight and daily inspections.
2. Landing grounds — i.e. LG60, Fuka, LG09.
3. Tobruk at the time of the song was in *Allied* hands being cut off by the Axis partners. Tobruk fired at *all* aircraft, friend or foe!

*

ingtons bombing Villa-
airfield, January 1944

cessful attack on the
gio Emelia aircraft factory
orth Italy, January 1944

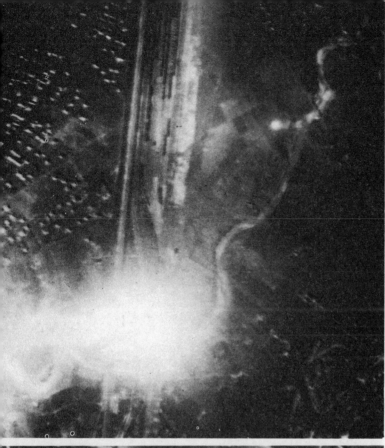

A raid on the marshal
yards at Sophia, March 19

Daylight bombing operat
by 205 group in April 19
partisans surrounded Germ
forces in Nicsik, Yugosla
and requested that the to
be bombed. 11 Wellingto
carried out the mission a
all aircraft returned safely
Foggia

Song to tune of 'Lili Marlene'
(The 'Lili Marlene' song was often played on the German radio
and enjoyed equally by the Allied servicemen.)

There's a certain Squadron, way up in the blue,[1]
We don't need any orders, we know what to do.
We go bomb Benghazi every night,
And when we don't, we all get tight,
We're going to bomb Benghazi, we're going there tonight.

Wing Commander Simpson leads us on our way
Leads us when we're working, leads us when we play,
Give him a ladle[2] when he's tight,
And eight five-hundred pounders[3] the following night,
He's going to bomb Benghazi, he's going there tonight.

1. The Desert was called 'The Blue'.
2. Wing Commander Simpson's 'party piece' late at night was to
   take a large soup ladle, fill it with scotch, and down it in one
   gulp! (He later became Air Commodore and AOC 205 Group.)
3. 500 lb General Purpose bombs.

Song to tune of 'Over the Rainbow'
Somewhere over Benghazi, way down low,
There's a Wimp on one engine
Chased by a one one oh.[1]
Somewhere over Benghazi, Heinkels fly,
They fly over Benghazi,
Why then oh why must I?
(*Note: there were other verses and songs!*)

1. Messerschmitt 110.

*

26th December 1943
This morning there was an intelligence officers' conference at
Group HQ. The afternoon was one of pouring rain and in the
evening the mess was made untenable by a smoking fire.

30th December 1943
We moved today and our squadron will now operate from Foggia
Main (Gino-Lisa).

31st December 1943: New Year's Eve
A wet night was followed by an unforgettable day of constant
heavy rain. There is mud and water everywhere and most tents
erected yesterday are now in poor shape. A gale added to our
misery but this abated towards nightfall and the weather did not
prevent an enormous and spontaneous celebration of the New
Year by every serviceman who had access to a revolver, rifle or
gun. Machine-guns, 20mm cannons, Bofors light AA guns and
even heavy AA guns fired live ammunition into the weeping skies
completely heedless of the consequences in terms of falling
shrapnel and shell splinters. I cursed the unknown idiots and
reached for my tin hat as metal pieces pattered down around me.

1st January 1944
We woke to a gloomy day, wet and cold with a strong east wind.
The large mess tents and kitchen tents were flat to the ground and
I offered the Intelligence tent for meals. We used this for 24 hours
until conditions improved sufficiently for the other tents to be
re-erected. Gumboots arrived from base and a rum issue was made
which was very popular.

3rd January 1944: General Montgomery Leaving Italy
A sunny day at last to help dry things out. The ground is sodden
everywhere but the mountains with their snow cappings look
magnificent in the sunshine. I was issued today with oilskins and
a leather jerkin for my motorcycling and night work. The war
news is excellent with Berlin raided again last night and the
Russians are nearing their own western frontier. Optimism is
so much in the air that Guy Britton and I laid bets — he is
alcoholically optimistic tonight and insists that the war will be
over by 30th June. We are all encouraged by the news and by
Monty's statement that 'The end is in sight'. Monty is returning to
Britain and has handed over to Lieutenant General Sir Oliver
Leese.

5th January 1944: Italian Winter
After a terrible night of wind and driving rain all the good done
by the brief spell of sunshine has been ruined. It rained all day and
we now have great pools of water and slush between the tents.
Rum was issued again tonight.

6th January 1944
Snow covered the ground in the camp when we wakened today
and all hills and lower slopes have a thick white blanket over them.
A bitterly cold wind blew from the north across the Plain of
Foggia bringing more snow during the morning. The Group
Captain decided that this particular day was a good one to shift
camp so in the miserable conditions we took down our tents
and worked like slaves to put them up again on a drier site about
a mile away.

7th to 17th January 1944: Reggio Emelia Success
This was a period of hard work in grim conditions with almost
daily conferences and briefings. A raid on Reggio Emelia aircraft factory on the night of 7th/8th January produced excellent
results and the Opsum was substantiated by our own night photographs and subsequent daylight photographs by the American
Fortresses. The Intelligence routine established at Foggia was for
me to fly each day with the Group Captain in our wing's Fairchild
'puddle jumper' to an airfield near Group HQ where we were
picked up by staff car and taken to the SASO's conference on the
target for the day. The Group Captain generously allowed me to
fly the aircraft for part of each trip and this was extremely enjoyable. Coming back was less enjoyable as I had to write out information reports about the target with duplicate carbon copies for
each of the squadron commanders. On one occasion I was allowed
to fly the plane while 'Paul' tried to shoot ducks from the window
of the cockpit!

17th January 1944
News of my father's death was contained in a letter received today
from D.

18th January 1944
When the Group Captain and I arrived at the Fairchild this morning
it was u/s with a fractured exhaust pipe which had caused blacken-
ing of the front of the fuselage from the flame. It was lucky for us
that it had been noticed as it might have caused a fire in the air.
Eventually the Beechcraft came over for us (piloted by Pilot
Officer Rippengal ex. 40 Squadron) and we had a pleasant trip to
No 3 airfield over the green and orderly countryside crossed by
two meandering rivers. Roads and railways across the plain are
straight for long distances and the towns show up white or browny-

white against the green of the land. Map reading from the air is very easy.

After the conference and our return to Foggia Main we had a further conference in the Ops. trailer with the Group Captain, squadron commanders, navigation officer and intelligence officers — briefed by the G/C and myself. Our Wellingtons are attacking airfields to prevent Luftwaffe action against a new landing by American and British troops behind the front line.

19th January 1944

The puddlejumper was serviceable again this morning and the G/C and Group Captain Beare indulged in fighter tactics of close formation flying en route — causing some nervous twittering among the passengers. On the way back 'Paul' kindly gave me some dual flying training and completed it by giving a description of his own landing procedures and making a wizard landing which quite surprised him! (So he said!)

Two of our crews were missing from last night, one from each squadron; ours was Pilot Officer Puddephat and crew whom I recently interrogated with a PRO Officer listening, when they came in from the Sofia raid of 10th/11th January. A nice chap Puddephat, only recently commissioned, but an experienced pilot. He and his crew had nearly finished their tour of operations.

20th January 1944: Tragedies

Tonight an American officer came into our mess after performing a dismal duty — he had brought back five bodies from the crew of 'V for Victor' of 40 Squadron which had been found on top of the mountain ridge of the Gargano Promontory. 'K for King' of 104 Squadron (Puddephat and his crew), had also been located in a similar position but the bodies were unidentifiable. These tragedies were the result of the weather conditions that night (18th/19th) with cloud covering the Gargano plateau which rises sharply to over 3,000 feet from the Foggia Plain to the south and west, which itself is only some 200 feet above sea level.

21st January 1944

One surprise in the mail today was a Christmas parcel from the townsfolk of Blandford Dorset — including a letter from the Mayor. I felt very pleased at the kindness of the home folk — this is the first time I've seen a 'British Comforts Parcel' while the Australians, New Zealanders and Canadians seem to have them frequently from their homelands. Briefing today was for an interesting target — port facilities at Fiume.

22nd January 1944: Anzio Landing

The Fiume attack was successful with fires started and some good photographs of the port. Today the Allied convoy of assault troops and equipment was able to reach the Anzio beaches un-observed from the air. This means that our recent bombing of enemy airfields has been effective.

24th January 1944

Air Marshal Sir John Slessor chaired today's conference at Group HQ. With his rows of medals, greying hair and rather stern visage he was an impressive figure and seemed a sound and decent com-mander from what he said to our assembly of AOC, group captains, wing commanders and lesser ranking intelligence and operations officers.

It was a bumpy journey back to Foggia Main. When we arrived at our field we were held up for sometime while the Fortresses took off for an operation and formed up overhead into their powerful formations. The Group Captain observed to us that he always played safe, i.e. he always landed into the wind rather than use the runway in a crosswind. He proceeded to land across the runway and badly shocked a truck driver who mis-calculated our landing direction. However, we landed safely and some other air-craft had *not* — there was another puddlejumper pranged just off the runway and a Hudson also damaged by landing across the wind. Tonight the operation was cancelled because of the weather.

26th January 1944

This morning the Group Captain took off across the runway deliberately because of the rough crosswind and driving rain-storms. We set course for the cathedral in the distance and I was allowed to fly the aircraft myself all the way. The G/C made a wizard landing across the runway and then we watched the Beech-craft come in and bounce all over the place in the crosswind. It could easily have pranged. After the conference we had a bumpy passage back through rain showers while I tried to write out the carbon copies for the squadron COs. Then we made another very good landing into the squally wind of 25 to 30 mph at Foggia Main.

Heavy rain and strong winds caused the cancellation of operations tonight. Our new site looks like becoming as wet as the earlier one, as water poured into the officers' mess and threatened to put out the fire.

31st January 1944
Africa Star ribbons were presented to all ranks by Group Captain P.I. Harris at a parade today.

10th February 1944
Nothing much has happened recently because of bad weather and the puddlejumper has been unserviceable for most of the time. Snow is thick on the mountains but soon melts on the airfield and camp areas. Gumboots have become permanent footwear.

Today the puddlejumper was OK and we took off after a long wait for the big US day bombers to come in from a mission. They called for an ambulance for one crew hit by flak. We wondered how many were missing. Conditions were bumpy but the country-side looked very green and beautiful with plough patterns showing up on the plains and the mountains and foothills standing up sharp and white with their snow cover. We landed on one wheel in the crosswind at No 3 and had some nasty moments before straightening up.

After the conference we took off from a taxi path between two Wellingtons and I did my usual secretarial tasks while we bumped up and down in the turbulent air. We made another one-wheel landing at Foggia Main — whew!

Operations were cancelled tonight which is a great pity because things are looking serious at the Anzio bridgehead and this weather is preventing our use of air superiority.

12th February 1944
The Adjutant rang up today to congratulate me on a 'Mention'. I'm not particularly excited having seen others get it, but I expect that D. and my mother will be pleased. We had a bit of a party in the mess at night but in view of double-sorties in support of the Army at Anzio, and the resultant night work for Intelligence, celebration was strictly limited.

13th February 1944
It's been an exhausting 24 hours with about three hours sleep last night. Snow is now rushing past borne on a bitterly cold wind. We had a conference at Wing today with Psychological Warfare Branch

American friends — Captain Lyons, Lieutenant Whitney and Lieutenant Price — and our intelligence officers. Later I had a good yarn with Whitney and Price about America. They hail from North Carolina and we talked of the Mason-Dixon Line which they say is real enough between Pennsylvania on the north and Virginia to the south. The line is named after two surveyors who were responsible for demarcation of the State borders between North and South.

In the afternoon we dealt with 'nickels'. There are double-sorties to the battle area again tonight. The situation at Anzio is said to be so serious that we may be forced to withdraw.

14th February 1944
My 'Mention in Despatches' was in today's DROs.

15th February 1944: Monte Cassino Monastery Bombed
Today the daylight heavy bombers blasted the ancient hill-top monastery at the request of the Army. Photographs show that the bombing was superbly accurate but the decision to bomb caused a lot of debate in the mess. We are thankful not to be involved.

17th February 1944: Accidents
Two of our aircraft were lost last night. 'A for Apple' (104 Squadron) dived in while in the circuit after returning from the operation. It buried itself in the ground and no-one had an earthly chance to get out. The pilot was talking to Flying Control a second or so before the crash. One theory is that the Wellington had iced up coming down through the clouds. 'T for Tommy' (40 Squadron) was later found crashed on a hillside SW of Foggia with all burned beyond recognition. The operation itself was successful with several good photographs taken.

Work went on normally today and then while we were at dinner in the mess tonight there was an ominous noise from the flare-path direction and someone said, 'There's been a crash at the end of the runway'. We dashed outside and could see the usual red fire and smoke. There was one dull explosion and then a fearsome crack that made us all wince and up went the bombload. It was 'B' of 40 Squadron (Flying Officer Lyon) which had gone in near the main road, killing some civilians and a soldier in addition to the Wellington crew — except for the rear-gunner, who was blown clear in his turret.

Flying Officer Irwin was down on the crew list as navigator but he fell sick at the last minute and a Flight Sergeant Pellinger took his place. What curious fate ordains such things? And this is our third crew lost in the last 24 hours. Tonight we are again giving all-out assistance to the Army by close support bombing around the Anzio bridgehead where the Germans yesterday began a heavy counter-attack.

18th February 1944: Farewell Party

Work as usual and then I went to Wing Commander Bagnall's farewell party at 40 Squadron mess. It was great to say goodbye to old 'Bags' and know that there is another first class commander who has survived and will be available as a future leader in the RAF. He did some extremely courageous and accurate bombing attacks during his tour and set high standards. He demanded much from his crews — and from his Intelligence Officers! Don Crossley has gone and Don Saville has gone, but 'Bags', 'Micky' Mount, Harold Turner and others survive to carry on.

From the party I went on to help Ralph with the interrogations. There was another case of icing-up tonight and Warrant Officer Bradshaw — a Canadian — ordered his crew to bale out over the aerodrome and they did so. His own parachute slipped out of his reach so Bradshaw stuck to the controls and managed to bring the aircraft down safely on his own — a very good effort!

20th to 24th February 1944

Little to report except that the situation at Anzio has stabilised at last and we can return to strategic targets. On the 24th the target was an aircraft factory at Steyr in Austria and I did both squadron briefings myself for a change.

25th February 1944: Bombing Raid Reports in The Press — Steyr

The attack on Steyr was not very successful because only two aircraft definitely reached the target. Flying Officer Ashbaugh (a Canadian on his second tour) took a wizard photograph showing a fire burning in the factory as he arrived — a fire resulting from the American daylight heavies attack in the morning. Flight Sergeant Holmes, also of 104 Squadron, located and bombed correctly but the others were mainly west of target and bombed the marshalling yards and built up areas up to 30 miles west.

Here is the story of the raid as told by Associated Radio Press on the 26th February:

Two engined RAF Wellington bombers specialists in mopping up operations by night after American Flying Forts and Liberators have bashed a target by day have joined the Italy-based assault on Hitler's aircraft industry Thursday night with a blow at Steyr Austria already bathed in fires from two days of American pounding. Making their deepest foray yet against the enemy from Med. bases the British Work Horses concentrated on the Daimler factory at Steyr pouring their bombs down accurately by light of leaping fires and scattered other explosives over built-up areas and railroads serving the Manufacturing Centre.

Why on earth should reporters write such utter tripe? — why can't the truth be written soberly and sensibly? It makes me sick!

27th and 28th February 1944: Italian Civilians
On these two days of 'stand down' due to weather I worked in the mornings and spent the afternoons exploring the countryside on the Indian motorcycle. I went along the Naples road each day in the dull rainy conditions down the dangerous and steep hill leading to the beautiful River Cervaro valley. The roads were slippery due to mud but the scenery was splendid with hills and mountains on either side of the pebbly river bed. The road and railway changed sides occasionally and crossed each other as they followed the general line of the valley. Here and there, hill torrents came down to join the main river, fed by the melting snow on the mountains which had been well covered in recent days.

The railway is an electrified line and I saw several electric locomotives drawing trains and one 2—8—0 steam locomotive pounding along the valley in fine style with a high plume of dirty white smoke over the train and trailing behind. The only sad thing to remind me of the war was the number of Italians trudging along the roads and the railway line. There were soldiers, sailors and civilians including women old and young, many with bundles on their heads or carrying cases. One or two were bare-footed. Some of the girls were quite presentable and obviously wanted a lift. The Italian people are certainly suffering for the foolishness of their ruler in getting them involved in this war.

On the second day I diverted from the main Foggia—Naples road and climbed up a narrow track leading towards Greci which I knew was perched up on a hill top on the north side of the Cervaro valley. Snowdrifts across the road were two to three feet deep in places and I had to paddle through or charge the drifts and sometimes trample down a track before I could get the bike through. It was fun and eventually I got to the muddy street of Greci where the village youngsters clustered around me and I had a talk with a large pleasant looking man with a horse.

I said *'Buon Giorno'* and he beamed and said, 'Good Afternoon.' He spoke broken English and told me he had been to America and lived in Cleveland. I asked why he. hadn't stayed there and he told me that he had come back to see his people in 1911 and been caught by the Great War in which he fought and was wounded. He said he hadn't had his pension for six months and that there was no work and no money. How did he live? Well, he had some peas, beans and other vegetables and he lived on these.

He continued, 'I should like you to come to my house but I have nothing to offer you.'

I sympathised and said that things would improve when we captured Rome and a government was established there again.

Giving this friendly man all my cigarettes I rode along the main street amidst the shouting children, one or two of whom could speak a little English. I gave out a few sweets which was all I had and then ambled down the winding road with its hairpin bends back to the main road.

Talking in the mess later to Flying Officer Archer (Flying Control) and 'Doc' Gimson about the hungry and sad procession of Italians along the roads, 'Arch' told us of his own recent experience. In Naples he had been asked for a lift to Foggia by two women and a pretty young girl in her teens. The women pointed to the girl and told Archer he could 'fuck fuck' all the way to Foggia. He was in a convoy and couldn't take them but it shows what a sad state many of them are in – starving and desperate in their attempts to get a lift. When I argued that lifts should be given by service transport where there was room, Doc insisted that the rule had been made because so many were infested with lice and could spread typhus among the troops.

It makes me miserable in that we appear to be neglecting humanitarian principles in our treatment of the Italian people. And this also applies to our choice of some bombing targets, e.g. when we attack road sections in built-up areas and town centres. Now that the Italians are our allies – how can we do these things?

1st March 1944: A Play — 'Quiet Weekend'

We operated again tonight on a battle area target. After briefing, ten of us from the wing mess went to see *Quiet Weekend* played by the full West End cast, including Marjorie Fielding, George Thorpe, Margaretta Scott, Mary Llewellin, Robert Harris, Stuart Lindsell and Jeanne Stuart. It was strange and yet heartening to find that this pleasant and quiet play about peacetime life was just the sort of thing we all wanted as an antidote to war and bombing and violence in general.

We all thoroughly enjoyed the evening and the skilful acting — even though the place was crowded and we had to stand for the entire performance. Margaretta Scott was the young married girl with a youngster and Jim Brent the husband was mad on golf! I thought of D. and myself and our youngsters, now a boy and a girl, and how madly keen I was on golf back in the Blandford Dorset days of peace.

When we arrived back at Foggia Main our Wellingtons were already circling overhead and coming in to land which meant that my work would soon be beginning in the Intelligence section. From peace and a *Quiet Weekend* it was back quickly to interrogation and war.

2nd to 10th March 1944

In general the weather was bad during this period and for some days the airfield was completely unserviceable and several officers were allowed to go on leave.

11th to 14th March 1944: Leave in Bari

Although the airfield was officially declared unserviceable the American heavies ignored this and took off on the 11th for a mission, throwing up clouds of spray from the puddles and pools as they roared down the runway. However the airfield was still u/s for 205 Group night bombers and Archer, Braybrook and I were allowed to go on leave to Bari where we lunched at the Officers' Club after imbibing several Vermouths in the bar. As I remembered it afterwards the lunch was mediocre but the effects of a bottle of thickish sweet wine, golden in colour, were extraordinary. We all swayed happily as we stood up and I had a feeling of floating and steering my way to the door and being very doubtful if I could get through without bumping into the sides. We soon recovered well enough to visit Group HQ in the afternoon. Next morning, the 12th, we attended the morning conference. General

Twining himself was there and General Boon plus our own AOC and SASO etc. What we most appreciated was a running buffet with delicious coffee and cakes served by very red-lipped and pretty Italian girls obviously specially chosen for their looks. At night we dined at Group and then went to *Services Cocktail* — a good variety show at the Garrison Theatre.

I shared a room at the American hotel with a Lieutenant Smith, a tour expired Californian pilot of a P38 Lightning. We had some enjoyable talks together and found that we agreed on many matters. I haven't met many fighter-pilots and perhaps expect them to be different from my bomber pilot friends. Lieutenant Smith was quiet and thoughtful and would have fitted into our mess perfectly.

On the 13th we went shopping and I found a toy motorcycle for Duncan. In the afternoon I called on a friend, Sub-Lieutenant Marshall, who commands an ML which was in the harbour. He showed us round his little ship which made me think MLs are as fragile and dicey as aircraft. Going ashore in a dinghy I was nearly decapitated by a rope hawser which I didn't see in time to avoid.

The others went to a club party in the evening while I chose the flicks after dinner at the hotel. It was Fred Astaire in *The Sky's the Limit* and I enjoyed it and met a curious looking Russian who was heavily bandaged. When I asked what he had been doing he said, 'Truck turn over — many killed. I'm happy, I not killed.' We returned to camp on the 14th. Our airfield is still unserviceable.

15th March 1944: Flying Incidents
On 15th March the Fortresses and Liberators bombed the town of Cassino which was held by German troops. Even after the complete destruction of the town the enemy survived in numbers sufficient to hold on to the rubble for another two months.

The latter half of March was a busy time of operations. The volcano Mount Vesuvius was in furious eruption and everyone seemed to have seen it except me. The weather was frequently rough and windy but the Group Captain and I had almost daily flights to conferences in the puddlejumper. 'Paul' told me one day that I was getting quite good at flying, which pleased my ego! On the 18th just after I'd taken over there was a tremendous bang and the kite shook violently. We saw a cloud of brown and grey smoke rising from a field about 200 yards away and realised it was probably a Liberator jettisoning its bomb load for we had seen two American planes returning early as we took off.

On the 27th we nearly had an accident after making a left-hand circuit, keeping a good lookout for other aircraft as we came in to land on the runway. Out of the corner of my eye I saw a Liberator doing a right hand turn with wheels down. Judging it to be just far enough away to allow us to get in first I said nothing until we got down and then told the Group Captain we were being followed in by a Liberator. He accelerated so much that we nearly took off again and we turned off quickly by the control tower. As we did so, a huge Liberator — it looked enormous — rushed by us with engines roaring as it went round again. Later we found out that the correct circuit at this airfield is a right-hand circuit. We didn't make the mistake again!

4th April 1944: The Beales of New Zealand

Last night's attack on Budapest was a good operation confirmed by photographs taken with bombing. Unfortunately four of 205 Group Wellingtons are missing including that flown by Squadron Leader Harry Beale, an old friend of 104 Squadron days in 1942. The Beale family from New Zealand deserve a book to themselves. Harry is a squadron leader and a flight commander in a Wellington Bomber Squadron. Very broad and strong, he can only be described as a wonderful fellow in every way. Arnold is in the New Zealand Infantry — also broad and strong but a little shorter than Harry. The 'little brother' is very tall and slim and in the Long Range Desert Patrol and Commando trained. He is quietly spoken and more reserved than the other two. I met all three brothers in 104 Squadron mess and at Kabrit on various occasions in 1942.

5th April 1944: Cross-Country

As it was a 'stand down', the Padre, the 'Colonel' (Squadron Leader Britton), Gordon and I decided to have a day in the mountains — using the Padre's 15 cwt gharry. In fact we went along the Naples road to Ariano then north through Montecalvo, Montefalcone and San Bartolomeo to Volturara on the Lucera road. It sounds easy but five bridges en route had been blown and we got stuck on numerous occasions until we were rescued by oxen and villagers and finally towed by two army trucks up a steep bank from a river bed. We arrived back in camp too late for a proper meal, tired, dirty and dishevelled after all our strenuous efforts — but thoroughly happy after a day in the fresh air amidst good scenery. The expedition had another side in that it showed us clearly why the land war is proceeding so slowly — the mountainous country is ideal for defence and hazardous for the attacker.

6th April 1944

The Group Captain and I went by truck today to our usual target conference at the new site for Group HQ. It was well laid out with new tents and a white-washed building for Intelligence with walls already decorated with useful maps of various fronts.

In the afternoon I checked on a security problem raised by the G/C and found that the particular Italian was trusted by the squadron adjutant and the chaps living near the place.

At 16.10 hours there were two huge bangs — two delayed action bombs went up causing Gregg and myself to get down smartly — then he went off as Armament Officer to find that it was caused by spontaneous explosion of one delayed action bomb setting off another. The Indian motorcycle has just been returned by Corporal Sandy Holmes of 104 Squadron and the engine ticks over like a steam engine with a gentle chuff chuff from the exhaust. It is absolutely enjoyable to talk cars and bikes with Sandy because he knows so much about them and they respond to him like a human being does to a good doctor.

8th April 1944: Daylight Mission — Niksic

To Group again by bike and this time we were all thrilled and also worried because we had a daylight target — a town, Niksic in Yugoslavia, which was said to be held by the Germans and surrounded by the Partisans. It was a hell of a scramble to brief and get off in time using eleven Wellingtons carrying 4,000 lb bombs. Wing Commander Turner went again, as he always does when any 'op' is apparently risky. Our job was to bomb the German HQ in the centre of the town which had a clearly defined road pattern on the target maps and was therefore easy to identify.

The bombing was well done and the photographs taken with bombing were excellent. All our aircraft returned safely and were not attacked by fighters. At night we had demands for extra prints of the photographs. The night operations were cancelled due to weather.

12th April 1944

Briefing for Budapest.

13th April 1944: Spectacular Crash

The Budapest attack was successful but Squadron Leader Mervyn

Jones went missing on the second 'op' of his second tour. Later we had the excellent news that he and all his crew had been picked up safely from their dinghy after ditching in the Adriatic.

Today we had a very spectacular aircrash right in the camp area. I was sitting on the latrine in the afternoon sunshine when I heard a plane diving and the engine note continuing to rise. Eventually I saw that it was an American Lightning fighter high up which was behaving oddly as though out of control — diving and pulling up and then stalling and falling away towards the earth with both engines apparently flat out. I got up very hastily and went towards my trailer thinking that this aircraft looked dangerous and could come down within our camp. It did! Getting into a vertical dive with smoke trailing from the screaming engines it came down straight at us at about 600 mph and hit the ground with a tremendous crump and a sheet of flame leaping above the crater to about 100 feet.

Tanks and ammunition all went up together and then all that was left was a large fire with black smoke and small explosions from ammunition and Very lights — and a smaller fire some distance away. Something else came whistling and tumbling down on the other side of our mess — a long range tank from the Lightning. I was between the two — the crashed aircraft and its extra tank.

Almost immediately there were sirens blowing and our camp was invaded by half a dozen American jeeps, a fire engine and several motorcycles — all appearing from nowhere. If the pilot had been in the Lightning there would be little left of him, I thought, and wondered if he had managed to get out. Looking up I saw a white dot some thousands of feet above us and later could see the pilot hanging limply from his harness — he had probably been injured or killed by contact with the tailplane in baling out.

17th April 1944: Good Troupers
A day of the usual work was relieved in the evening by a visit to Foggia to see a really good ENSA show — Florence Desmond and her party. Johnny Lockwood, the comedian of the show, started off with some jokes which were near the bone but new to me and quite funny. He warned the Foggia girls 'to look before they jeeped' or they would be 'Yanked into maternity' and the one about the American soldier who insisted on walking into a long railway tunnel because he was sure there were some beautiful women in there. Why? Because the trains go 'Whoo-oop' before entering and at the other end they came out puffing.

I suppose in wartime we are a good audience and easily amused — and certainly appreciate women performers who come out to entertain us. We saw two excellent dancers, a pianist, and then Kay Cavendish of 'Kay on the Keys' who sang and played delightfully. Then Florence did her imitations of Katherine Hepburn, Marlene Dietrich, Frances Day, Evelyn Laye and Cicely Courtneidge.

While she was singing 'Sally' in the Gracie Fields style and everybody was enjoying things, there was an almighty 'woomph' of an explosion which shook the whole theatre and brought down pieces of debris from the roof and lots of dust. Bob Wright, who was with me, and I looked at each other and at our watches — it was take-off time and we knew only too well what it meant. Florence had flinched and run to the back of the stage but encouraged by handclapping and shouts she came back like a good trouper and finished her act. The show ended with the usual enthusiasm and Florence thanked us and said that service shows like this thoroughly spoilt the artists for the audiences were so different from the usual civilian theatre audience.

Going out into the street we could see a red glow and a huge plume of smoke rising over the houses. There was another explosion and all the inhabitants were out at their doorways talking anxiously. My motorcycle was stopped near the aerodrome by MPs who said all traffic was stopped because a 4,000 lb bomb was expected to go up at any minute. I persuaded the police that as an IO my presence was urgently required and was allowed to proceed at my own risk.

Going round the back of the hangars and across the end of the runway I saw that the blaze was halfway along the flarepath. It had been a burst tyre and consequent swing off the runway by 'K King' of 40 Squadron which involved two other Wellingtons waiting for take-off, one 'G for George' with a 4,000 lb bomb. Pilot Officer Payne and his crew in 'K King' (4,500 lb bomb load) managed to get out but four were badly burned. 'K King' and 'G George' with their bombs, petrol tanks, flares, ammunition etc. were destroyed but no other crew members were injured.

Less than half the aircraft detailed for the operation (Plovdiv) got away and this reduced night work in the Intelligence section where I also had the help of Flying Officer Kirkby who is under training as an IO — previously a cipher officer and an old friend of some two year's standing. Later Flying Officer Emery of 'K' crew died from his burns and was buried in the town cemetery which now holds the remains of several crews from each of our squadrons, and other crews from the sister squadrons of the Wellington Group.

20th April 1944
There was another blow-up on the airfield today with the tell-tale fire, explosions and plume of black smoke, but this time it was an American Fortress.

21st April 1944
Delightful surprise on my birthday of a parcel from D. containing books and *Punches* and a heavenly long letter.

Tonight we had two prangs in succession on the runway, both due to burst tyres. Aircraft 'P for Peter' and 'K for King' both of 104 Squadron were damaged and 'K's' starboard engine wouldn't stop and roared on for twenty minutes or so. But neither Wellington caught fire and the crews got out safely, thank goodness. Prangs are getting too plentiful — tonight only three aircraft were airborne as a result.

22nd April 1944
We were given a 'stand down' today to allow repair of the runway damage and some improvements to be made.

27th April 1944
Another day of heavy rain during which I cleared up the 'In Tray', arranged security lectures and dealt with kit left behind by two chaps sent home.

In the evening I played table tennis in the Intelligence tent and managed to beat L.A.C. Clark — just! He used to play No 2 for Oxfordshire. Later I took 100 lire from 'Colonel' at the game. We were both a little 'vinoed' and afterwards played phoning and imitating certain senior officers' voices — good fun but rather dangerous!

30th April 1944: Verbal Reprimand
Squadron Leader A.B. Read, the Group Intelligence Officer, tore a strip from me this morning over the late arrival of our wing signal about last night's operation. Both of us got very huffy — and we are normally good friends. I apologised to him later and he to me, as it was due to a complaint by Group Captain Powell, relayed to Wing Commander Mills, relayed to A.B., amplified en

route at each stage and then passed on to me. Some ass at 15th Air Force HQ had refused to take down an earlier flash report I had passed to Group at 05.45 hours.

2nd May 1944: A Good Target and a Good Party

Today has been very busy but enjoyable with a good target to attack. Group sent a plane to HQ 15th Air Force for new target maps and we sent a despatch rider to MAPRC for copies of recent photographs. All arrived safely in time for briefings and the briefing went very well. I returned to camp on the Indian motorcycle in pleasant evening sunshine with a threat of rainstorms in the distance and thought to myself that everything had gone far too well — the operation would probably be scrubbed. It was, as a report came from Met that cloud had increased at the target.

There was an unusually wild party in the mess at night owing to the scrubbing of the operation and also to the fact that 'Colonel' Britton had at last obtained a supply of the 'Muscato' that some of us prefer to other wines. 'The Colonel' gave me a large glass of wine to start with after we'd played a few games of table tennis in the Intelligence section. The Group Captain was having a bit of a party at the bar and he quickly provided another full glass for me so that by the time we ate my thoughts were slightly but pleasantly affected by the vino. Paul was also a little merry and I laid him a bet of 100 lire, my standard stake, that the invasion would start before June. I will not try to record the happenings *after* dinner.

I noticed that dentist Blackwell took out his teeth and gave them to the barman Corporal Payne who already had my glasses for safe keeping. Somehow I eventually got to the operations trailer and Bob Wright very kindly assisted me to retire to bed.

3rd May 1944

I rose early feeling rather as if I'd been run over by a steam roller, otherwise OK. A cut on my knee and a small tear in my trousers in addition to the wounded hand, are the only visible scars from last night. At breakfast I found that the rest of the mess seemed to have enjoyed the party and no one bears any ill will. Jock Simpson did not appear at breakfast — he had his nose damaged in a game of rugby in the mess after I'd left. They played with a small bomb fin container box used normally as our mail box. Blackwell threw a pass too high for Jock and hit him bang on the nose. It's quite a change for Jock to get hurt, usually he lays others out e.g. the adjutant of 104 Squadron still has cartilage trouble as a result of a wrestle with Jock. A good job that I left the mess last night when I did!

Tonight we briefed for Bucharest but a strong crosswind prevented all but the essential flare droppers from getting off at Foggia Main.

4th May 1944

Last night's bombing was scattered but effective. Tonight we are going to a marshalling yard at another Balkan capital, Budapest. We are visiting all the Balkan capitals these days — Sofia, Bucharest, Budapest, and also dropping mines into the River Danube.

5th May 1944

Last night's bombing was again scattered and this time there was opposition. Aircraft 'E for Edward', 104 Squadron, is missing, Flying Officer Avery (pilot) and Flying Officer Ziegler (navigator), a Czech professor from London University — decent chaps both and a good crew altogether.

Another Wellington, 'M for Mother', Flight Sergeant Wasson (40 Squadron) was attacked by a night fighter and hit in the wing, tail, hydraulics and fuselage — but the crew drove off the enemy aircraft and undeterred went on to drop their 4,000 lb bomb on the target. Tonight we had another interesting target — the second largest oil refinery in Rumania (at Campina northwest of Ploesti) with a capacity of 1¼ million tons a year out of a total of about 9½ million tons of crude oil which can be handled by Rumanian refineries. I did the briefing for Ralph's 40 Squadron tonight as he was moving house. It was enjoyable doing the briefing with so much information to give and I was able to draw a sketch map of the plant and the storage tanks. The crews were keen and interested — this is the sort of target that seems worthwhile.

6th May 1944: Oil Refinery Fires at Campina

Interrogations started at 04.30 hours and there were no lights on at the Intelligence tent so I started work in the light from my truck's headlamps. Ralph turned up late — no one had called him. The lights eventually came on and we interrogated all the crews who reported most excellent results with three large fires burning among the storage tanks. Two Wellingtons were attacked by night fighters without crew members being hurt, but 'R for Robert'

(Flight Sergeant Royle) is missing and an aircraft was seen shot down over the target. I returned to Wing to complete the Opsum and was then warned by phone of a special briefing at 10.30 hours. There was barely time to shave before going to this briefing which was given by Bob Pountney still in his pyjamas but suitably covered! The other aircraft of the squadrons were given a different target — Bucharest. I dashed off to Group to get the details and returned later to brief both squadron commanders.

Next the special target was cancelled and two bridges were substituted.

I spent the afternoon preparing the main briefing (for Bucharest) and gave this for 104 Squadron. When I came back to Wing for dinner the 'special' map arrived and I rushed off to deliver it to Wing Commander Turner who is going after one of the two bridge targets (Siliasi). Today's work has occupied 16½ hours and I'm on duty again tonight for interrogation and Opsum as usual.

7th May 1944: Bridge Difficulties

It was another hectic day here starting with Wing Commander Harold Turner and his bridge. Harold spent an hour at 600 to 1,000 feet searching valleys for the Filiasi bridge which he eventually found and after careful dummy runs proceeded to bomb. The 4,000 lb bomb was placed dead on the bridge but failed to explode after all their searching and preliminary work. Harold went up to 2,000 feet to take photographs and brought back two good ones which will be used for target maps for tonight's repeat performance. The second bridge was not located but the crew bombed another unimportant bridge. They missed the bridge but, of course, their bomb went off OK.

The bombing at Bucharest was scattered but useful. Two Wellingtons 'Q for Queenie' (Flight Sergeant Martin) and 'O for Orange' (Warrant Officer Coape-Smith) were missing after this operation. Night fighters were active and presumably got our two crews.

This afternoon I did the briefing on Bucharest again for my old Squadron 104 and being the third briefing running I felt more at ease. On the two previous occasions I felt quite nervous and out of practice.

I asked Harold Turner, the Wing Commander, to take me with him as witness of his bridge busting — he's going again tonight. He wouldn't play as he has already stood down the captain of the aircraft he is taking — but he agreed to take me next trip. It's time I

did another operation. It definitely does have beneficial results in
the effect on relations between an IO and the aircrews. These
chaps in the squadron now are all new and don't know that I've
ever flown in an aircraft let alone been on a few operations. The
trouble is, too, that the fewer risks one takes, the less inclination
there is to take any risk.

8th May 1944: Night Fighters
The operation on Bucharest was a good one but we suffered pretty
heavy losses. Flight Lieutenant Williams DFC (Willie of the school-
girl complexion and many party songs) and Flying Officer Douglas
Calvert — another very nice chap — are missing in 'X for X-Ray' of
40 Squadron — Flight Sergeant Creasey and crew of 104 are
missing — and there were many combats reported and six aircraft
seen to go down.

The night fighter opposition has increased significantly in the
raids on long distance Balkan targets and is now the most serious
we have ever encountered. One of our crews reported seeing a
Halifax with one engine on fire being chased by two fighters. The
Halifax blew up in mid-air. Also missing last night, and on what
must have been nearly their last operation of this tour, was
Warrant Officer Bradshaw, the Canadian, and his crew in 'T for
Tommy' of 40 Squadron, who were attacking one of the bridge
targets. This is the crew who iced up over Foggia in February and
had to bale out before Bradshaw managed to bring the aircraft
down safely on his own. They are a first class crew, known as
experienced and excellent flare droppers, and keen and competent
in everything they do. One can only imagine that in going low to
make sure of the bridge they were hit by light flak or affected by
the blast of their bomb.

Wing Commander Turner and his crew got their bomb to burst
near the Filiasi bridge they were attacking for the second time but
the photograph shows no apparent damage to the structure. He
should have taken me with him for luck!

The weather outlook for tonight was bad, and in consequence
we had a 'stand down'. We made use of this by exploring the Man-
fredonia area for a good bathing spot. The 'Colonel', Doc and I
found a beautiful little pebbly cove with beach and caves overlooked by a 100 foot cliff, and spent a happy time sunbathing and
having the first swim of the year. It was pretty cold so the swim
was brief.

9th May 1944
It was a busy day with two operations — one called Joyride involved supply dropping for the Partisans in Yugoslavia while the other target for the main force was at Genoa.

10th May 1944
Genoa was reasonably successful with all our aircraft returning safely. Joyride was a washout due to terrible weather in the target area with cloud down to 2,000 feet with severe icing and electrical storms. Squadron Leader Richards of 104 Squadron had static electricity build up and explode in his aircraft causing minor damage — the electrical phenomena burned fabric off the wing tips. Flying Officer Johnny Huggler — a grand chap and on his last operation of this tour — is missing with the crew of 'H for Harry' (40 Squadron). A fire was seen among the mountains and it looks as if he bought it among the hills trying to get beneath the cloud — or perhaps he got iced up. Two other aircraft which got to the area reported seeing rifle fire on the ground.

Tonight's briefing was for Budapest.

11th May 1944: Army Offensive
All aircraft got back safely from Budapest. On the night of 11th/ 12th the Army started a new offensive heralded by what is said to be the heaviest artillery barrage yet seen in Italy and to include three times the number of guns used at Alamein. If so, that's quite a barrage!

Battle area support by our aircraft was ordered for tonight and there was news of the air war being stepped-up.

12th May 1944
'V for Victor' (40) Pilot Officer Cleeve was missing from last night's operation and is believed to have gone down off Lesina as a glow was seen and a red Very light. A search found no trace. One theory is that 'V' was shot down by an intruder.

Battle area targets are again on for us tonight.

Today I had a thorough medical examination by the Doc who is required under AMO 377 to supply a medical certificate that I am fit to go on operational flights. He passed me A3B — aircrew standard, and said I am a first class life for insurance purposes — all very nice to know.

13th May 1944
This morning I was shocked to hear that Wing Commander Turner was missing in 'B for Beer' of 104. Happily in this case, and to the vast relief of everyone because Harold is such a wizard type, he had managed to make a crash landing near Naples and tonight he is back with the squadron having suffered nothing worse than cuts. All the crew are safe – but 'F for Freddie' (Flying Officer Gooch) is missing and there is no news of this jolly nice crew whom I know well. We are having a bad period for losses in the squadrons at the present. [Flying Officer Gooch and crew later turned up safely.]

14th May 1944
The 13th/14th was the fifth night running of work without extra sleep to compensate but there is some hope of a break in the workload soon because I've been selected for an Intelligence course in Cairo.

19th May 1944
Bob Pountney celebrated his flying officer rank by inviting Ralph Dunning and me to 104 Squadron for dinner.

20th May 1944
'Stand down'. I played L.A.C. Clark at table tennis in Intelligence and found him much too good. He won 3 games to 0.

21st to 29th May 1944
A series of nightly operations followed by a 'stand down' on the 29th.

30th May 1944: Wellington Accident
Flying Officer R.L.W. Cheek DSO was killed this afternoon in a Wellington crash near Group. Apparently he was low flying and pulled up quickly to about 1,000 feet where possibly an engine cut out because the aircraft stalled and dropped like a stone. Nothing was left of the Wellington which was a 57 RSU machine being air tested with the Engineer Officer of 57 on board and two corporals from the Group mess. This sad accident cost four lives including that of one of 205 Group's most daring and brilliant bomber pilots. Flying Officer Dick Cheek did some 43 operations with 40 Squadron between 9th June and 13th November 1943. He received the award of DSO on 31st October after a series of

accurate bombing attacks frequently followed by low level machine gunning of targets such as enemy aircraft in dispersals.

31st May 1944: Medical Board at Naples
In spite of Squadron Leader Gimson's thorough medical test on 12th May I have been ordered to Naples to undergo a Medical Board inspection before being granted official permission to go on further operational flights. Today I had an excellent trip to Naples in Wellington 'J for Johnny' of 40 Squadron, through the courtesy of Flying Officer Long who is training crews in the use of navigational aids.

We made a good take-off and set off SW over Troia a hill top village I've visited on the motorcycle. Benevento looked smaller than I expected and as the Calore River disappeared we came over the Naples plain and saw the huge mass of Vesuvius with its grey sloping crater lips. The eruption is over. We made a good landing at Capodichino, thanked the crew, and Flight Lieutenant King and I set off to find transport into the city. Wing Commander Le Grand of MAAF Plans — formerly SIO of 236 Wing, gave us a lift to the transit hotel. After high tea and a walk along the front we had a quick bath and change before going to the flicks, *The Road to Morocco*, with Bob Hope, Dorothy Lamour and Bing Crosby — very suited to our frame of mind.

1st June 1944
Today I went out to Portici to go before a Medical Board of four doctors — eye specialist, ear nose and throat, heart lungs etc., and the President of the Board. It was a thorough examination and I was very interested and noted carefully what was tested and the results where I could find out what these were.

The tests confirmed exactly what Squadron Leader Gimson had found in his earlier examination. I was passed A3B and told I was very fit and up to aircrew standard. A certificate was issued to me stating that I was fit for combatant passenger duties.

I hitched back to Capodichino aerodrome and met Flight Lieutenant King again and we were then treated most generously by Wing Commander Bodman DFC, the Canadian CO of the Communication Squadron and a friend of mine from the days when he was on operations with us as a flight commander of 40 Squadron. He agreed to fly us back to Foggia in a Cessna Crane — a small four-seater twin-engined aircraft. We were given parachutes of seat pattern and the Wing Commander himself took-off and climbed to 4,000–5,000 feet before setting course for Benevento and Foggia. After Benevento I was allowed to fly the Cessna and told not to get us lost! The Wing Commander told me that I was sitting in the seat of the famous for two days ago General Alexander had sat in my seat and was flown up to the battle front at 50 feet by one of the Communication Squadron flight commanders. The General, too, had taken over the controls for part of the trip. The Cessna was beautiful to fly — very light and responsive on the controls. Coming down after the mountains the speed got up to over 140 mph and Wing Commander Bodman laughed and pulled my leg that this would blow the wings back. He then took over and made a perfect approach and landing. We couldn't thank him enough for his kindness and it was a delightful ending to a very pleasant break from the routines of duty.

2nd to 8th June 1944: Tiber Bridge Target

It has been back to work with a vengeance and operations on each night. The most interesting mission was on the night of 3rd/4th June when we were suddenly switched to a new target as our Wellingtons were about to start up engines for take-off. The crews were called back to the briefing rooms and given a tactical target

a bridge over the River Tiber between Ostia and Rome. The object of the raid was to break this bridge and cut off part of an enemy force trapped south and south-west of Rome. The Wellingtons duly attacked and severely damaged the bridge and its approaches, rendering it impassable. *And Rome was captured on the 4th June!*

We received a message of congratulation from General Twining, the Commander of 15th Air Force on a fine piece of work — also a message from the General Commanding Tactical Air Force — and a message from our own Air Officer Commanding 205 Group. It really was a splendid effort by all concerned. Our crews love something exciting and different and this Tiber Bridge provided such a target.

The war news is exciting — our boys are in Rome and British, Canadian and American troops landed in Normandy (D-Day) 6th June 1944.

9th June 1944: Hang-Up

At 04.40 hrs as I was cleaning my teeth outside my tent in the pale dawn light before dashing over to interrogation, a Wellington came in to make a good landing — then suddenly blew up with a

tremendous crack and bang followed immediately by leaping
fire and the horrible crackling noises so typical of a 'prang'.

Obviously a hang-up had dropped off and exploded underneath
the tail and I couldn't see how anybody could get out of the
inferno which developed quickly and shot off Very lights and
dazzling white lights as some flares ignited.

I learned shortly afterwards that it was 'Z for Zebra' (104
Squadron) piloted by Flight Sergeant Bailey, and that he and the
bomb aimer were OK though suffering from shock. The navigator
had a leg blown off and died later in hospital and the wireless
operator was very seriously injured and was operated upon later in
the day. The bomb had burst under the rear turret and blown this
and the rear gunner to pieces. The aircraft carried on for a
hundred yards or so under its momentum and without its tail wing
but the fin ended up amongst the wreckage as though the fuselage
had folded like a concertina.

11th June 1944

The Intelligence course at HQME has become a fact and today I
visited RAF Movements Foggia and the Air Transport Command
office at Foggia Main to arrange an air passage to Cairo.

13th June 1944: Intelligence Course at Cairo – ending 8th July

The course at HQ RAF Middle East included lectures on the
German Air Force, Bulgaria and Rumania, a visit to Alexandria to
observe Coastal Air Force AHQ Eastern Med. and the Anti-Aircraft
and Searchlight units using new techniques against attacking
aircraft from the Palestine Operational Training Units – and a visit
to Palestine to see the training units in operation at Qastina and
Aqir. During the course I was asked whether I would be interested
in a coming vacancy for a squadron leader post in Intelligence at
Qastina No 77 OTU in Palestine – to take charge of the training
programme in Intelligence at that unit as an experienced SIO
coming direct from an operational wing in Italy.

I thought a great deal about this offer before making a decision.
It means leaving the wing and squadrons with whom I've been
happy for two and a half years. However, I'm beginning to feel
that I've gone past my best as an operational intelligence officer
and am increasingly aware of losing many of my squadron friends
due to enemy action and aircraft accidents. The new post would
give me a lighter loading of work and new challenges as an
educationist to find the best lecturing techniques and aids to

teaching while making some use of my long experience in the bombing squadrons. At Qastina I would be working under my former commanding officer at Kabrit and in Malta, Group Captain J.A.P. Harrison DFC, and with some of my old friends from the squadrons who are now flying instructors at the OTU.

I'll accept the post if it is offered.

6th July 1944: Air Battle over Feuersbrunn, Austria
The operation on Freuersbrunn airfield while I was in Cairo was a major air battle. Our bombers destroyed 19 aircraft on the ground including 17 Me109s and the force of some 50 enemy aircraft was prevented from attacking the American daylight formations operating on the following day against oil installations in Germany. The operation earned a strong commendation from General Twining of 15th Air Force. Unhappily 104 Squadron lost 'B for Bertie' (Flight Sergeant MacDonald) with Flight Lieutenant Cruden as navigator. Cruden, a quiet good-tempered giant of a man, was very well liked in the mess.

Feuersbrunn was a costly success for 205 Group. We lost 13 bombers out of 61 aircraft attacking the airfield — 10 Wellingtons, 2 Liberators and 1 Halifax. Night fighters were active and many bombers were involved in combat. One Ju88 was claimed shot down by a 37 Squadron Wellington.

12th July 1944
We operated tonight from Foggia Main sodden with recent heavy rains. Only six aircraft got off and the others were bogged.

14th July 1944
An old friend of mine, 'Judy' Garland, now of 142 Squadron, was missing from last night's operation to Brescia and one Wellington of 104 Squadron was also missing.

17th July 1944: Take-off Tragedy
Tonight's target was oil storages, shipping and port facilities at Fiume. I asked to go with Johnny Johnson but permission was refused. I did the briefing which went reasonably well because the target was interesting and the crews could see that the attack could be valuable to the war effort in preventing or hampering delivery of fuel and other supplies to the German Army in Italy.

At the last minute when the Wellingtons were almost ready to start up their engines some new information was received and I went around the aircraft on my motorcycle to each crew in turn, checking that they understood the change and pointing this out on the target map. I chatted cheerfully with Warrant Officer Gerty and his crew underneath the dark shape of 'D for Donald' knowing them as an experienced and sound crew; and they knew me because I've been Wing Intelligence Officer throughout their period of some months with 104 Squadron and I've often done the briefing and/or their interrogation after a mission. With a wave to them I went on the next crew — and so on until I had completed the round of the airfield.

Shortly afterwards I stood at the entrance to my tent in the dusk and watched the take-off — feeling particularly interested because I had tried to go on the 'op' myself. Wellingtons taxied in line along the paths leading to the Chance Light and as they received the green light from control they opened up their two Hercules engines into a smooth deep roar and gathered speed down the flarepath and slowly rose and disappeared in the distance. Things appeared to go normally until a sudden terrific flash lit up the sky to the north followed by Very lights, and firework effects amidst a huge cloud of smoke mushrooming upwards. A few seconds later the crack of the explosion reached us showing that the crash was not far away. I learned that it was 'D for Donald'. Sparks had been seen coming from one engine at take-off and then almost immediately the Wellington ploughed in and blew up with its 4,000 lb bomb exploding on contact.

The tragedy somehow confirmed me in my desire to leave the Wing. These losses have become too personal to me — and you can't wage war efficiently if losses are taken in this way.

21st July 1944
Wellington 'M for Mother' (104 Squadron) on its return from an operation over Yugoslavia reported an unusual experience. Both engines cut out over Yugoslavia and the captain gave the order 'prepare to bale out'. The engines subsequently picked up and the aircraft was brought back safely to base but the rear gunner was missing from his turret.

22nd July 1944: Posting to HQ RAF ME
The Wing Adjutant informed me that my posting to Middle East for Intelligence duties has been received.

24th July 1944: Farewell Party
This was my last night in 236 Wing mess and I had a party to

which came Group Captain Paul Harris and Wing Commander Harold Turner, Squadron Leader A.B. Read, Flight Lieutenant Davies, Flying Officer Rhodes, Flying Officer Bob Pountney and Flying Officer Ralph Dunning among others. A very good time was had by all but Ralph was ill this time and Pilot Officer Wood subsequently broke up a tent at the squadron and threw things at Jock Brody! (Jock, our ex-CID policeman, is a very hefty chap.) Johnny Johnson and Flying Officer Murphy came from the squadron and Johnny later took us up to the squadron mess for a drink and a snack which he produced from nowhere. It was a sadly happy occasion and I could hardly take in the implications — nor did I want to.

25th July 1944
I was up early and surprisingly none the worse for last night's party, thank goodness. With Flight Lieutenant King, Flying Officer Gooch and Flight Lieutenant Davidson, I left by road for Bari, myself en route for Cairo and HQ RAF ME for posting to new Intelligence duties.

*

Number 236 Wing and its Squadrons 40 and 104 continued to operate from Foggia until the end of the war. Group Captain P.I. Harris DFC remained as Commanding Officer until 4th August 1945 when he returned to England on the expiration of his overseas tour. Early in 1945 the squadrons were re-equipped with Liberator bombers instead of the familiar Wellingtons. On 14th February 1945 104 Squadron did their first operation with Liberators. Their last operation of the war was 25th/26th April to bomb marshalling yards at Freilassing near Salzburg.

CHAPTER TEN

Epilogue

The epilogue is mainly a summary of opinions, ideas and 'theories' about some particular aspects of the air war. These are based on war experience and discussion with fellow officers who served in 205 Group together with some reading and research among documents and war histories.

Aircrews

These young men came from all walks of life and from all strata of society and some were straight from school. In those who completed their first tour of operations an unusual maturity had developed, one that perhaps no other form of experience in life could have produced. By their training, operational experiences, sense of duty and responsibility to their fellow crewmen, they learned to act calmly and to overcome fear in times of danger. (Some aircrew personnel have stated that their minds became 'conditioned' to accept the risks and catastrophes of war, almost as normal occurrences.) Perceptibly they changed into men older than their years and for many this was the only maturity that fate allowed them.

The isolated tented camps of the 205 Group squadrons encouraged a renewal of the ancient art of conversation. Language was colourful, technical and typical of the RAF and Allied air forces. Aircrews would raise all kinds of subjects and speak in a language of their own — of erks, flighties, wingcos, groupies, ground loops, goons, gongs, prangs, dicy dos, shaky dos, sprogs, vegetables, gardening, heavies, cookies, roddies, fans, flaps, kites, jinking, belt ups, beat ups, and shoot ups, of 'going for a Burton', 'getting the chop' and 'buying it', of 'binding bastards' and 'gabardine swine', and of the ubiquitous gremlins, the mysterious, mischievous spirits born in 'Fremlin' beer bottles. These poltergeists of the RAF were blamed for putting u/s (unserviceable) for no apparent reason, guns, turrets, radio equipment, and every form of aircraft paraphernalia.

Operational tactics, operational experiences, the odds relating to their chances of survival and occasionally their thoughts and expectations about their return to 'civvy street', were frequent topics.

Graphic descriptions of operational experiences over heavily defended targets often emerged, told with an air of nonchalance, without dramatics and with the view that they were only to be expected, although some 'ops' were relatively smooth. Fortunately, no one knew what might lie ahead, as they told of their past moments of tension and relief. Their philosophizing was of a special brand — amusing and interesting. Some wag would always intervene if things got too serious. 'Belt up, you blokes, what did you join up for?' The rejoinder would be 'to hurl back the Hun, of course!' and 'to strike a blow for liberty!' 'Well, that's fine as long as we all get the Victory Medal.'

Despite the 'dicy dos' and 'shaky dos' aircrew were not in general a pessimistic lot. A period of intensive operations such as that during the Army retreat to the Alamein Line could increase normal anxieties and strain. However all had hopes of eventually returning to civilian life, and it was doubtful if many of them went on an 'op' with the thought that this would be 'it'. There was safety in numbers, they thought, and despite the high percentage of losses during the time it would take them to get through a tour, each 'op' had to be treated separately so far as the rate of losses was concerned. One 'op' completed meant one less to do. They believed that there was no way of determining the chances of survival by mathematical calculation — the law of averages did not apply in this kind of business.

There were certain points unanimously accepted. To have a chance, every member of the crew had to be efficient and vigilant, and of course, an element of luck was essential. Both the highly experienced and the less-experienced crews went missing — there was no discrimination so far as a well directed burst of flak was concerned — *that* was a matter of luck!

Not all aircrew showed signs of superstition but some did. One was meticulously careful about making up his bed before he took off, others wore good luck symbols. Some of the more fatalistic would argue that if a bullet had your name on it you had had your chips anyway, but the more logical ones would counter this by saying that there was no point in taking evasive action if such were the case, and every pilot did this without exception.

Desert conditions made for a homogeneous way of squadron life and a good deal of fraternisation took place amongst all ranks.

In particular, a great deal of goodwill and breezy camaraderie existed between the aircrews and the maintenance crews whose efforts were nothing short of prodigious when note was taken of the conditions with which they had to contend. Armourers, refuellers, riggers, radio technicians and the general maintenance teams were constantly on the go and sometimes involved in dangerous tasks — defusing unexploded bombs, fire fighting blazing Wellingtons and repairing airstrips in between enemy bombing attacks.

Great pride and interest was taken in the operational performances and results achieved by the aircraft they maintained, and a lot of light hearted banter was directed at aircrews if an 'op' had not been completely successful.

In response the aircrews did everything possible to make the lives of the airmen more interesting — they would be taken up on air tests, allowed to handle the control column and given lifts when going on leave.

The humour and back chat of these aircraft maintenance boys was remarkable. Many of them had creative ability in the entertainment side of life — rollicking songs and amusing recitations about war time conditions and types came out in a constant flow when they 'got together'.

Aircrews and the Targets
The men who crowded into the briefing room or tent were trained to accept orders from higher up the chain of command. It was not their place to question the target but to operate against it. If anyone didn't like the target he cursed 205 Group who had passed on the target but probably in most cases had not originally chosen it. We might curse also HQ RAF ME or the 15th Air Force but no one argued about the target — it was now *our* target, to deal with as best we could.

The squadrons and wings were the delivery end of the chain of command and decision. From our tents the long trains of trolleys could be seen with bombs being loaded into the bays of the deep-bellied Wellingtons. It was our job to deliver the bombs as accurately as target information, aircraft equipment and crew training allowed us to do.

Sometimes the targets did not appear worthwhile or they seemed so well-defended or distant that the effort might bring greater losses to the squadrons than material damage inflicted on the enemy. Crews preferred an interesting or unusual target such

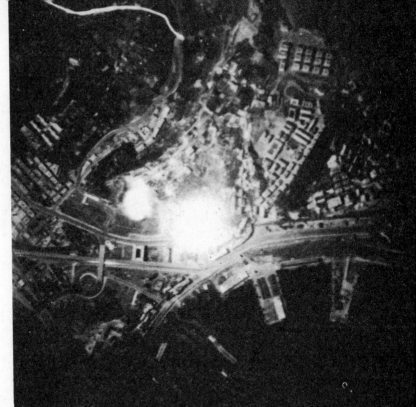

illuminating an attack
noa Docks, May 1944

attack on Feuersbrunn,
1944.
craft were destroyed on
ground and enemy
rs were prevented from
ing American daylight
tions

205 GROUP ROYAL AIR FORCE

PALERMO · PANTELLARIA · SYRACUSE · MESSINA · SALERNO · ANZIO · VITERBO · GUILIANOVA · VERONA · TURIN · PISA · LEGHORN · TRIESTE · MILAN · SOFIA · BUDAPEST · STEYR · VALENCE · MUNICH · FIUME · BUCHAREST · PLOESTI · DANUBE

ALBANIA · JUGOSLAVIA · BULGARIA · SYRIA · IRAQ · RHODES · CRETE · PIRAEUS · CORINTH · LEROS · DABA · CAPUZZO · FUKA · HALFAYA · EL ADEM · MARTUBA · TOBRUK · BENGHAZI · TRIPOLI · MARETH · GABES · CAPE BON · TUNIS

GERMANY · AUSTRIA · HUNGARY · POLAND

FRANCE

RUMANIA · BULGARIA

TURKEY

YUGOSZAVIA · ALBANIA · GREECE · CRETE

SYRIA · CYPRUS · PALESTINE · EGYPT

ITALY · SICILY · PANTELLARIA · MALTA · CORSICA · SARDINIA

WESTERN DESERT

MEDITERRANEAN

TRIPOLITANIA · TUNISIA · ALGERIA

In the 1939 – 1945 World War, 205 Group provided the only mobile force of heavy night bombers in the Mediterranean theatre. During the North African and Italian campaigns the Wellingtons, Halifaxes and Liberators of the Group, operating as a tactical force, attacked communications and concentrations of Rommel's Afrika Korps and of the Italian armies during their advance to the Quattara Depression, the Battle of El Alamein and during their retreat until their final capitulation in Tunisia. Without respite they operated against Kesselring's army during the invasions of Sicily, Italy and the South of France. As a strategical force their targets – ports, airfields, marshalling yards, oil refineries and factories – ranged over the Mediterranean area and Europe. Aid was given to patriots in France, supplies and arms were dropped to Partisans in the Balkans and to the patriots in Warsaw. The Danube was mined persistently.

Shining courage is the epitaph of those who died.
We will remember them.

JUNE 1940   MAY 1945

as a bridge, an aircraft factory, an airfield with many aircraft known to be dispersed around its perimeter, an oil refinery which would produce large fires or a marshalling yard with photographic evidence of likely ammunition trains and other war supplies, or a section of the battle area where we knew our bombs would affect the enemy directly as they crouched near their parked transport, guns and tanks. The bomber crews were naturally not so keen on a heavily defended harbour target like Benghazi or Tobruk or Sousse where many bombs fell into the water and ships were hard to see and to hit. However, the crews could see the strategic sense of bombing ports to restrict enemy supplies. No one liked bombing roads in built-up areas or the centres of towns said by those who set the targets to be essential to delay the enemy withdrawal through these urban areas. We knew that many towns possessed ring roads which avoided the town centres so that damage in the town did not necessarily disrupt enemy transport or tank withdrawal.

It was the job of the squadron commander and the intelligence officer at briefing to show that a target was worthwhile and that our attack was essential or at the least a valuable contribution to the war effort. An IO who felt involved with the crews was unhappy in conscience if he had to brief on a target for which the information available was insufficient to give clear justification for the attack.

Much depended upon how the briefing was done and upon the relationship between the squadron commander and his briefing team of various specialist officers on the one hand, and the 'audience' of captains and crews on the other. Officers doing the briefing for a bombing mission looked into the eyes of men who were about to risk their lives to undertake the task which was being outlined to them. No one could be insensitive to the drama and vital importance of the occasion.

Aircrews and the Effects of a Tour of Bombing Operations
War situations brought constant competition between training and the immediate fears induced by contact with the enemy. Aircrew training emphasized that efficiency in attending to the technical details of flying and safety was the sound way to preserve the aircraft and crew from the dangers of the environment and the enemy. 'P/O Prune', the beginner pilot who made all the silly mistakes, was lampooned in the training manuals and posters. The inference was that 'Prune' deserved to be shot down or to

crash, but that efficient pilots and crews would escape or not even get into difficulties. One tended to accept this viewpoint because it was a positive approach and encouraged crews to become efficient. In actual fact it was clear that there was a good deal of luck in survival and that even the finest crews were sometimes shot down or lost through no fault of their own.

The Empire Air Training Scheme was a fine concept because it brought together some of the best, carefully selected, intelligent young men from each of the Allied nations and from a variety of home backgrounds — and they learned to like and respect each other. Mixed crews were usually happy crews and devoted to each other so that no one would think of letting down his crew or his own nation by showing cowardice over a target. What would an 'Aussie' say if a 'Pommy' showed he was frightened or vice versa? Could the ex-public school boy show his frailty to the miner's son or vice versa? Or could the new crew on their first 'op' with their wing commander as captain of the aircraft do anything but perform according to training and the textbook? Even the IO had to behave according to the book rather than show his inward fears when flying with a squadron crew on an operational flight or being taken on an air test flight by a young pilot eager to show-off his flying skills. There must have been nervous people among the aircrews but they bravely managed to conceal it.

Did anyone break down under the strain? Some of the accidents with crew members jumping out of aircraft that seemed likely to crash were clearly cases of nerves strained to breaking point. A few baled out thinking that their aircraft was going down but it was brought back safely. It seems that under strain they misinterpreted warnings as orders to bale out or anticipated such orders.

Very occasionally a crew jettisoned their bombs for insufficient reason and returned to base instead of attacking a target. There were some cases of crews who bombed outside the flak at Tobruk rather than go over the target. It was not possible immediately to identify such a crew unless a crew member talked out at interrogation or in private to intelligence officers or their flight commander. However, if such off-target attacks were continued it was likely to be detected or suspected because of the lack of photographs of the target normally taken with bombing.

The RAF referred to such rare cases as LMF, i.e. they were said to be 'lacking in moral fibre', but when they could be identified, the commanding officers were anxious to help them by sending them on extra leave to recover or sometimes by taking them off operations before the tour had been completed and posting them to administrative posts or for retraining into some duty other than flying. We had no official LMF cases during my period of duty with the squadrons, but at one time I was very worried when I had some hints from crew members and one accusation from a young pilot that a senior pilot of one squadron was 'yellow' and did not press home attacks on given targets. The man was a kindly, friendly, gentlemanly and altogether delightful chap in the mess and a good pilot. I was never able to fly with him to test the accusations and never revealed the matter to the wing commander of the squadron. It was my fervent hope that it was uncharacteristic and if true was the result of the strains of duty. There were no good photographs of targets from him but he was granted a long period of sick leave when he left operations which was evidence of the severe strain under which he had operated during his second tour.

Periods of intense operations, often involving double and even triple sorties on battle area targets during army crises which demanded all out support from the RAF, occurred in 1942 and 1943 in North Africa and in Italy in 1944. At times like these aircrews were working close to the limits of human endurance and physical signs appeared of the very severe nervous strains and tensions. As indicated in the diaries the characteristic signs were — twitches of the facial and eye muscles and occasionally jerky movements of an arm or shoulder, inability to sleep, over-indulgence in alcohol or smoking, greying or whitening of the hair, attachment to mascots and other eccentricities of behaviour. We tended to refer to severe cases as 'going round the bend', getting 'bomb happy', or becoming 'op tired', and the wing commander would sometimes discuss particular cases with intelligence officers and the Doc, in order to take measures to stave off a man's breakdown in health through severe operational strain. Most of our commanding officers when dealing with cases of overstrain were essentially humane and considerate. Sympathetic handling of the problem sometimes led to excellent results and successful completion of operational tours.

Occasionally a problem arose among the members of a bombing crew if they were not all in full agreement with the captain's method of attack. For instance, some of our more daring young pilots after having bombed the target liked to dive down low to machine-gun aircraft parked around the perimeter of an enemy airfield. This method of attack was often successful in setting fire to parked planes and a crew would come into interrogation beaming and laughing from the fun of delivering such an attack. However, there were other cases where some crew members would voice their unhappiness in being forced to take part in such activities which they thought were unnecessarily risky and crazy. There was one case where a wireless operator was permitted to leave one crew and join another as he didn't agree with some of the methods of attack by the first crew.

Attacks on bridges were often performed at low altitudes to make sure of accuracy but these were planned attacks authorized by the Commanding Officer and not therefore the cause of any crew disagreement.

Aircrew Survival

Aircrews on their second or third tour of operations were easy to pick out in the squadrons by their rank, decorations and maturity. New crews looked up to them and so did Intelligence Officers for we could depend more upon their opinions of the success or failure of attacks. Those officers who survived for a third tour were then usually wing commanders of squadrons, or flight commanders or navigation or signals or gunnery officers — and former sergeant aircrew members became flight sergeants, warrant officers or were newly commissioned officers.

The overall survival rate in 205 Group was probably higher than in Bomber Command but reliable statistics are not available to me. I once took careful note of what happened to 25 crews of 104 Squadron in 1943 from start to finish of their operational tour of some 30 to 40 operations. 18 crews survived to be rested, while 7 crews, or 28% of this particular intake, were lost in a period of some three to four months. However, this quarter of 1943 was one of relatively *low* operational losses and it seems more typical that between one-third and one-half of Wellington crews in 205 Group were killed or went missing during their first tour.

A congratulatory message to 205 Group squadrons dated 25th August 1943 from General James Doolittle USAAF, Commander of the Northwest African Strategic Air Force, referred to 3020 sorties by the Wellingtons between 1st July and the fall of Sicily on 17th August. The average operations of 205 Group were given as 62 sorties per night and the percentage losses per sortie as 1.71%.

Accidents took not infrequent toll of aircraft and crews while weather conditions were an occasional hazard, e.g., causing the heavy losses on the Turin operation of November 24/25, 1943. In 1944 on long distance targets in the Balkans, enemy night fighters caused regular and worrying losses to the attacking bombers.

In the face of the *probability* of their own deaths in action if the war were prolonged, the aircrews of the Wellington squadrons stood up remarkably cheerfully under the strains of their hazardous occupation and showed that courage and training can conquer fear.

Post war examples suggest that some aircrew members who reacted bravely to the horrors of war, have suffered breakdowns in mental health in later years.

Ground Personnel and the Effects of War Service

Because the administrative and maintenance staffs were not engaged directly in flying operations the tensions of war service were much lighter than for the aircrews. In 1942 RAF units in the Western Desert and the Canal Stations were subjected to many bombing attacks by enemy aircraft. After 1942 such bombing attacks were rare and in Italy we were possibly safer than the civilians in Kent and London who in 1944 and 1945 suffered severely from the VI pilotless flying bombs and V2 rockets.

In general then, apart from the real hazards of handling and living close to explosives and the accidents always associated with aircraft and war, ground personnel survived with nothing more serious than the tensions and worries resulting from very long periods without their families and friends. The overseas tour for ground personnel was three years and this was frequently exceeded.

Intelligence officers with operational night bombing squadrons were subjected to unusual strains because of periods of intense activity with little sleep. Some officers suffered nervous breakdowns and others would readily admit to having felt thoroughly worn out from the pace of life and the long contact with the tragedies and strains of squadron life.

Leadership and the Operational Efficiency of the Squadrons

During the period of operational service as IO with 104 Squadron (under 236 and 238 Wings) and as SIO of 236 Wing, it was my privilege to serve under seven wing commanders of the squadron and six group captains commanding 236 or 238 Wings. In addition, if the partnering squadrons working for a time with 104 Squadron

are included, there were close associations with three wing commanders of 40 Squadron, two wing commanders of 148 Squadron,
one wing commander of 462 Squadron and one of 108 Squadron.
By the nature of the job intelligence officers were constantly
exchanging information with the commanding officers of the
squadrons or wings and meeting with them in the mess and on
social occasions.

In the Royal Air Force as I knew it, the Lord Acton dictum
that all power corrupts and absolute power corrupts absolutely,
didn't seem to be true. It may apply more to politicians and
leaders in business and commerce in times of peace than to service
leaders in war time. Among these men of courage and quality I
thought I could recognise two types of leadership. Type 1 would
let everyone know what was expected of them and make frequent
efforts to check that his orders were being carried out. He would
be authoritarian in dealing with aircrews and intelligence officers
and eager to raise efficiency through further training and exercises.
He might be a little aloof and reserved in the Mess and briefings
would be formal with emphasis on efficiency in time and heading
over the target and getting into the target area without any
excuses. The emphasis was based on the theory that training and
efficiency produce the best results in operations. The CO would
go on the worst targets and showed clearly that he would not
expect the crews to go anywhere unless he himself was prepared
to share the dangers. There might be some tendency to under-
state or brush aside enemy opposition but he would be prepared
to acknowledge and praise good efforts in bombing. If he thought
it would be useful he could occasionally use the lash of his tongue
to condemn some slackness and spur on the crews to new efforts.
The general impression was one of tight control of the air operations,
the crews and the ground personnel by the commanding officer.

Type 2 would somehow be able to inspire the impression that
this was a group of friends (or Nelson's band of brothers?) and he
would lead the squadron by quiet example. He would be inclined
to work through his flight commanders. He liked to discuss targets
and tactics and ideas in general with his flight commanders, technical officers and intelligence officers. He would listen to com-
plaints and deal firmly but pleasantly with offenders. He would be
willing to take the IO on operational missions and take care to put
himself on targets he regarded as difficult and requiring his presence
and example. He would be warm and friendly in the mess and able
to relax happily at 'stand downs' and drink with his aircrews and

ground officers. He would show a sense of humour and interest in all that was going on in the squadron and in the world outside. The general impression was one of humanity and warmth spreading from the leader throughout the squadron and linking air and ground staff to the common duty of working together for the war effort.

These are stereotypes and individual commanding officers would be seen somewhere along the line in between these two types. It is an interesting fact that one would not be able to argue that one type of leader was more successful than the other. Occasionally, however, a leader with outstanding charisma appeared in command at a time when that squadron was outstanding in the bombing results of the group. Such a leader could perhaps make things hum a little more efficiently with good results in bombing and in the happiness and confidence of the crews. Competition between the squadrons was never emphasized but intelligence officers would sometimes have opinions about which squadron had the best records of the moment. Sometimes one squadron, sometimes another would appear to be the crack squadron of the group. [It is equally true that under weak, unfair, unpopular 'leadership' a squadron could conceivably quickly fall apart and develop problems of poor discipline and inefficiency. Such conditions were extremely rare and I can recall only one possible example and not in our squadrons.]

While there were runs of successes, there were equally unfortunate runs of bad losses in operations and from accidents in take-off and landing. Luck seemed to play a part in squadron efficiency and losses.

(I had an illogical feeling that some aircraft letters were unlucky probably because several friends were lost in a succession of losses of 'R for Robert' in 104 Squadron. When looking through the squadron records for 1942–45 I checked on the letters of aircraft lost by enemy action or by misfortune during an operation and they numbered approximately one hundred (97). 104 Squadron aircraft with letters A, B, F, R and V each recorded either seven or eight losses. 104 Squadron aircraft with letters J, K, O, Q, X and Y recorded one loss only.)

Was War Bombing Effective?
In 1941 examination of the results of Bomber Command attacks on Germany had revealed that the bombing was well scattered and only a small percentage dropped on a given target. These results

were subsequently much improved by the use of Pathfinder techniques with flares and markers dropped by selected crews aided by radar devices. Photographs and ground examination of Tobruk and Benghazi showed in both cases that our bombing was also widespread around the target area of the harbour.

The use of special flare droppers from among the experienced crews helped to improve 205 Group bombing and commanding officers like Group Captain P.I. Harris DFC of 236 Wing insisted that crews practise their bombing skills and aimed at high standards.

The efficiency of bombing in achieving results damaging to an enemy is difficult to assess and this is not the place to do more than quote examples.

(a) Reports from POWs after Alamein indicated that the harrying of the enemy by RAF bombing by day and by night was effective in lowering morale. Even if night bombing in the battle areas in North Africa and Italy did no more than 'keep their heads down' it must have been a terrifying experience for enemy troops and would affect their fighting powers.

German resistance at Monte Cassino may counter this opinion.

(b) A Wellington raid on Aquino airfield Italy on night of 19th/20th July 1943 produced some twenty fires which appeared to be burning aircraft. PRU photographs showed 36 aircraft destroyed or damaged plus much damage to building and hangars.

(c) A Wellington raid on the aircraft factory at Reggio Emelia on 7th/8th January 1944 produced excellent results confirmed by subsequent daylight photography.

(d) A 205 Group attack on Feuersbrunn airfield on 6th July 1944 destroyed 19 enemy aircraft including 17 Me109s, and prevented a force of 50 fighters from attacking the American daylight formations on the following day when they were en route to oil installations in Germany. This attack received official commendation by a special signal to the Group from General Twining of 15th Air Force. Two of the attacking planes were lost at Feuersbrunn.

(e) The Luftwaffe made a very successful raid on 2nd December 1943 on shipping crowded into Bari harbour. A force of about 100 Ju88s came in at low level in a surprise attack which caused fires and damage to a number of ships. In all

some 17 ships were destroyed or sunk and over 1,000
service and civilian personnel were killed for the loss
of two of the attacking aircraft. (Source: Infield: *Disaster
at Bari*).

(f) An attack on Luqa airfield Malta on 18th December 1942
by some 30 German bombers destroyed 7 Wellingtons and
damaged 3 others for the loss of one attacking aircraft
shot down.

Marshal of the Royal Air Force, Sir Arthur Harris, who commanded Bomber Command from 1942 to 1945, has said that
bombing pressure by Bomber Command and the US 8th Air Force
won the war's biggest land battle. He quoted from the memoirs
of Albert Speer that the land battle had been won by forcing the
German Air Force on the defensive and tying down vast quan-
tities of men and guns needed desperately on the Russian and
Western fronts. Sir Arthur Harris added that Germany had to be
prepared to defend every major city and this involved apart from
air defence units, some 900,000 soldiers, 20,000 88 mm guns,
24,000 light flak guns continually on standby, plus 250,000
tradesmen to repair bomb damage.

The weight of the air offensive amounted to a second front
over the whole of Germany. Bomber Command alone lost 47,000
men killed or missing in achieving this result but it is impossible
to estimate how many casualties in the invading armies were saved
by the bombing offensive. [In 1944 and 1945 the Allied air
offensive against German controlled Europe was strongly supported by the 15th USAAF and 205 Group RAF bombers from
Foggia.]

Are Wars Futile?

The best anti-war play that I've seen was *X=0* where the killing
of a soldier on the battlements by one side is avenged by a similar
killing by the other side. The first world war led to plays about
trench life and the horrors of shelling and going over the top. The
second world war plays and films successfully portray the tensions
of men in battles on land and at sea and in the air.

We expected the second world war to mark the doom of mankind by bombing and to some degree the towns which were blitzed
by one side or the other must have felt they were experiencing
the end. Bombing culminated in attacks on Hamburg, Dresden,
Hiroshima and Nagasaki — but mankind survived because the war
came to an end in 1945.

I had not the slightest argument with conscience in joining the RAFVR in the war against Hitler and his Germany, yet in the Vietnam War I took part in anti-war demonstration marches and was thankful that one of my sons was medically unfit at call-up.

Are there righteous wars and wars which are without justification? Perhaps in the present state of the world this is so, and our consciences will sometimes allow us to participate, and sometimes not.

Frankly I can't see how Hitler and his ideas could have been stopped without recourse to war. Another dictatorship of either right or left may justify going to war. But it won't be a war of squadrons and intelligence officers but one of isolated teams in concrete pens or the hulls of nuclear submarines pressing the buttons of world destruction.

Our war of 1939—45 provided some examples of magnificent courage and fortitude by servicemen and civilians. Let us hope that so many did not die in vain and that man can survive to solve disputes by means other than war, for war with modern weapons is probably also world suicide.

Appendix

205 Group Royal Air Force — formed 23rd October 1941 at Shallufa, Egypt.

At various times during the Middle East—Mediterranean campaigns the following squadrons operated under 205 Group command —

RAF	SAAF	RCAF	RAAF	USAAF	FAA
14					
37	31	420	462	American	Albacores
38	34	424		Halverson	
40		425		Detachment	
70				Liberators	
104					
108					
142					
147					
148					
150					
159					
160					
178					
227					
614					

205 Group Order of Battle at El Alamein, October 1942

231 Wing 37 and 70 Squadron

236 Wing 108 and 148 Squadrons

238 Wing 40 and 104 Squadrons

242 Wing Liberators

245 Wing, 14, 227 and 462 RAAF

205 Group Order of Battle based at Gardabia, February 1943

40 Squadron attached directly to 205 Group H.Q.

231 Wing 37 and 70 Squadrons

236 Wing 104 and 462 RAAF

205 Group Order of Battle based at Kairouan, July 1943
231 Wing 37 and 70 Squadrons.
236 Wing 40 and 104 Squadrons
330 Wing 142 and 150 Squadrons
331 Wing 420, 424 and 425 Squadrons RCAF

205 Group Order of Battle based at Foggia, August 1944
231 Wing 37 and 70 Squadrons
236 Wing 40 and 104 Squadrons
330 Wing 142 and 150 Squadrons
240 Wing 178 (Liberators) and 614 (Halifax Pathfinders) Squadrons
SAAF No. 2 Wing, 31 and 34 Squadrons (Liberators)
(In February 1945 the Wellington squadrons of 205 Group were converted to Liberators.)

205 Group Aircrew Slang

Bandit,   an enemy aircraft.

Beau,   Beaufighter aircraft, twin engined fighter.

Beat up,   also shoot up, Buzz (USAF). Extreme low-level flying for fun over personnel or ground objects, strictly forbidden by the RAF.

Belt up,   Let there be no further discussion on the subject, shut up.

Binding bastards,   personnel who never stopped complaining.

Blue (the),   the desert.

Bomb happy,   personnel who have been rather shaken by constant or frequent enemy bombing.

Bumph,   paper work such as DROs, originating from the expression "bum fodder".

Bumphlets,   propaganda leaflets.

Bumphleteering,   the dropping of propaganda leaflets over enemy territory.

Burton (to go for a),   also to have "bought it" or to have "got the chop". To have been killed on operations.

Chai, Chai up, tea,   make some tea.

Chop rate,   the percentage of losses for bomber operations.

Clapped out (kite),   a poorly maintained or obsolete aircraft unsuitable for operations.

Clapped out (aircrew),   aircrew tour expired operationally.

Cookie,   a 4000 lb blockbuster bomb.

Deck (the), the runway,   the ground in general.

Dicy do, also Shaky do, a close shave during bombing operational involvement.

Desert happy, also Round the bend,   to act peculiarly due to overlong desert exposure.

Desert lily,   improvised camp toilets made from kerosene or other cans.

Drink (to ditch in the),   to crash land in the sea.

Erks,   aircraftmen for the servicing and maintenance of aircraft.

Fans,   aircraft propellers.

Flap,   a state of excitement due to some unexpected occurrence calling for urgent operational action.

Flightie,   a Flight-Sergeant in charge of ground personnel.

Flying can opener,   a tank buster Hurricane aircraft armed with a cannon.

Fort,   Flying Fortress (USAF).

Gabardine swine,   HQ Administrative Officers.

Gardening,   an aerial mine laying operation.

Gen (duff or pukka),   information either unsound or sound.

Gen (type),   an experienced RAF type, operationally or otherwise.

Gremlin,   an imaginary mischievous sprite alleged to cause mishaps, said to have been born in a Fremlin beer bottle.

Gong,   a gallantry decoration.

Goons,   brash or stupid inexperienced aircrew personnel.

Ground loop,   an unintentional aircraft swing on the ground through a complete circle on take-off or landing, due to the lack of pilot control.

Groupie,   Group Captain.

Halibag,   a Halifax four engined bomber.

Hangar doors (to close the),   stop talking "shop".

Heavies,   1000 lb bombs.

Hurribird,   a Hurricane fighter aircraft.

Intruder,   an enemy aircraft sent to shoot down aircraft on take-off or landing at base.

Jinking,   a cork-screwing weaving manoeuvre adopted by pilots to avoid attack by night fighters and flak.

Kite,   an aircraft.

Kitty,   a Kittyhawk fighter aircraft.

Lib,   Liberator four engined bomber.

Mae West,   inflatable life jacket.

Mail Run (the),   bombing operations on Benghazi, a frequently bombed target in 1942.

Morning prayers,   a Flight Section's morning briefing for the allocation of aircrews and aircraft for that night's operations.

Mossie,   a Mosquito twin engined reconnaissance aircraft.

Nickels,   propaganda leaflets.

Op,   abbreviation for a bombing operation.

Piss-poor (effort),   an unsuccessful bombing operation.

Prang,   an aircraft landing accident or other accident involvement.

Piece of cake, a relatively easy target.

Ropey (kite),   an old or obsolete aircraft considered unfit for operational use.

Roddie,   a bomb with a rod screwed onto its nose to cause it to explode above the ground.

Strip (to tear a strip off some one),   a stiff reprimand by a senior officer.

Shit (coming up),   flak coming up over the target area.

Shit storm,   a Khamsin, desert sand-storm.

Sprog,   a newcomer, inexperienced operationally.

Spit,   a Spitfire fighter aircraft.

Stringbag,   a Sword-fish carrier-based aircraft.

Shop (to talk),   subjects pertaining to the RAF or one's job therein.

Tinned fish,   a torpedo.

Vegetables,   aerial marine mines.

Wimp, Wimpy, Wimpey,   a Wellington bomber. So called after the famous *Popeye* cartoon character.

Wingco (or Wing Co),   Wing Commander.

Wog,   Egyptian — said to be derived from 'Worthy Oriental Gentleman' — any native.

Wop,   Italian

German Aircraft

88   a Junkers JU88 twin engined bomber or night fighter.

109   a Messerschmitt single engined fighter.

110   a Messerschmitt twin engined fighter.

190   a Focke-Wulf single engined fighter.

List of Abbreviations

AA	Anti-aircraft fire or Flak
A/C	Aircraft
AC	Aircraftman
ACM	Air Chief Marshal
AHQ	Air Headquarters
ALG	Advanced Landing Ground
AM	Air Marshal
AOC	Air Officer Commanding
AOC in C	Air Officer Commanding-in-Chief
ASP	Air Stores Park
AVM	Air Vice Marshal
CO	Commanding Officer
DFC	Distinguished Flying Cross
DFM	Distinguished Flying Medal
DRO's	Daily Routine Orders
DSO	Distinguished Service Order
E/A	Enemy Aircraft
ENSA	Entertainment National Service Association
EPIP	Egyptian Pattern Indian Produced — a large square marquee or tent
ETA	Estimated Time of Arrival
F/Lt	Flight Lieutenant
F/O	Flying Officer
F/Sgt	Flight Sergeant
Flt/Cdr	Flight Commander
G/C, G/Capt.	Group Captain
GIO	Group Intelligence Officer

HQ	Headquarters
HQRAFME	Headquarters Royal Air Force, Middle East
IFF	Identification Friend or Foe (radar device)
IO	Intelligence Officer
KRRC	The King's Royal Rifle Corps
LG	Landing Ground
MAAF	Mediterranean Allied Air Forces
MAPRC	Mediterranean Airforces Photographic Reconnaissance Centre
MBE	Member of the Order of the British Empire
ME	Middle East
NASAF	Northwest African Strategic Air Force
NATAF	Northwest African Tactical Air Force
NCO	Non-Commissioned Officer
NZ	New Zealand
OBE	Officer of the Order of the British Empire
OPSUM	Operational Summary (Intelligence)
OTU	Operational Training Unit
P/O	Pilot Officer
POW	Prisoner of War
PRO	Public Relations Officer
PRU	Photo Reconnaissance Unit
Q Site	Dummy Airfield or Flarepath
RAAF	Royal Australian Air Force
RAF	Royal Air Force
RAFVR	Royal Air Force Volunteer Reserve
RCAF	Royal Canadian Air Force
RE	Royal Engineers
RNZAF	Royal New Zealand Air Force
RSU	Repair and Salvage Unit

SAAF	South African Air Force
SASO	Senior Air Staff Officer
SIO	Senior Intelligence Officer
SL	Searchlight
S/Ldr	Squadron Leader
U/S	Unserviceable
USAAF	United States Army Air Force
W/Cdr	Wing Commander
W/O	Warrant Officer

Index